The Karabakh Conflict Between Armenia and Azerbaijan

M. Hakan Yavuz · Michael M. Gunter

The Karabakh Conflict Between Armenia and Azerbaijan

Causes & Consequences

M. Hakan Yavuz
Department of Political Science
University of Utah
Salt Lake City, UT, USA

Michael M. Gunter
Department of Sociology and
Political Science
Tennessee Technological University
Cookeville, TN, USA

ISBN 978-3-031-16261-9   ISBN 978-3-031-16262-6 (eBook)
https://doi.org/10.1007/978-3-031-16262-6

© The Editor(s) (if applicable) and The Author(s), under exclusive license to Springer Nature Switzerland AG 2023

This work is subject to copyright. All rights are solely and exclusively licensed by the Publisher, whether the whole or part of the material is concerned, specifically the rights of translation, reprinting, reuse of illustrations, recitation, broadcasting, reproduction on microfilms or in any other physical way, and transmission or information storage and retrieval, electronic adaptation, computer software, or by similar or dissimilar methodology now known or hereafter developed.

The use of general descriptive names, registered names, trademarks, service marks, etc. in this publication does not imply, even in the absence of a specific statement, that such names are exempt from the relevant protective laws and regulations and therefore free for general use.

The publisher, the authors, and the editors are safe to assume that the advice and information in this book are believed to be true and accurate at the date of publication. Neither the publisher nor the authors or the editors give a warranty, expressed or implied, with respect to the material contained herein or for any errors or omissions that may have been made. The publisher remains neutral with regard to jurisdictional claims in published maps and institutional affiliations.

This Palgrave Macmillan imprint is published by the registered company Springer Nature Switzerland AG

The registered company address is: Gewerbestrasse 11, 6330 Cham, Switzerland

Contents

1	Introduction	1
2	The Historical Background to the Continuing Conflict Over Nagorno-Karabakh	13
	Introduction	13
	Origins of the Conflict	16
	Russian Rule	18
	Soviet Rule	20
	Further Analysis of Soviet Rule	22
	Conclusion	26
3	The Causes of the First Nagorno-Karabakh War	33
	The Sociopolitical Causes of the Karabakh Conflict	35
	"Azerbaijanis as Turks": The Karabakh Conflict as Continuing the 1915 "Genocide"	40
	Suffering and Identity	42
	Tracing the Events of the Conflict	44
	The First Stage (1987–1991)	46
	The Sumgait Riots	47
	The Second Stage (1991–1994)	53
	Khojaly as the Nanjing of Azerbaijan	53
	Truce Agreement and the Composition of the Official Claims (1994–1995)	58
	Conclusion	60

4 The Consequences of the First War on Armenia and Azerbaijan 67
Armenia 69
   The Rise of the Karabakh Clan 70
   The Tension Between the Hayastanti and the Karabakhsis 72
   Perpetual War Economy, Regional Exclusion,
   and Migration 76
   Changes in Armenian National Identity
   and the Genocide Rhetoric 77
   The Impact on Foreign Policy: Russia as Chief Patron 78
Azerbaijan 82
   The Consequences of the War on Azerbaijan 82
   Securitization 83
   Victimhood 84
   A New Sense of Nationalism 86
   The Azerbaijani View of Russia 89
   Azerbaijanism as Identity 91
   State-Building and the Military 94
   Single-Issue Foreign Policy: Liberation of Karabakh 96
Conclusion 98

5 Failed Negotiations 107
Iran 114
United Nations 116
Minsk Group/Process 116
Renewed Conflict 122
Conclusion 123

6 Self-Determination or Territorial Integrity? International Legal/Political Doctrines in Opposition & Their Implications for Karabakh 135
Introduction 135
Additional Reasoning 138
Future Possibilities 141
Conclusion 144

7 The Second Nagorno-Karabakh War: Causes and Consequences 153
Causes of the Second Karabakh War 155
Aliyev versus Pashinyan 157

Turkey's Role and Erdoğan's Determination	164
Russia's Enduring Yet Declining Influence	167
Armenia's "Clash of Civilizations"?	170
The Ceasefire: The Transformation of the Conflict	172
SocioPolitical Implications of the Second War	174
The Impact on Azerbaijani State and Society	175
The Impact on Armenian State and Society	176
Debate Over the Final Status of Karabakh: Independence, Autonomy or Minority Rights	180
Conclusion	185
8 Conclusion	195
Selected Bibliography	201
Index	221

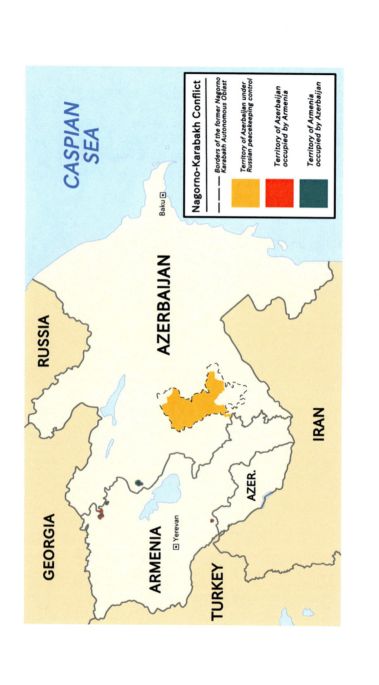

RESULTS OF ARMENIAN AGGRESSION

The occupied territories of the Republic of Azerbaijan

Former Nagorno Karabakh
Autonomous Oblast - NKAO(1923-1991)

Territory: 4.388 sq. km
Population (1989): 189.085
- Armenians: 145.450 (76,9%)
- Azerbaijanis: 40.688 (21,5%)
- Russians: 1922 (1%)
- Others: 1025 (0,5%)
Adm.territorial div.: Mardakert, Askeran, Shusha, Martuni, Hadrut districts

SHUSHA district
Territory: 290 sq. km
Population (1989): 20.579
- Azerbaijanis: 19.036 (92,5%)
- Armenians: 1.377 (6,7%)
Date of occupation: May 8, 1992

THE OCCUPIED TERRITORIES OF THE REPUBLIC OF AZERBAIJAN OUTSIDE FORMER NKAO

	date of occup.	area (in sq.m)	popul. at the time of occup. (1989)	current popul. (2011)
Lachyn	18.05.1992	1.840	51.594	70.900
Kalbajar	02.04.1993	3.050	57.756	83.200
Aghdam	23.07.1993	1.150	132.170	180.600
Fuzuli	23.08.1993	1.390	88.729	118.900
Jabrayil	23.08.1993	1.050	48.949	72.700
Gubadli	31.08.1993	800	28.111	30.700
Zangilan	29.10.1993	710	31.330	40.500

*after administrative-territorial changes of 1992

GAZAKH district*

			ARMENIA
Baghanis Ayrym	24.03.1990		
Kheyrymly	08.03.1992		
Ashaghy Askipara	12.03.1992		
Barkhudarly**	27.04.1992		
Sofulu**	27.04.1992		
Gyzylhajyly	11.05.1992		
Yukhary Askipara**	08.06.1992		

*the population of the occupied territories of Gazakh dist. was purely Azerbaijani.
**"enclave villages.

SADARAK dist., NAKHCHYVAN AR

	date of occup.	population (1989)	ethnic comp. (1989)
Karki enc.village	15.01.1990	333	100% aze

Victims of aggression (approximately):
killed: 20.000
disabled: 50.000
missing: 5.000

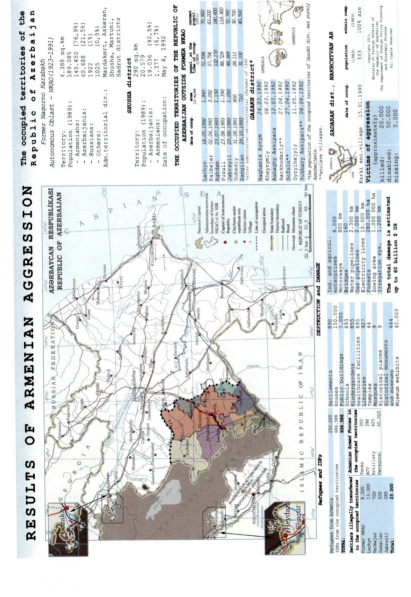

AZƏRBAYCAN RESPUBLİKASI
REPUBLIC OF AZERBAIJAN

DESTRUCTION and DAMAGE
Ind. and agricul. enterprises	6.000
Motorways	800 km
Bridges	160
Water pipelines	2.300 km
Gas pipelines	2.000 km
Electricity lines	280.000 ha
Sowing area	1.000.000 ha
Irrigation sys.	1.200 km

The total damage is estimated up to 60 billion $ US

Settlements	890
Houses	150.000
Public buildings	7.000
Schools	693
Kindergardens	855
Healthcare facilities	695
Libraries	927
Temples	44
Mosques	9
Historical places	9
Historical monuments and museums	464
Museum exhibits	40.000

Refugees and IDPs
Refugees from Armenia	250.000
IDPs from the occupied territories	686.586
TOTAL:	936.586

Settlers illegally transferred to the occupied territories
Former NKAO	15.000
Lachyn	13.000
Kalbajar	8.500
Zangilan	520
Jabrayil	280
Total:	23.000

Armenian Armed Forces in the occupied territories
Tanks	350
ACV	398
Artillery	425
Personnel	45.000

Copyright 2011
Ministry of Foreign Affairs of
the Republic of Azerbaijan
the Department of Strategic Policy Planning
and Strategic Studies
All rights reserved

Introduction

The conflict over Nagorno-Karabakh (Mountainous Karabakh) in the Caucasus is about an important, long-running, post-Soviet, frozen/unfrozen ethnic struggle between the Indo-European-speaking Armenians and Turkic-speaking Azerbaijanis. Nagorno-Karabakh is a relatively small, but symbolically important area in the Caucasus, which lies between the Black and Caspian Seas, athwart Europe and Asia, at the northern edge of the Middle East, and near one of the ends of the fabled Silk Road where today China's imaginatively bold Belt and Road Initiative reaches Europe. An incredible ethnic and linguistic diversity lies within this rather small, but geographically divided and largely mountainous region. Indeed, depending on how they are counted, there are as many as 50–200 different ethnic groups and 5 different language families (not just languages) including Indo-European (Armenian being one small example) and Turkic (Azerbaijani being a larger representative). The ancient and now assimilated Caucasian Albanians and Iberians—who had nothing to do with their spurious namesakes in Europe to the west—add to the mixed, ethnic confusion. A further, but unrelated aspect of the controversy the term Caucasian can foster arises from its usage as a synonym for the White race as semantically this meaning is clearly misleading.[1]

Nagorno-Karabakh has significant relevance for ethnic conflict studies in general, post-Soviet conflict studies in particular, and great power struggles involving Russia, Turkey, Iran, and even further afoot including among others, the United States and the European Union. Karabakh also has implications for the international oil market transfer from Azerbaijan (rich in oil from time immemorial) to outlets around the world. Continuing conflict over Nagorno-Karabakh might damage important international oil markets seeking to operate in, from, and to Baku, the capital of Azerbaijan. As such, the oil market and commerce in general demand a solution to the Nagorno-Karabakh problem since continuation of the conflict or even uncertainty regarding it would jeopardize oil transport.

The most recent war over Nagorno-Karabakh (September–November 2020) was won by Azerbaijan largely by using drones as a very important weapon. This implies that drones might be a very critical ingredient of fighting future wars.[2] Thus, this interdisciplinary study of the post-Soviet ethnic conflict over Nagorno-Karabakh will impact many subject areas that are widely taught and researched. This study's importance also lies in its originality because, in addition to its broad, inter- and multi-disciplinary purview, it will be one of the first ones written subsequent to the paradigmatic-changing war fought in September–November 2020. Earlier studies are now more than a decade old, and thus dated in their analyses. This new study will remedy this gap in our knowledge.

Karabakh itself is a small, landlocked area of varying sizes, depending on whose precise narrative one hears, in the South Caucasus, now usually referred to as Transcaucasia as distinct from the Russian North Caucasus or Ciscaucasia. Many would divide Karabakh into three areas: Nagorno-Karabakh, Lowland Karabakh to the south, and the eastern slopes of the Zangezur Mountains. Karabakh often is equated with the administrative boundaries of the former Nagorno-Karabakh Russian oblast of 4,400 square kilometers/1,700 square miles. However, the area of the entire region comprises some 8,223 square kilometers or 3,175 miles.[3] The region has been known as Karabakh (Black Garden) since the thirteenth century. Since the end of the Second Karabakh War in November 2020, the Azerbaijani authorities prefer simply to refer to the entire region as Karabakh as this implies the reintegration of the territory with Azerbaijan and maintenance of its territorial integrity. The term Nagorno-Karabakh is no longer used. However, this book will continue to employ the term when appropriate since it has long been so widely used.

It is the smaller part known as Nagorno-Karabakh, with its ethnic Armenian majority, that was granted autonomy as an enclave within

Turkic-majority Azerbaijan in the early years of the Soviet Union. As long as the Soviet Union remained strong and unified, this arrangement worked. However, as Ernest Gellner, the renowned scholar of nationalism, warned, "not all nationalisms can be satisfied ... because the satisfaction of some spells the frustration of others."[4] In words that seem to have been written precisely for Nagorno-Karabakh, Gellner continued, "This argument is further and immeasurably strengthened by the fact that very many of the potential nations of this world live ... not in compact territorial units but intermixed with each other in complex patterns. It follows that a territorial political unit can only become ethnically homogeneous, in such cases, if it either kills, or expels, or assimilates all non-nationals. Their unwillingness to suffer such fates may make the peaceful implementation of the nationalist principle difficult."[5]

When the Soviet Union broke up in 1991 and the Armenians won the ensuing war against Azerbaijan over Karabakh, the unrecognized de facto state that the Armenians eventually carved out not only included the entire area of greater Karabakh, but seven more surrounding districts of Azerbaijan. In fact, the Armenian-occupied area of Nagorno-Karabakh covered 4,400 square kilometers, and with the occupied territories it came to approximately 12,000 square kilometers, representing 20 percent of Azerbaijan's total area. Before the First Karabakh War (1988–1994), some 120,000 Armenians lived in the smaller Nagorno-Karabakh region. On the other hand, an estimated 800,000 Azerbaijanis were forced from the greater Karabakh region and the occupied territories as a consequence of the Armenian invasion of the Azerbaijani territories. At the end of the First Karabakh War, Armenian forces completely ethnically cleansed Azerbaijanis from their homes. Conversely, the same Karabakh conflict was the reason that more than 200,000 Armenians from Azerbaijan were forced to leave their homes. The Sumgait (just north of Baku on the Caspian Sea) pogrom in 1988 resulted in murdering at least 26 (probably more) Armenian civilians,[6] while the Khojaly (a small town in northern Nagorno-Karabakh) massacre in 1992 saw Armenian militias massacre 613 Azerbaijani civilians.[7] Both sides poignantly remember their tragedy, but seldom even mention the other's. The war resulted in major human sufferings on both sides. Specific numbers are often disputed because as the old saw explains, "the first casualty when war comes is truth."

The occupying Armenian forces refused to use the term Karabakh since it was an Azerbaijani name for the region, instead referring to it as the Republic of Artsakh, an Armenian term. Not even the kin-state of Armenia legally recognized this de facto situation whose successful precedent would have challenged the territorial integrity of every state on earth including of course Azerbaijan and even Armenia on another day in the name of secessionist self-determination. Numerous UN General Assembly and Security Council resolutions have recognized this situation.[8] For example, UN General Assembly Resolution 62/243 adopted on March 14, 2008 declared that it:

> *Reaffirms* continued respect and support for the sovereignty and territorial integrity of the Republic of Azerbaijan within its internationally recognized borders; 2. *Demands* the immediate, complete and unconditional withdrawal of all Armenian forces from all the occupied territories of the Republic of Azerbaijan; 3. *Reaffirms* the inalienable right of the population expelled from the occupied territories of the Republic of Azerbaijan to return to their homes [Armenian and Azerbaijani] ... [and] 5. *Reaffirms* that no State shall recognize as lawful the situation resulting from the occupation of the territories of the Republic of Azerbaijan, nor render aid or assistance in maintaining this situation.[9]

All this is a far cry from the Armenian propaganda that repeatedly paints the Turkic Azerbaijanis as the aggressors and perpetrators of genocide continuance in the present situation.

Thus, pro-Armenian support largely stems from the residual sympathy for what many perceive as genocide committed against Armenians during World War I. Although the Armenians did indeed suffer greatly in that struggle, so too did the Turks and other Muslim groups. As a result, some question whether the term genocide is appropriate for the Armenian experience during World War I.[10] Of course, whatever historical interpretation one might give to these earlier events, it would not justify blatant Armenian aggression a century later. Thus, the past Armenian experience is largely beyond the scope of this book. Nevertheless, much of the Armenian position on Karabakh implicitly rests on the belief that the Azerbaijani position today regarding Karabakh is simply a continuance of what the Armenians and their many supporters claim was an earlier genocide. This book does not agree with these Armenian and pro-Armenian interpretations. Indeed, this book calls upon the Armenians to accept a reasonable solution based on respect for Azerbaijani territorial integrity and abandon revanchism. Nonetheless, this book recognizes how this tortured history affects the current situation and calls upon the now stronger Azerbaijani side to offer the Armenians a magnanimous solution that benefits both sides in the future. Otherwise both sides will continue to be condemned to repeat their tragic pasts.

Determined to regain its occupied territory after the First Karabakh War (1988–1994), but long stymied not only by its opponents but its own divisions, Azerbaijan finally recovered its lost territory in the Second Karabakh War won in 2020. However, illustrating the most recent deadly results of this conflict that suddenly unfroze in September–November 2020, Russian president Vladimir Putin declared "there were more than 4,000 killed in both countries … including civilians, 8,000 wounded and thousands driven from their homes."[11] At the present time, there is only another temporary cease-fire and truce. Unless a more permanent arrangement can be reached, the two sides will probably be condemned to future wars over the same issue.

The meanings of the Karabakh region and conflict differed significantly between Azerbaijanis and Armenians. For Azerbaijan, the earlier loss of Karabakh and the defeat in the first war signified their national humiliation, wounded national identity, shattered ideals of territorial integrity, and the failure of their state project. Azerbaijanis negatively gauged their state and the success of its political leadership against the loss of Karabakh and prior defeat. For Armenians, however, the First Karabakh War symbolized their victory to protect what they saw as a key historical center and to consolidate Armenian national identity and state-building. Using a longer historical lens, the Armenians saw the earlier victory as revenge for Armenian massacres, also called "genocide," at the hands of the Ottoman Turks in the early twentieth century. Armenia's military victory against Azerbaijan in the First Karabakh War also emboldened the ties with the diaspora of Armenian communities. The Armenians perceived it as an act in which they, the earlier victim, had become the victor and managed to achieve retribution.

Thus, the Karabakh defeat constantly reminded the Azerbaijanis what they had lost, while the Karabakh victory reminded the Armenians what they could achieve as they sought a strategy of "new wars, new territories." In the prior conflict, the victorious Armenian army, along with the self-proclaimed Armenian "Republic of Artsakh," fostered an image of becoming the most powerful army in the Caucasus. Yet, this military victory also facilitated a continuing flow of Armenians emigrating to Russia, Europe, and the United States. While Armenia wanted to expand its borders, many Armenians, especially those who were upper-middle class and well educated, left their country for good.

The conflict between Armenia and Azerbaijan progressed through several stages. The first concluded with the 1994 cease-fire agreement. Although skirmishes and military movements continued along the contact lines, many experts labeled the situation as a "frozen" conflict. The Organization for Security and Cooperation in Europe (OSCE)'s Minsk Process with its subsequent Madrid Principles assured the status quo in favor of Armenia for more than a quarter of a century. The main issues with which they supposedly dealt with were the return of the occupied territories surrounding Nagorno-Karabakh; the future status of Nagorno-Karabakh; the return of Azerbaijani refugees; and the status of the "Lachin Corridor" connecting Nagorno-Karabakh to Armenia.

During this period, while Armenia attempted to consolidate its military occupation and aggravate the situation with humiliating rhetoric directed against their enemy, Azerbaijan deployed its resources to prepare for an eventual repeat of the war to liberate their territories and resuscitate their national pride and identity. Azerbaijan cultivated its own rhetoric of humiliation targeting Armenia. In short, Armenia won the war, but not the peace and the conflict drained resources from both countries. Neither the mediators nor the hegemon, mainly Russia, sought to change the dynamics of bilateral relations and instead exploited the conflict for their own interests by selling weapons or pitting one side against the other.

The second, relatively minor stage of the conflict was triggered as a result of a confrontation between the two armies in early April 2016. Still, this was the largest confrontation since the 1994 cease-fire. It lasted for four days and resulted in a few very minor gains for Azerbaijan, which had tried repeatedly to unfreeze the conflict. Therefore, a key question to be explored in this book is when and under what conditions do conflicts frozen in tension thaw and unleash a new round of military activity? Another is how did Armenia's negative framing of the Azerbaijanis as continuing what the Armenians viewed as the earlier genocide in World War I as well as the Azerbaijanis being lazy, backward, unpatriotic, and corrupt, in turn, shape Armenian military and foreign policies?

The Nagorno-Karabakh conflict also has regional implications. Russia and Iran have traditionally supported Armenia, whereas Turkey and Israel have backed Azerbaijan. Russia historically supported Armenia as a fellow Christian state, while Shiite Iran ironically did so to check perecived Azerbaijani territorial aims on Azeri parts of northwestern Iran. On the other hand, Turkey supported Azerbaijan because of strong ethnic ties and residual fears and animosities toward the Armenians. Israel supported Azerbaijan as a way to gain a listening post next to its greatly feared Iranian foe.

Casting his purview even further, Zbigniew Brzezinski, among the most prominent geostrategists of the contemporary era, recommended Western support for Baku when he explained that "Azerbaijan, with is vast energy resources, is also geopolitically critical. It is the cork in the bottle containing the riches of the Caspian Sea basin and Central Asia."[12] Elaborating, Brzezinski argued how "an independent Azerbaijan, linked to Western markets by pipelines that do not pass through Russian-controlled territory, also becomes a major avenue of access from the advanced and energy-consuming economies to the energy rich Central Asian republics."[13] Therefore, to check Russia's position in the Caucasus, strengthen the Western geostrategic position and access to energy resources, and appeal to the Turkic populations in Central Asia, a strong and independent Azerbaijan was a catalyst.

On the other hand, Armenia believes that it has no option but to depend on Russia, as Armenia sustains a deep, ingrained suspicion toward Turkey and Azerbaijan. Russia exploited this animosity and today major industries and public utility firms in Armenia are owned by Russia. Russia protects the borders of Armenia (but not Nagorno-Karabakh) and, in turn, Armenia provides the locations for Russian military bases. Russia would not prefer Armenia to develop closer economic and political ties with the West. The continuation of the Karabakh conflict serves Russian interests to control Armenia and Azerbaijan. This explains why Russia will hesitate to resolve the Karabakh issue, indeed continue it in its own interests of keeping intact its access to what is perceived as its historical territory via its role as a mediator.

In addition, the Nagorno-Karabakh conflict[14] also constitutes the most recent example of the continuing clash between the oft-opposed international legal/political doctrines of self-determination and territorial integrity.[15] Put simply, self-determination refers to the right of a people to choose their own form of government (usually independence), while territorial integrity means the right of a state to maintain its existing borders.[16] The United Nations Charter includes specific references to self-determination in Articles 1(2) and 55, and to territorial integrity in Article 2(4). Thus, in the case of Nagorno-Karabakh, Armenia has supported the doctrine of self-determination because the vast majority of its population is ethnic Armenian. On the other hand, Azerbaijan has maintained the doctrine of territorial integrity because Karabakh is part of Azerbaijan.[17]

As stated above, in this up-to-date study, the authors analyze the subject from all the main sides in light of the most recent war over Nagorno-Karabakh that raged from September to November 2020. Although there are past studies, no one has analyzed Nagorno-Karabakh in light of this later war and in such a broad perspective that gives weight to all sides of this conflict. As already noted, this is a very appropriate time to reconsider Nagorno-Karabakh in light of its significant importance for ethnic conflict in general, the post-Soviet Caucasus specifically, and the most recent war just fought over the area from September to November 2020. Thus, the main themes will stress these points as well as the importance of the Nagorno-Karabakh issue for the future by considering its precedents and implications for other secessionist wars, how such wars begin and end, the international legal precedents of self-determination vs. territorial integrity, its implications for post-Soviet developments and conflicts in such other regions as Ukraine in 2022 and earlier, and the latest successful weapons developments lessons from the recent war involving drones, and energy-strategic access to oil. Clearly, this up-to-date analysis of Nagorno-Karabakh has importance in a number of different areas.

Following this brief introductory chapter, the present study consists of seven more chapters. Chapter 2 deals with the historical background to the struggle, while the third considers the causes of the First Karabakh War (1988–1994). Chapter 4 details the consequences of the First Karabakh War, while Chapter 5 analyzes the failed OSCE Minsk Process negotiations following the first war. Chapter 6 examines the conflict in terms of the conflicting principles of territorial integrity vs. self-determination. Chapter 7 assesses the causes and consequences of the Second Karabakh War (September–November 2020). The final, eighth chapter summarizes the book's main findings, while making the existentially important fact that international law clearly held that Nagorno-Karabakh belonged to Azerbaijan despite misleading arguments to the contrary about supposed Armenian rights of self-determination often parsed into claims of some type of internal and/or remedial self-determination. Chapter 8 also assesses the all-important leadership role of Azerbaijani president Ilham Aliyev, and looks to a brighter future for both sides based on a magnanimous implementation of the results of the Second Karabakh War in late 2020.

Notes

1. The term Caucasian as a racial synonym for Whites was apparently first introduced in the 1780s by the German anatomist and member of the Gottingen School of History Johann Blumenbach following his impressionistic visit to the region and subsequently flawed attempt at racial categorization. This usage was picked up in the United States and stuck even though literally it only referred to the ethnically mixed, indigenous populations living in the Caucasus, not the White Europeans who were then spreading around the world. Further discussion of this matter is beyond the scope of this book.
2. On this important point, see Seth J. Frantzman, *Drone Wars: Pioneers, Killing Machines, Artificial Intelligence, and the Battle for the Future* (New York and Nashville: Post Hill Press, 2021); Ash Rossiter and Brendon J. Cannon, "Turkey's Rise as a Drone Power: Trial by Fire," *Defense and Security Analysis*, https://doi.org/10.1080/14751798.2022.2068562, Routledge, published online May 4, 2022, pp. 8–9; Stephen Witt, "The Turkish Drone That Changed the Nature of Warfare," *The New Yorker*, May 9, 2022, https://www.newyorker.com/magazine/2022/05/16/the-turkish-drone-that-changed-the-nature-of-warfare?utm_source=nl&utm_brand=tny&utm_mailin, accessed May 9, 2022; and Robyn Dixon, "Azerbaijan's Drones Owned the Battlefield in Nagorno-Karabakh—And Showed Future of Warfare," *Washington Post*, October 11, 2020, among others.
3. On these figures, see by Robert H. Hewsen, "The Meliks of Eastern Armenia: A Preliminary Study," *Revue des etudes Armeniennes* NS: IX (1970), p. 288; and *Armenia: A Historical Atlas* (Chicago: The University of Chicago Press, 2001), p. 264.
4. Ernest Gellner, *Nations and Nationalism*, 2nd ed. (Blackwell, 2008), p. 2.
5. Ibid.
6. As an Armenian retrospect concluded, "it is certain that the anti-Armenian pogroms at Sumgait constitute a genocide as defined by the UN Convention on the Prevention and Punishment of Genocide." Samvel Shahmuratian, compiler and editor, *The Sumgait Tragedy: Pogroms Against Armenians in Soviet Azerbaijan. Eyewitnesses Accounts*, Vol. I (New Rochelle, NY and Cambridge, MA: Aristide D. Caratzas and Zoryan Institute, 1991), p. 1. "The current situation in the region … can be traced back to Sumgait." Ibid., p. 10. Of course, Azerbaijanis would argue

that the current situation stemmed from earlier Armenian demonstrations demanding that Nagorno-Karabakh be ceded to Armenia.
7. While all Azerbaijanis know about Khojaly and stress the civilian massacre that occurred there as proof of Armenian genocide against them, few in the West have even heard of this tragedy. Thomas Goltz, *Azerbaijan Dairy: A Rogue Reporter's Adventures in an Oil-Rich, War-Torn, Post-Soviet Republic* (Armonk, NY: M.E. Sharpe Press, 1998) is a rare exception. "Apparently, the idea that the roles of the good guys and bad guys had been reversed was too much: Armenians slaughtering Azeris?" Ibid., p. 124.
8. See, for example, UN Security Resolutions 822, April 30, 1993; 853, July 29, 1993; 874, October 14, 1993; and 884, November 12, 1993, which all called for "the withdrawal of all occupying forces from ... occupied areas of the Republic of Azerbaijan" as Resolution 822 put it.
9. UN General Assembly Resolution 62/243, March 14, 2008 on "The situation in the occupied territories of Azerbaijan."
10. For background on this situation, see Michael M. Gunter, *Armenian History and the Question of Genocide* (New York: Palgrave Macmillan, 2011); and M. Hakan Yavuz, "The Turkish-Armenian Historical Controversy: How to Name the Events of 1915?" *Middle East Critique* 29 (May 2020), pp. 1–21. For a sample of the voluminous pro-Armenian literature, see Taner Akcam, *A Shameful Act: The Armenian Genocide and the Question of Turkish Responsibility* (New York: Henry Holt and Company, 2006); and Donald Bloxham, *The Great Game of Genocide: Imperialism, Nationalism, and the Destruction of the Ottoman Armenians* (New York: Oxford University Press, 2005).
11. "Hundreds of Dead Armenian Soldiers Shown in Nagorno-Karabakh," Novinite.com (Sofia News Agency), November 13, 2020, https://www.novinite.com/articles/206519/Hundreds+of+Dead+Armenian+Soldiers+Shown+in+Nagorno-Karabakh, accessed November 14, 2020.
12. Zbigniew Brzezinski, *The Grand Chessboard: American Primacy and Its Geostrategic Imperatives* (New York: Basic Books, 1997), p. 46.
13. Ibid., p. 47.
14. For background on Karabakh, see Svante E. Cornell, *The Nagorno-Karabakh Conflict*, Report no. 46, Department of East European Studies, Uppsala University, Sweden, 1999; Thomas de Waal, *Black Garden: Armenia and Azerbaijan Through Peace and War* (New York: New York University Press, 2003); Thomas Goltz, *Azerbaijan Dairy: A Rogue Reporter's Adventures in an Oil-Rich, War-Torn, Post-Soviet Republic* (Armonk, NY: M.E. Sharpe Press, 1998); Michael Kambeck and Sargis Ghazaryan, eds., *Europe's Next Avoidable War: Nagorno-Karabakh* (New

1 INTRODUCTION   11

York: Palgrave Macmillan, 2013); Ohannes Geukjian, *Ethnicity, Nationalism and Conflict in the South Caucasus: Nagorno-Karabakh and the Legacy of Soviet Nationalities Policy* (Farnham, England and Burlington, VT: Ashgate, 2012); and Arsene Saparov, *From Conflict to Autonomy in the Caucasus: The Soviet Union and the Making of Abkhazia, South Ossetia and Nagorno Karabakh* (London and New York: Routledge, 2015), among others. More recently since the Second Karabakh War in 2020, see M. Hakan Yavuz and Michael M. Gunter, eds., *The Nagorno-Karabakh Conflict: Historical and Political Perspectives* (London and New York; Routledge, 2023); Laurence Broers, *Armenia and Azerbaijan: Anatomy of a Rivalry* (Edinburgh: Edinburgh University Press, 2021); and Fariz Ismailzade and Damjan Krnjevic Miskovic, eds., *Liberated Karabakh: Policy Perspectives by the ADA University Community* (Baku, Azerbaijan: ADA University Press, 2021).

15. Other recent examples that involve various elements of the inherent contradiction between these two conflicting doctrines, but in each case have their unique characteristics it should be noted, include Kosovo, Eritrea, Western Sahara, East Timor (Timor-Leste), Belize, Gibraltar, the Falkland Islands (Malvinas), the Basques, Biafra, Catalonia, Chechnya, Eastern Ukraine, the Kurds, Northern Cyprus, and Scotland, among numerous others. For background on over 40 self-determination conflicts including Karabakh outside the colonial context that have appeared virtually impossible to settle, see Marc Weller, "Settling Self-determination Conflicts: Recent Developments," *The European Journal of International Law* 20:1 (2009), pp. 111–164. For many further possible examples, see James Minahan, *Nations Without States: A Historical Dictionary of Contemporary National Movements* (Westport, CT: Greenwood Press, 1996).

16. The legal doctrines of sovereignty meaning unlimited power or better just independence, and uti possidetis meaning that old administrative colonial boundaries would remain legal international boundaries upon independence are closely related to and tend to reinforce the concept of territorial integrity. In general, see Peter Malanczuk, *Akehurst's Modern Introduction to International Law*, 7th revised ed. (London and New York: Routledge, 1997), pp. 17–18 and 162, 163. The most comprehensive analysis of statehood creation in international law is arguably James R. Crawford, *The Creation of States in International Law*, 2nd ed. (Oxford: Oxford University Press, 2006).

17. As Svante Cornell noted when the present conflict was still in its earlier stages: "The Armenians invoked the principle of peoples'

right to self-determination, and the Azeris defended the principle of territorial integrity." *Nagorno-Karabakh Conflict*, p. 25. Thomas de Waal concurred: "A resolution of the issue had to reconcile the competing claims of Azerbaijan's territorial integrity and Karabakh's self-determination (or, in blunter language, de facto secession)." *Black Garden*, p. 255.

CHAPTER 2

The Historical Background to the Continuing Conflict Over Nagorno-Karabakh

Introduction

The Caucasus contains a bewildering number of ethnic groups with their own histories, current needs, and conflicting ambitions. The struggle over Nagorno-Karabakh involves an important, long-running, frozen/unfrozen conflict between the Armenians and Turkic Azerbaijanis over a relatively small, but symbolically important area in the Caucasus. This continuing conflict also has heavily involved Russia and Turkey, among others. Since Nagorno-Karabakh was part of Azerbaijan during Soviet times, Azerbaijan now claims it according to the international legal principle of territorial integrity. However, since the vast majority of its population is ethnic Armenian, Armenia claims it according to the principle of self-determination.

To implement its claim, Armenia invaded and conquered Nagorno-Karabakh and seven more surrounding areas in Azerbaijan upon the breakup of the Soviet Union in the late 1980s and early 1990s. Thus, as mentioned above, this conflict has important implications for such international law concepts as territorial integrity (maintained by Azerbaijan), self-determination (advocated by Armenia), and peaceful settlement of disputes in general as well as international legal practice regarding United Nations (UN) obligations that "all Members shall refrain in their international relations from the threat or use of force against the territorial integrity … of any state" (UN Charter Article 2(4)), the Helsinki Final

© The Author(s), under exclusive license to Springer Nature Switzerland AG 2023
M. H. Yavuz and M. M. Gunter, *The Karabakh Conflict Between Armenia and Azerbaijan*, https://doi.org/10.1007/978-3-031-16262-6_2

Act of 1975 on the finality of international borders in post-World-War-II Europe, various decisions of the International Court of Justice (ICJ) regarding existing borders, and the international legal doctrines of state sovereignty, succession, and uti possidetis, among others.[1]

Karabakh also has significant relevance for ethnic conflict studies in general, post-Soviet conflict studies in particular, and great power struggles involving Russia, Turkey, Iran, and even further afoot, including among others, the United States and the European Union. In addition, Karabakh has implications for the international oil market transfer from Azerbaijan (rich in oil from time immemorial) to outlets around the world. Continuing conflict over Karabakh might damage important international oil markets seeking to operate in, from, and to Baku.

The most recent war over Karabakh (September–November 2020) reversed the results of the earlier one 30 years earlier and was won by Azerbaijan largely by using drones as a very important weapon. This implies that drones might be a very critical ingredient in fighting future wars.[2] Indeed, Uzi Rubin, the director of the Israel Missile Defense Organization, described this war as "the first post-modern conflict ... in which unmanned aircraft [drones] overwhelmed a conventional ground force, grinding it down to the point of impotency and paving the way for the Azeri ground forces to roll in."[3] Specifically, drones implemented "electronic [wizard] warfare that blinded Armenian radar, thus facilitating the destruction of its air defense batteries."[4] Once the Armenian air defenses were neutralized, the Azeri drones then successfully went after the [Armenian] armor, artillery, and logistical trains, which eventually enabled the Azerbaijani ground forces to regain their occupied territory.

Clearly, this interdisciplinary review of the origins of the conflict over Karabakh will impact many subject areas that are widely taught and researched. Given the importance of Karabakh and the continuing dispute over its origins, this chapter will attempt to present a historically objective analysis that will provide a background upon which to help interpret the current situation and accurately place it within current Middle Eastern studies.

The historical background of the continuing conflict regarding Karabakh—over which those involved tread on the thinnest of ice that periodically shatters into ethnic violence and war—mirrors the ethnically complicated and controversial background of the Caucasus in which Karabakh is located. Ethnic leaders from both sides maintain opposing mythomoteurs (constitutive myths that give ethnic groups their sense of purpose) that buttress their group's identity by invoking provocative historical memories and symbols of victimization. However, as Ernest Gellner, the renowned scholar of nationalism, warned, "not all nationalisms can be satisfied … because the satisfaction of some spells the frustration of others."[5] When this occurs, one might stumble upon the very DNA of Hell. How then to even begin this dark, enigmatic tale? Is it true, as Winston Churchill once reputedly advised, "In wartime, truth is so precious that she should be attended by a bodyguard of lies." With these caveats, this chapter will endeavor to separate one from the other, and when uncertain so advise.

As already pointed out above in the Introduction, the Caucasus lies between the Black and Caspian Seas, athwart Europe and Asia, at the northern edge of the Middle East, and near one of the ends of the fabled Silk Road, now being modernized in the guise of China's Belt and Road Initiative. An incredible ethnic and linguistic diversity lies within this rather small, but geographically divided and largely mountainous region. Indeed, depending on how they are counted, there are as many as 50–200 different ethnic groups and 5 different language families including Indo-European—Armenian being one small example—while the Azerbaijani language belongs to the Turkic language family.[6]

Karabakh (Karabagh) itself is a much smaller, landlocked area of varying sizes in the South Caucasus, now usually referred to as Transcaucasia as distinct from the Russian North Caucasus or Ciscaucasia. Many would divide Karabakh into three areas: Nagorno/Nagorny (Mountainous) Karabakh, Lowland Karabakh to the south, and the eastern slopes of the Zangezur Mountains. Karabakh often is equated with the administrative boundaries of the former Nagorno-Karabakh oblast of 4,400 square kilometers/1,700 square miles. However, the area of the entire region comprises some 8,223 square kilometers or 3,175 miles.[7] The region has been known as Karabakh since the thirteenth century.

When dealing with Karabakh, one must be careful about whether the issue is that of the larger area of Karabakh or the smaller part of it known as Nagorno-Karabakh. It is the smaller part known as Nagorno-Karabakh that was granted autonomy within Azerbaijan in the early years of the Soviet Union. However, when the Soviet Union broke up in 1991 and the Armenians won the ensuing war against Azerbaijan over Karabakh, the unrecognized de facto state that they eventually carved out not only included the entire area of greater Karabakh, but in effect seven more surrounding districts of Azerbaijan. This "greater" Armenian-controlled

Karabakh was eliminated by the results of the war won by Azerbaijan in 2020. The Azerbaijani authorities now prefer to use the term Karabakh rather than Nagorno-Karabakh because the first usage implies that full Azerbaijani territorial integrity has been restored.

The word Karabakh is usually said to be a combination of the Turkic word *kara* (black) and the Iranian word *bagh* (garden). Thus, Black Garden. However, a few linguists and historians point out the etymology for *kara* might also be large, not just black.

On the other hand, the less known Armenian name for Karabakh is Artsakh.[8] Folk etymology says that this term is derived from the personal name Ar (Aran) and *tsakh* (woods or garden). Thus, the Armenian name Artsakh would mean the gardens of Aran Sisakean, who was the first nakharar, the hereditary title of the highest order given to the house of the ancient and medieval Armenian nobility of northeastern Armenia.[9]

The ancestors of today's Turkic Azerbaijanis (Azeris) arrived in the Caucasus later, although, as with the Armenians, there is debate about a precise date.[10] Thus, Karabakh did become a home to various nomadic Oghuz Turkish tribes, among others, from the eleventh century onward. Today's Azerbaijanis argue for a much earlier date. They also claim partial descent from the Medes, who date from the seventh century BCE as well as Caucasian Albania and to the south, Aturpatkan (Atropatene), which also meant land of fire in allusion to its Zoroastrian heritage, both dating from the fourth century BCE.[11] However, there is much uncertainty about how these various ethnic groups interacted and assimilated.[12] For example, both Azerbaijanis and Armenians argue that they assimilated the earlier Caucasian Albanians and Iberians, and both are probably partially correct.

Origins of the Conflict

Over the centuries a bewildering procession of rulers in Mountainous Karabakh included the Arab Umayyad and Abbasid caliphates, Bagratid Armenia, the Mongol Ilkhanate and Jalayirid sultanates, the Turkic Kara and Ak Koyunlu, the Beylerbeylik states of the Persian Safavid empire, and even the Ottoman empire between 1578 and 1605 and again from 1723 to 1736. To strengthen their control over these new borderlands when it took them over early in the nineteenth century, Christian Russia resettled Christian Armenians and oversaw the deportation of Muslims.

Thus, demographics can tell very different stories depending on whom one is listening to and what period one is examining.

From 1501 to 1736, Karabakh owed ultimate allegiance to the Persian Safavid Empire. Under the Safavids, the five semi-independent Armenian melikdoms (principalities)—also known as the *Khamsa*, from the Arabic for five—were Armenian feudal-type entities headed by meliks (princes) that existed on the territory of modern Nagorno-Karabakh and adjacent areas dating from the dissolution of the earlier Armenian principality of Khachen. These five melikdoms of Gulistan, Jraberd, Khachen, Varanda, and Dizak existed in one form or another until Russia finally abolished them in 1822. However, these melikdoms already had begun to weaken by the mid-eighteenth century due to their internal quarrels.[13]

The Persian Empire's Nader Shah's assassination in June 1747, allowed Panakh Khan (1693–1759 or 1763), the leader of the Turkic Javanshir dynasty in Azerbaijan, in alliance with the Armenian melik of Varanda, to establish himself as the powerful khan (military ruler) of Karabakh. Panakh Khan built a mountain fortress in Shusha (known as Shushi by the Armenians). This city for at least the past three centuries has had broad and deep symbolic meaning to both Armenians and Azerbaijanis. In 1795 and 1826, it famously withstood two long sieges by Persian armies, the first one even costing the Persian shah Agha Mohammad Khan his life.

Panakh Khan died at the hands of the Persians in 1763 (but his tombstone lists 1759). He was succeeded by his son Ibrahim-Khalil Khan (1732–1806), who ruled over most of Karabakh and like his father became one of the most powerful potentates in the Caucasus. On the eve of the Russian conquest, various other khanates, all still under varying degrees of Persian suzerainty, constituted the remainder of Transcaucasia. On May 14, 1805, under the provisions of the Kurekchai Treaty, Ibrahim recognized Russian allegiance and permitted a Russian garrison to be stationed in Shusha. The following year, Ibrahim rejoined the Persians, only to die at the hands of the Russians apparently instigated by his grandson. The Russians then appointed Mehdigulu Khan Javanshir (1763–1845), a son of Ibrahim, as the new and last khan of Karabagh.[14] Although fascinating, further analysis of these earlier times is beyond the scope of the present study.

Interestingly, however, Zaur Mammadov, the present-day descendant of the last khan of Karabakh, is a major general in the special forces of the Azerbaijani armed forces. He participated in both the short, inconclusive Nagorno-Karabakh conflict of 2016 and also the recent, more important one in 2020, where he led the Azerbaijani forces in the battle for Shusha. For his services, Zaur Mammadov was awarded Hero of the Patriotic War on December 9, 2020. This is the highest honorary title in Azerbaijan. After the war, he was also appointed the first commandant of Shusha and marched with the victory flag that had been hoisted in Shusha in the subsequent victory parade in Baku.

Russian Rule

In 1813, under the provisions of the Treaty of Gulistan ending the Russo-Persian War (1804–1813), the Russians formally replaced the Persians as Karabakh's rulers. (The remainder of Transcaucasia fell under Russian rule in 1828 according to the provisions of the Treaty of Turkmenchai that followed the Russo-Persian War of 1826–1828.) Under Russian rule, Karabakh constituted approximately 13,600 square kilometers or 5,250 square miles. Its demographic composition has been open to much controversy and political manipulation. In addition, the changing administrative boundaries often make a direct comparison between ethnographic data from different time periods especially difficult. Furthermore, the population could be highly volatile because the nomad population would alter its grazing grounds due to war or famine, while even the sedentary populace might move because of raids, taxation, or disease. For example, in the first decade of Russian rule, Armenian immigration from Iran occurred. Thus, the numerical size and ethnographic composition could vary noticeably from year to year.

These changing, at times even conflicting, population figures were reflected by the following demographic data. In 1823, the Russians conducted an initial survey that counted the number of villages, but not people, for taxation purposes. According to the Russian census figures in 1823, the Armenian population in Karabakh represented just 9% (the Muslims 91%), but then grew to 35% in 1832, and constituted a majority of 53% by 1880.[15] However, an official census published in 1836 listed Mountainous (Nagorny) or Highland Karabagh as almost entirely Armenian,[16] while the population of the larger, former khanate, which included Lowland Karabakh, was mainly Muslim.[17] It should be noted that these censuses and surveys were taken in the winter and so did not count as inhabiting Nagorno-Karabakh thousands of Tartar (Azerbaijani) nomads who lived in the lowlands during the winter and then migrated to Mountainous (Nagorny) Karabakh for summer pastures.[18] What is more, these seasonal Tartar migrations contributed to conflicts with sedentary Armenians. The Russian imperial census of 1897 showed that the population of the Shusha *uezd* (district) that largely corresponded to Karabakh totaled 138,771, with the Armenians at 73,953 and the Azerbaijani Turks at 62,868. Russians accounted for a much smaller 1,504.[19]

In 1822, Russia abolished the Karabakh khanate in an apparent attempt to alter old loyalties and supposedly create new, more modern, pro-Russian ones. Karabakh was initially absorbed in the Kaspijskaya oblast, and then in 1846 constituted a portion of the Shemakha governorate. In 1876, Karabakh became part of the Elisabethpol governorate. This final administrative arrangement held until the Russian Empire collapsed in 1917.

Shusha—called the "Jerusalem of Karabakh"—was Karabakh's main city. Indeed, throughout Transcaucasia only Tiflis, Erevan, and Baku possibly surpassed it in importance. Thomas de Waal explains that Shusha was "not only a strategic fortress ... but also a place saturated with history ... as well, the cradle of Azerbaijan's music and poetry, the home of poets like Vagif and Natevan."[20] On the other hand, the city also had served as the center of one of the five, semi-independent, Armenian principalities mentioned above (Varanda) into the eighteenth century. As such it also had religious and strategic importance for the Armenians, housing the Ghazanchetsots Cathedral as well as the church of Kanach Zham, among others.[21]

During much of the nineteenth century, Shusha was one of Caucasia's most important and prosperous cities. George Keppel, a British aristocrat who visited the city in 1824, remembered, "The town is built on a huge mass of sloping rock of great height."[22] Three-quarters of the population were Azerbaijanis, while one-quarter were Armenians, making it confusingly an Azerbaijani majority within an Armenian majority within an overall Azerbaijani majority. "The language is a dialect of the Turkish; but the inhabitants, with the exception of the Armenians, generally read and write Persian."[23] Thomas de Waal cites the local Armenian archbishop Parkev that in the late nineteenth-century Shusha "had had forty thousand residents, six churches, two mosques and twenty newspapers."[24] More precise figures show that in 1886, the total population was 26,806 (15,188 Armenians and 11,595 Tatars/Azeribaijanis, a strong reversal of the ethnic percentages in the century's first decades). In the census of 1897, the number had slightly fallen from a decade earlier to a total of 25,881 (14,436 Armenians and 10,785 Tatars).[25] Nevertheless, under

Russian rule, the population in Transcaucasia nearly doubled between 1851 and 1897.

Communal, ethnic, and nationalist tensions rose as the nineteenth century wore on due in part to economic, geographic, and demographic changes both sides perceived as threatening.[26] The oil boom in Baku, competition for territorial rights and ownership, and population changes were specific examples. "Massive eruptions of violence in the form of mutual intercommunal massacres began with the 1905 Russian Revolution, and would reemerge each time the Russian state was in a condition of crisis or overhaul."[27] Both sides bore responsibility for "the 1905–6 ethnic clashes … known as the Armeno-Tatar war…. These serious episodes of conflict would leave bitter residues in both peoples' memories."[28] "With retaliation and counter-retaliation, the Armeno-Tatar War lasted until the Spring of 1906, involving approximately two hundred thousand people and leaving a trail of ruin, epidemic, and famine."[29] Indeed, "the atrocities of 1905–6 between the Armenians and the Azerbaijanis marked one of the important stages of their national consciousness."[30] Shusha never recovered from the violence and destruction that occurred with the collapse of tsarist rule. In 1926, its population was only 5,104 with just 93 Armenians remaining.[31] By 1959, the numbers had only grown to 6,117. In 2021, because of the fighting that had occurred with the end of the Soviet Union and then again in 2020, the city lay mostly in ruins and had seen its population decline to maybe 2,000. However, by the time the two authors of this book visited the city in April 2022, they saw reconstruction and revival. The famous Armenian Ghazanchetsots Cathedral was covered in scaffolding and undergoing controversial reconstruction.

Soviet Rule

Ethnic fighting broke out between the newly established republics of Armenia and Azerbaijan following the collapse of the tsarist Russian Empire in 1917 and failure of a Transcaucasian Federation. Initially, Ottoman troops invaded the region and even occupied Baku. British forces briefly followed. Both proved greatly over stretched and were soon withdrawn. The continuing, chaotic vacuum facilitated several short wars between Armenia and Azerbaijan over various regions including Karabakh as well as the eventual Bolshevik/Soviet conquest.[32]

Some argue that the current conflict over Nagorno-Karabakh stems in part from the notorious divide-and-rule decisions made by Joseph Stalin, who was the commissar of nationalities for the Bolshevik regime at the time. "By placing the region within the borders of Azerbaijan, the Armenian inhabitants could be used as potential 'hostages' to ensure the Armenian SSR's cooperation with the wishes of the Soviet leadership. By the same token, an 'autonomous' Armenian enclave within Azerbaijan could serve as a potential pro-Soviet fifth column in the event of disloyalty by the Azerbaijanis."[33] Although the future Soviet dictator later became infamous for his general manipulation of Russia's prison of nations and did play a role in regard to Karabakh, the evidence indicates that others on the Bolshevik Kavburo (Caucasian Bureau)[34] were probably the main decision-makers at the time. They operated according to more opportunistic reasons of immediate necessary compromise to facilitate hotly challenged Bolshevik rule and less from carefully crafted thoughts of diabolically playing the competing sides off against each other.[35] Moreover, as already illustrated above, the seeds of the conflict actually preexisted from centuries past. The Bolsheviks were just the latest and not the final overseers.

In July 1918, the Armenian assembly in Nagorno-Karabakh declared the region self-governing and created a national council and government. However, the British who were temporarily occupying Karabakh provisionally accepted Khosrov Bey (Bek) Sultanov, who had been chosen by the Azerbaijani government as the governor-general, pending a final decision by the Paris Peace Conference dealing with the results of World War I. The Armenians responded by declaring union with Armenia. In April 1920, while what there was of an Azerbaijani army was focused on battle against Armenian forces in Karabakh, the Bolsheviks entered Azerbaijan and easily established their rule, which they then extended to Armenia and Georgia after much back-and-forth fighting. To facilitate their victory, the Bolsheviks finally decided, as one of their many tactics, that Karabakh should remain within Azerbaijan, while giving the Armenians in Karabakh autonomy.

Economic geography probably also played a role since the mountains to the west where Armenia lay made Nagorno-Karabakh largely inaccessible from Armenia, while access from Azerbaijan to the east was much easier. Indeed, there was no direct road capable of wheeled transport connecting Armenia with Karabakh. It was quicker to travel from Erevan to Karabakh via Georgia and Azerbaijan than to cross the mountains of

Zangezur. Not until the mid-1920s was there even a road linking Armenia with Zangezur. Cart transport had to traverse the Azerbaijani exclave of Nakhichevan. In contrast, Baku enjoyed relatively convenient contact with Nagorno-Karabakh. The journey by railway and then along a paved road to Shusha took only two days. "Mountainous Karabagh was indisputably tied economically to Azerbaijan."[36] Thus, to circumvent accusations of bourgeoise nationalism, the ultimate, Marxist decision-makers could employ more ideologically sound economic and administrative efficacy rationales for keeping Karabakh part of Azerbaijan.

When the Bolsheviks officially proclaimed the Autonomous Oblast of Nagorno-Karabakh (AONK)[37] in 1923, with borders drawn to include Armenian villages and exclude Azerbaijani ones as much as possible, the oblast covered an area of 4,338 square kilometers and spread for 120 kilometers from north to south and 35–60 kilometers from east to west.[38] It had a population of 131,500, 94.4% Armenian and only 5.6 Azerbaijani or 7,400 people. By 1979, the population of Nagorno-Karabakh had only increased to 162,000, but the Azerbaijanis now accounted for 22.8% or 37,000.[39] In early 1987, there were 133,200 Armenians in the region (down to 74%) and 43,900 Azeris (up to 24.4%).[40] These figures illustrate that the percentages were increasing disproportionately in favor of the Azerbaijanis. Between 1959 and 1970 the Azerbaijani percentage increased by 37%, while the Armenian only by 1.6%. The more recent faster Armenian growth from 1979 to 1989 probably reflects the flight of Azerbaijani refugees when conflict began in the late 1980s. These changing numbers probably contributed to tensions as perceptive Armenians and Azerbaijanis could foresee the possible, eventual loss of the Armenian majority and, therefore, even the demise of its autonomous status due to the faster growth in the Azerbaijani population. What will the Azerbaijani victory in the war of 2020 bring?

Further Analysis of Soviet Rule

With this brief introduction to Soviet rule and how this affected Karabakh, what follows is a more detailed analysis of how this occurred. After the Bolsheviks reintegrated Transcaucasia into Russia by early February 1921, they quickly settled their external borders with Turkey under the provisions of the Moscow Treaty of March 16, 1921. (Interestingly, this agreement actually allowed Turkey, one of the losers of World

War I, to regain Kars and Ardahan, some of the territory it had lost in its war against Russia, in 1877–1878.)

However, the internal boundaries within Transcaucasia proved a much more difficult kettle of fish. The Kavburo naively had assumed that Armenia and Azerbaijan, as well as Georgia, would quickly reach an accommodation since they were now controlled by "fraternal" Bolshevik leaders. Interestingly, out of the huge welter of nationalities in the Soviet Union, only a few bore the prestigious appellation "titular nation" in reference to their sharing their ethnic name with that of their republic's. (The Armenians in the Armenian Soviet Socialist Republic (SSR) and Azerbaijanis in the Azerbaijani SSR were two of what eventually became only 15 titular nations.) However, illustrating the Marxist failure to appreciate the power of nationalism, the Tiflis (today's Tbilisi) conference called to draw these internal boundary lines failed miserably. On the other hand, Marxism's emphasis on conflict being inherent, undoubtedly corresponded more to reality and thus helped the Bolsheviks eventually overcome the opposition and implement their rule.

In the early 1920s, the Bolsheviks often seemed hopelessly weak and outnumbered in Transcaucasia. The Red Army lacked sufficient resources fully to control those areas it occupied. Thus, numerous anti-Bolshevik uprisings occurred despite the Red Army's initial victories. For example, rebellions took place in the Azerbaijani town of Ganja in May 1920 and then Shusha, followed by Zakatala in northwestern Azerbaijan the following month. In October 1920, the Zangezur region in what is now southeastern Armenia rebelled. Further revolts broke out in Armenia and southern Karabakh in February–April 1921. Only the divisions among their enemies and their revolutionary zeal allowed the Bolsheviks to persevere. To do so, however, they had to follow a policy of tactical short-term promises and concessions to the Armenians and Azerbaijanis to win their support. This led to inconsistency and confusion, altering decisions regarding the same issue on various occasions. The Armenian and Azerbaijanis often were able to take advantage of this weakness by trying to use Moscow against each other. Thus, the Kavburo was unable readily to implement its preferences, often becoming ensnared in its own contradictory promises to the two hostile sides.

In general, the Bolsheviks had two possible choices: approve the existing boundaries that included minorities of the one in the other's republic (in effect the international law principle of uti possiditis meaning that the old existing administrative boundaries would remain the new legal boundaries within the Bolshevik state, a principle closely related to the concept of territorial integrity) or redraw the borders so that the two ethnic groups each would inhabit its respective ethnic republic (in effect the principle of self-determination). The first choice would please Azerbaijan, but alienate the minority (in the case of Karabakh, the Armenian majority living there as a minority within Azerbaijan), while the second choice would satisfy the minority by joining it to its kin-ethnic republic, in this case, Armenia. Back and forth swung the proposed, opportunistic offers according to which seemed best at the moment for Bolshevik rule.

Thus, after initially Sovietizing Azerbaijan, the Bolsheviks strongly supported the Azerbaijani claim in an attempt to maintain their support. However, when the Bolsheviks were incorporating Armenia in December 1920, they impelled the Azerbaijanis to relinquish their claims over Karabakh. Then in May 1921, the Bolsheviks declared that Karabakh would be given to Armenia to undermine anti-Soviet resistance in Zangezur located in the southeast of today's Armenia. (The Bolsheviks used similar tactics in Abhazia and South Ossetia, smaller nations within the Georgian SSR. Russia and Georgia eventually fought a short war over this issue in 2008.) The political decision on Nagorno-Karabakh was finally made after a heated Kavburo session on July 5, 1921. By this time, the Bolsheviks had virtually completed their conquest of Zangezur, so there was no longer any reason to appease Armenia in a "war of laws" with insincere promises over ownership of Nagorno-Karabakh. Even so, political struggles continued between Armenian and Azerbaijani Bolsheviks within the now required Marxist ideological guidelines. The Armenians sought autonomy for Karabakh, while the Azerbaijanis argued that this was unnecessary. Thus, the formal declaration was only issued in June 1923 and the legal status and borders drawn in 1924–1925. The capital was moved from Shusha to Khankendi located just six miles to the east. The latter town's name was changed to Stepanakert to honor Stepan Shahumian, an Armenian Bolshevik from Baku, whom the Azerbaijanis claim led the killing of thousands of their kin during the March massacre of 1918.[41]

Given the problems getting to this point, Nagorno-Karabakh was the final region in Transcaucasia to obtain some type of official autonomy. Its designation of autonomous *oblast* (region) was lower than that of Soviet Socialist Republic (SSR) or Autonomous Soviet Socialist Republic (ASSR).[42] Nevertheless, Nagorno-Karabakh was the only autonomous area in the Soviet Union that had an ethnic-kin SSR (the Armenian SSR) to take up its interests at the highest possible levels in Moscow. This situation undoubtedly grated on the sensibilities of the Azerbaijan SSR, especially since the Azerbaijani minority within Armenia (and the Georgian SSR too) did not enjoy such status and rights. The eventual solution to grant the Armenians in Karabakh a low grade of autonomy within Azerbaijan only worked because of ultimate Soviet power that enforced it. When this declined in the late 1980s, the divisive autonomy solution of mines buried in the early 1920s quickly began to explode.

There are several differing interpretations of these earlier years that affected the Karabakh decision. Richard Pipes explained the Bolshevik success by their skillful manipulation of the nationality question to their own advantage. Their promises to minority groups were merely opportunistic ploys to win support, but never intended for implementation.[43] Thus, the Soviet autonomous nationality territories were merely nationalist in form, but socialist (i.e. Soviet) in content. The ultimate goal was for nationality to wither away and be replaced by Soviet identity. This, of course, did not occur, the fate of Karabakh being a prime example.

On the other hand, Ronald Suny suggested that the Soviet Union purposely recognized or even created genuine nationalities along its periphery for the ideological belief that they would speed up the advance of socialism but then naturally disappear.[44] Indeed, the steady official decline of Soviet ethnic groups from nearly 200 in 1926 to only 90 by 1979 presented evidence of the intended, natural assimilationist processes. The *korenizatsiaa* (indigenizaion or nativization) policy of affirmative action to develop national cultures and celebrate the ethnic diversity of minority groups waxed in the 1920s, but was dropped from the Soviet vocabulary by the 1930s. A new, over-arching Soviet citizen was supposedly replacing the earlier, increasingly irrelevant nationalities.

Svante Cornell offers yet another interpretation of the Bolshevik's intentions when he ironically argues that the very presence of autonomy that was supposed to forestall conflict in Karabakh instead fostered it.[45] This is because autonomous institutions like the Armenians had in Karabakh, strengthened their national identity and provided them with actual, state-like structures that could be and were used against the host republic, Azerbaijan, when Soviet power declined. Other more seemingly explanatory variables like cultural differences, ethnic national conceptions, earlier conflicts, myths about origin, difficult geographical terrain, relative demographic differences, existence of ethnic kin, economic viability, radical leadership, and external support proved less significant.

Interestingly, there were two autonomous regions in Transcaucasia not based on ethnicity. The Ajarian Autonomous Socialist Republic (ASSR) in southwest Georgia and the Nakhichevan ASSR exclave of Azerbaijan were created as a compromise with Turkey, who also had territorial claims on them, on the condition they were given autonomy. On the other hand, there were several large ethnic minority groups that were not given any autonomy status. Some of them had populations larger than smaller groups that did receive autonomy. The final Soviet census, for example, revealed that there were 123,987 Armenians and 307,556 Azerbaijanis, each settled rather distinctly as a unit in Georgia; 84,860 Azerbaijanis living in Armenia; and 171,395 Lezgins, 44,072 Avars, and 21,169 Talsyh inhabiting Azerbaijan.[46] Although some of them had grievances against their host republics, their absence of political autonomy might help explain their inability to initiate secessionist movements. Of course, the main reason the Bolsheviks did not give these groups autonomy in the first place was their lack of violence during the Sovietization process in the early 1920s.

Conclusion

This is a brief historical introduction to the ethnic conflict in Karabakh. It provides total vindication for neither side, but explanation for why each side maintains its continuing emotionally vested interest in the region's future. As George A. Bournoutian observed, "Unfortunately ... partisans of both sides produced polemical studies affirming their historical claims to the region."[47] Thus, we now are able to move forward to understanding better more recent events such as the two major wars between Armenia and Azerbaijan over Karabakh in the early 1990s and in 2020, along with the knowledge why ultimate compromise has been so difficult although necessary if the participants are ever to reach a solution that satisfies both.

Notes

1. For background on Karabakh, see Svante E. Cornell, *The Nagorno-Karabakh Conflict*, Report no. 46, Department of East European Studies, Uppsala University, Sweden, 1999; Thomas de Waal, *Black Garden:*

Armenia and Azerbaijan Through Peace and War (New York: New York University Press, 2003); Gerard J. Libaridian, ed., *The Karabakh File: Documents and Facts on the Question of Mountainous Karabakh, 1918–1988* (Cambridge: Zoryan Institute, 1988); and Thomas Goltz, *Azerbaijan Dairy: A Rogue Reporter's Adventures in an Oil-rich, War-torn, Post-Soviet Republic* (Armonk, NY: M.E. Sharpe Press, 1998). More recently, see Michael Kambeck and Sargis Ghazaryan, eds., *Europe's Next Avoidable War: Nagorno-Karabakh* (New York: Palgrave Macmillan, 2013); Ohannes Geukjian, *Ethnicity, Nationalism and Conflict in the South Caucasus: Nagorno-Karabakh and the Legacy of Soviet Nationalities Policy* (Farnham, England and Burlington, VT: Ashgate, 2012); and Arsene Saparov, *From Conflict to Autonomy in the Caucasus: The Soviet Union and the Making of Abkhazia, South Ossetia and Nagorno Karabakh* (London and New York: Routledge, 2015). More recently since the Second Karabakh War in 2020, see M. Hakan Yavuz and Michael M. Gunter, eds., *The Nagorno-Karabakh Conflict: Historical and Political Perspectives* (London and New York; Routledge, 2023); Fariz Ismailzade and Damjan Krnjevic Miskovic, eds., *Liberated Karabakh: Policy Perspectives by the ADA University Community* (Baku, Azerbaijan: ADA University Press, 2021); and M. Hakan Yavuz and Vasif Huseynov, "The Second Karabakh War: Russia vs. Turkey?" *Middle East Journal* 27 (Winter 2020), pp. 103–118.
2. Stephen Witt, "The Turkish Drone That Changed the Nature of Warfare," *The New Yorker*, May 9, 2022, https://www.newyorker.com/magazine/2022/05/16/the-turkish-drone-that-changed-the-nature-of-warfare?utm_source=nl&utm_brand=tny&utm_mailin, accessed May 9, 2022; Ash Rossiter and Brendon J. Cannon, "Turkey's Rise as a Drone Power: Trial by Fire," *Defense and Security Analysis*, https://doi.org/10.1080/14751798.2022.2068562, Routledge, published online May 4, 2022, pp. 8–9; and Robyn Dixon, "Azerbaijan's Drones Owned the Battlefield in Nagorno-Karabakh—And Showed Future of Warfare," *Washington Post*, October 11, 2020, among others.
3. Uzi Rubin, "The Second Nagorno-Karabakh War: A Milestone in Military Affairs" (Tel Aviv: Begin-Sadat Center for Strategic Studies, 2020), p. 5.
4. Ibid., p. 4.
5. Ernest Gellner, *Nations and Nationalism*, 2nd ed. (Blackwell Publishing, 2008), p. 2. In words that seem to have been written precisely for Karabakh and already mentioned above in the Introduction to this book, Gellner continues, "This argument is further and immeasurably strengthened by the fact that very many of the potential nations of this world live … not in compact territorial units but intermixed with each other in complex patterns. It follows that a territorial political unit can only become

ethnically homogeneous, in such cases, if it either kills, or expels, or assimilates all non-nationals. Their unwillingness to suffer such fates may make the peaceful implementation of the nationalist principle difficult." Ibid.
6. The ancient and now assimilated Caucasian Albanians and Iberians, who have nothing to do with their spurious namesakes in Europe to the west, add to the mixed, ethnic confusion. A further example of the controversy this subject can engender is revealed by the obsolete and misleading term Caucasian as a synonym for the entire White race.
7. On these figures, see by Robert H. Hewsen, "The Meliks of Eastern Armenia: A Preliminary Study," *Revue des etudes Armeniennes* NS: IX (1970), p. 288; and *Armenia: A Historical Atlas* (Chicago: The University of Chicago Press, 2001), p. 264.
8. More precisely, Artsakh refers to Upper or Mountainous Karabakh, while Utik denotes lower Karabakh. See Geukjian, *Ethnicity, Nationalism and Conflict in the South Caucasus*, p. 33.
9. For background, see by Robert H. Hewsen, *Armenia: A Historical Atlas*; and "Ethno-History and the Armenian Influence upon the Caucasian Albanians," in Thomas J. Samuelian, ed., *Classical Armenian Culture: Influences and Creativity* (Chicago: Scholars Press, 1982), pp. 27–40; Stephan H. Astourian, "In Search of their Forefathers: National Identity and the Historiography and Politics of the Armenian and Azerbaijani Ethnogenesis," in Donald V. Schwartz and Rezmik Panossian, eds., *Nationalism and History: The Politics of Nation-Building in Post-Soviet Armenia, Azerbaijan and Georgia* (Toronto: University of Toronto Press, 1994), pp. 43–45; Khachig Tololyan, "National Self-Determination and the Limits of Sovereignty: Armenia, Azerbaijan, and the Secession of Nagorno-Karabakh," *Nationalism and Ethnic Politics* 1 (Spring 1995), pp. 86–110; David M. Lang, *Armenia: Cradle of Civilization* (London: George Allen and Unwin, 1970); and for an Armenian view of the history of Karabakh, see Levon Chorbajian, Patrick Donabedian, and Claude Mutafian, *The Caucasian Knot: The History and Geopolitics of Nagorno-Karabagh* (London and New Jersey: Zed Books, 1994), pp. 51–108.
10. Before the twentieth century, today's Azerbaijanis (Azeris) were simply referred to as Tatars or Muslims.
11. For a discussion on the origins of the Azerbaijani Turks, see Audrey L. Altstadt, *The Azerbaijani Turks: Power and Identity Under Russian Rule* (Stanford, CA: Hoover Institution Press, 1992), pp. 1–26. Also see Peter B. Golden, "The Turkic Peoples and Caucasia," in Ronald Grigor Suny, ed., *Transcaucasia: Nationalism and Social Change*, rev. ed. (Ann Arbor: University of Michigan, 1996), pp. 45–67; Charles van der Leeuw, *Azerbaijan: A Quest for Identity: A Short History* (London: Curzon Press, 2000); Tamara Dragadze, *Azerbaijan* (London: Melisende, 2000); and

Suha Bolukbasi, *Azerbaijan: A Political History* (London and New York: I.B. Tauris, 2001). Altstadt places "Turkicization" as occurring "during the 4th to 6th centuries." *Azerbaijani Turks*, p. 173. Others would argue that linguistic Turkification occurred gradually and later. R.N. Frye, "Iran v. Peoples of Iran (1) A General Survey," *Encyclopaedia Iranica*, XIII/3, pp. 321–326.

12. Geukjian, *Ethnicity, Nationalism and Conflict in the South Caucasus*, pp. 17–36 provides a good overview of the Armenian and Azerbaijani ethnic past and myths of ethnogenesis.
13. For background, see Robert H. Hewsen, "The Meliks of Arc'ax," in Thomas J. Samuelian and Michael E. Stone, eds., *Armenian Texts and Studies* (Chico, CA: Scholars Press, 1984), pp. 52–53.
14. For background, see Muriel Atkin, "The Strange Death of Ibrahim Khalil Khan of Qarabagh," *Iranian Studies* 12, No. 1/2 (Winter/Spring 1979), pp. 79–107.
15. Svante E. Cornell, *The Nagorno-Karabakh Conflict* Report no. 46, Department of East European Studies, Upplala University, Sweden, 1999, p. 5.
16. George Bournoutian, "The Politics of Demography: Misuse of Sources on the Armenian Population of Mountainous Karabakh," *Journal of the Society for Armenian Studies* 9 (1996–1997), pp. 99–103.
17. Svante Cornell, *Small Nations and Great Powers: A Study of Ethnopolitical Conflict in the Caucasus* (Richmond, Surrey, England: Curzon, 2001), p. 54. One Russian survey of 1832 listed for the entire population of Karabakh, 64.8% Azerbaijanis and only 34.8% Armenian. Altstadt, *The Azerbaijani Turks*, p. 293/n. 20. Also see by George Bournoutian—cited just above for listing a large Armenian majority in Nagorno-Karabakh—an Azerbaijani majority for the entire population of Karabakh. "The Ethnic Composition of and Socio-Economic Condition of Eastern Armenia in the First Half of the Nineteenth Century," in Suny, ed., *Transcaucasia: Nationalism and Social Change*.
18. For further population figures, see Anatoly N. Yamskov, "Ethnic Conflict in the Transcaucasus: The Case of Nagorno-Karabakh," *Theory and Society* 20:5 (October 1991), pp. 644–653.
19. See Table 3.1 in Altstadt, *The Azerbaijani Turks*, p. 30.
20. Thomas de Waal, *Black Garden: Armenia and Azerbaijan Through Peace and War* (New York: New York University Press, 2003), p. 185.
21. For background, see George A. Bournoutian, *Armenians and Russia, 1626–1796: A Documentary Record* (Costa Mesa, CA: Mazda Publishers, 2001). "The retention of the mountain fortress is a guarantee of their security—and almost no Armenians will countenance the return of Shusha's Azerbaijani inhabitants in an eventual peace deal." De Wall, *Black Garden*, p. 185. Unfortunately, in their zeal to control the city, both

ethnic groups have largely laid waste to each other's achievements and heritage.
22. George Keppel, *Personal Narrative of a Journey from India to England* (London: Henry Colburn, 1827), p. 188; as reprinted by Elibron Classics replica edition, 2005.
23. Ibid., p. 194.
24. De Waal, *Black Garden*, p. 193. However, the Armenian-Tartar war in 1905, followed by the wars in 1920, 1992, and 2020 laid much to waste.
25. These statistics were garnered from Arsene Saparov, *From Conflict to Autonomy in the Caucasus: The Soviet Union and the Making of Abkhazia, South Ossetia and Nagorno Karabakh* (New York: Routledge, 2015), p. 112/n. 8.
26. For background, see Firuz Kazemzadeh, *The Struggle for Transcaucasia (1917–1921)* (Birmingham: Templar Press, 1951). For general background, see Donald L. Horowitz, *Ethnic Groups in Conflict* (Berkeley: University of California Press, 1985).
27. Tadeusz Swietochowski, "The Problem of Nagorno-Karabakh: Geography Versus Demography Under Colonialism and in Decolonization," in Hafeez Malik, ed., *Central Asia* (Basingstoke: MacMillan, 1994), p. 145. See also Nigar Gozalova and Eldar Amirov, eds., *Armenian-Azerbaijani Conflict of 1905–1906 According to "The New York Times" Coverage* (Baku, Azerbaijan: Elm, 2021); and Nigar Gozalova and Eldar Amirov, "The South Caucasus in 1905–1906 According to "The New York Times" Coverage," *Review of Armenian Studies*, Issue 43 (2021), pp. 83–108.
28. Geukjian, *Ethnicity, Nationalism and Conflict in the South Caucasus*, p. 45.
29. Anahide Ter Minassian, "The Revolution of 1905 in Transcaucasia," *Armenian Review* 42 (Summer 1989), p. 11.
30. Geukjian, *Ethnicity, Nationalism and Conflict in the South Caucasus*, p. 46. Also see Kazemzadeh, *Struggle for Transcaucasia*, pp. 18–19. The Muslim-Armenian massacres in the Ottoman Empire during World War I—deemed genocide by the Armenians—further contributed to these ethnic animosities. However, further analysis of these events is beyond the scope of the present analysis.
31. These statistics were listed in Saparov, *From Conflict to Autonomy in the Caucasus*, p. 112/n. 8.
32. For background, see Saparov, *From Conflict to Autonomy in the Caucasus*; Jamil Hasanli, *The Sovietization of Azerbaijan: The South Caucasus in the Triangle of Russia, Turkey, and Iran, 1920–1922* (Salt Lake City: University of Utah Press, 2018); and by Richard G. Hovannisian, *Armenia on the Road to Independence, 1918* (Berkeley: University of California, 1967); *The Republic of Armenia: The First Year, 1918–1919*, Vol. I (Berkeley: University of California Press, 1971; *The Republic of Armenia:*

From Versailles to London, 1919–1920, Vol. II (Berkeley: University of California Press, 1982); and *The Republic of Armenia: From London to Sevres, February–August 1920*, Vol. III (Berkeley: University of California, 1996). In addition, see Nigar Gozalova, "Massacre of the Azerbaijani Turkic Population (1918–1920) According to the Documents of the British Diplomats," *International Crimes and History*, Issue 18 (2017), pp. 37–53.

33. Michael P. Croissant, *The Armenia-Azerbaijan Conflict: Causes and Implications* (Westport, CT: Praeger, 1998), pp. 19–20. Also see Caroline Cox and John Eibner, *Ethnic Cleansing in Progress: War in Nagorno-Karabakh* (London: Institute for Religious Minorities in the Islamic World, 1993), p. 31; and Cornell, *Nagorno-Karabakh Conflict*, pp. 8–9, who claims that "Stalin's tendency to divide the Caucasian peoples to prevent unified resistance … must have been welcome." Geukjian speculates, "Perhaps Stalin aimed to leave Armenia and Azerbaijan volatile in order to frustrate their potential challenges to Soviet authority," adding, "Apparently, they had created enclaves within Armenia and Azerbaijan capable of generating ethnic strife in the future if any possible ethnic tension was caused by economic and cultural deprivation by the dominant nationality." *Ethnicity, Nationalism and Conflict in the South Caucasus*, p. 76. See also, Nigar Gozalova, "The Karabakh Issue in Relation with Armenia and Azerbaijan (1918–1920)," *AVIM Conference Book*, No. 24 (2019), pp. 37–53.
34. The Caucasian Bureau was created on April 8, 1920 to represent the Central Committee of the Russian Communist Party (Bolsheviks) as the Bolsheviks' primary policy and decision-making organ in the Caucasus. Its members included Sergo Ordzhonikidze, Sergei Kirov, Amayak Nazarpetian, Mamia Orakhalashvili, Ivan Smilga, and, subsequently, Joseph Stalin, among others.
35. Stalin's original absence from Kavburo membership seemingly supports this later interpretation as do official records. See the discussion by Saparov, *From Conflict to Autonomy in the Caucasus*, pp. 90–114 and 125–137.
36. On this important point, see Hasanli, *The Sovietization of Azerbaijan*, p. 144. See also Saparov, *From Conflict to Autonomy in the Caucasus*, pp. 91, 123.
37. The name was changed to Nagorno-Karabakh Autonomous Oblast (NKAO) in 1937.
38. Hratch Tchilingurian, "Nagorno-Karabakh: Transition and Elite," *Central Asian Survey* 18:4 (1999), p. 435. Nagorno-Karabakh was divided into five administrative areas: Martakert, Martuni, Shusha (Shushi), Hadrut, and Askeran.
39. These figures were taken from A. N. Yamskov, "Ethnic Conflict in the Transcausasus [sic]: The Case of Nagorno-Karabakh," *Theory and Society*

20:5 (October 1991), p. 644. These numbers appear reasonably accurate as Yamskov gathered them from various Soviet sources. For slightly different figures, see Table 7.2 in Saparov, *From Conflict to Autonomy in the Caucasus*, p. 163. This table shows that in 1926 the Armenians constituted 111,700 or 89.1% of the population, while the Azerbaijanis totaled 12,600 or 10.5%. In 1939 the percentages showed very little change, but by 1959 the now 110,053 Armenians had declined to 84.3%, while the now 17,995 Azerbaijanis had risen to 13.8%. These percentages kept changing so that by 1979, the Armenians were now down to 75.8% (still more than three times that of the Azerbaijanis it should be noted), while the increasing Azerbaijani percentage now stood at 22.9%.
40. Ibid., p. 645.
41. Yusif Gazıyev, "Karabakh in 1920–1980," *Virtual Karabakh*, 2009; as cited in "When Was the Nagorno-Karabakh Autonomous Oblast (NKAO) Created?" https://karabakh99.com/2020/10/31/when-was-the-nagorno-karabakh-autonomous-oblast-nkao-created/, accessed January 29, 2021.
42. An individual's ethnic nationality was listed in his/her internal passport. It was transmitted by descent and did not depend on place of residence. Rogers Brubaker, *Nationality Reframed: Nationhood and the National Question in the New Europe* (Cambridge: Cambridge University Press, 1996), p. 32. In this way, argued Brubaker, "the USSR inadvertently created a political field supremely conducive to nationalism." Ibid., p. 17. For further background on Soviet nationality policies, see Bohdan Nahaylo and Victor Swoboda, *Soviet Disunion: A History of the Nationalities Problem in the USSR* (New York: Hamish Hamilton, 1990); and Simon Gerhard, *Nationalism and Policy toward the Nationalities in the Soviet Union from Totalitarian Dictatorship to Post-Stalinist Society* (Boulder: Westview Press, 1991).
43. Richard Pipes, *The Formation of the Soviet Union: Communism and Nationalism, 1917–1923*, rev. ed. (Cambridge, MA: Harvard University Press, 1997).
44. Ronald G. Suny, *The Revenge of the Past: Nationalism, Revolution and the Collapse of the Soviet Union* (Stanford: Stanford University Press, 1993).
45. Svante E. Cornell, "Autonomy as a Source of Conflict: Caucasian Conflicts in Theoretical Perspective," *World Politics* 54:1 (January 2001), pp. 245–276.
46. For these figures, see Saparov, *From Conflict to Autonomy in the Caucasus*, p. 9.
47. George A. Bournoutian, *Two Chronicles on the History of Karabagh* (Costa Mesa, CA: Mazda Publishers, Inc., 2004), pp. ix–x.

CHAPTER 3

The Causes of the First Nagorno-Karabakh War

> Because of the Karabakh conflict, Armenians not only made themselves a servant of Russia, but they also made us Azerbaijanis hostage to Russian policies![1]
>
> In the Caucasus, Russia always relied on Armenians. Armenians, in return, always regarded Russia as their savior at the expense of their neighbors. Thus, both Georgians and Turks consider Armenians Russian agents.[2]

Azerbaijan is the most important state in the sub-regional system of the Caucasus, which borders the following three historical empires and their associated civilizations: Russian, Persian, and Ottoman.[3] Insofar as these three civilizations merge into one another in this region, their central trait remains diversity. Clashes among these three empires have also left a lasting legacy, which underpins contemporary regional conflicts and the existing patterns of relations. Just like the Balkans, the Caucasus thus remains a diverse amalgamation of ethnic and religious groups.

In the Caucasus, the twentieth century has been defined by the collapse of three major empires. The Russian empire first collapsed in 1917, and then in 1991 (as did the USSR); the Ottoman empire collapsed in 1920; and the Qajar state collapsed in 1924. Inasmuch as these imperial cultures mixed with one another in the Caucasus, their collapses also ensured that the region would remain riddled with external interventions throughout its history. With Russia having been the most influential of these three empires, it has also had the deepest penetration into this region.

Indeed, the Caucasus remains one of the most Russian penetrated sub-systems due to its internal fragmentation and ongoing ethnic and territorial conflicts. Russia has enjoyed a full monopoly on shaping the Caucasus borders, institutions, ethno-territorial boundaries, and elite political norms. This dominant Russian presence has always been a source of instability in the Caucasus; indeed, this instability has also allowed Russia to dominate the area. Since the collapse of the Soviet Union in 1991, Russia has imposed its will on the region by manipulating ethnic conflicts and through its "peacekeeping" role. The Russian legacy of local conflicts and interstate rivalries has been so deep that no other power has been capable of imposing its own will on any Caucasus state.

Armenians have usually remained pro-Russian—they have certainly been the most pro-Russian of the three regional nations—and were instrumental in expanding the Russian empire into the Caucasus. Even after the collapse of the Soviet Union in 1991, Armenia volunteered to host Russian military bases and asked Russia to help protect its external borders. Azerbaijan and Georgia, in contrast, used every opportunity to move toward the West and distance themselves from Russia.

While the Azerbaijanis and the Georgians have tended to regard Russia as a source of instability, the region failed to dodge top-down Sovietization. Within the Soviet system, both these nations were given the status of a republic; however, their ethnic identities had remained in direct conflict with socialism. Ethnic nationalism had thus become the most potent source of solidarity inside these republics. Once the Soviet Union became history, that ethnic nationalism morphed into a nation-state ideology and became the central ideology of legitimacy, a source of identity, and a motivating force for economic and social development inside these newly minted nation-states.

Due to their recent origins and mixed nature, each group has since taken an extreme nationalist position to prove the purity of its own identity. Given that the regional communities had consisted of more primordial rather than civic ties, a centralized state has been hard to take shape. The post-Soviet republics had to build themselves as distinct nations, states, and market economies. These three simultaneous transformations have not always been successful; people in the region are still dealing with the aftermath of the Soviet Union's collapse—the power vacuum it left behind—and other manifestations of Soviet legacy. In the case of the Karabakh conflict, the constructed collective memories about

3 THE CAUSES OF THE FIRST NAGORNO-KARABAKH WAR 35

the past still shape the identities of the concerned post-Soviet communities: The Armenian community especially seems trapped in its past and a trauma-based identity that it has adopted.

After examining Russia's dominant role in the making of nationalities and their political borders along with its current policy of maintaining its hegemony through a "peacekeeping" role, this chapter focuses on the following questions: What are the main theoretical approaches to explaining the causes of the Armenian separatist movement? How have ethnic Armenian entrepreneurs and nationalists contributed to the Karabakh conflict? What have been the effects of the First Karabakh War and the unfolding conflict generally on how Azerbaijan and Armenia respectively articulated themselves as nations and states? How did the Armenian depiction of Azerbaijanis as "backward, Oriental, Asiatic, Muslim, and Turk" shape the Karabakh conflict? How have these images helped Armenians ally themselves with the Orientalist discourses outside the region to rally the Christian public opinion to their cause? How did these images affect diplomacy intended to address the Nagorno-Karabakh issue? One must explore the role of modern Armenian nationalism as the main driver of the Karabakh conflict. I examine the ideological makeup of Armenian nationalism in the first section of this chapter.[4] In the second section, I discuss the key regional developments that unfolded through the 1987–1994 period to highlight the consequences of the First Karabakh War. The third and last part of this chapter briefly focuses on the cease-fire negotiations and agreements.

THE SOCIOPOLITICAL CAUSES OF THE KARABAKH CONFLICT

In order to grasp the causes of the Karabakh conflict, one must come to terms with the factors responsible for the Armenian separatist nationalist movement. I would argue that a weakened Soviet Union, the new political context of perestroika, and the rise of an Armenian political elite determined to compete for power with the old Armenian elite were the forces that fueled the Armenian separatist formulation of nationalism. A new layer of the Armenian elite, mostly ethnic entrepreneurs, used the Karabakh issue to gain political status and positions—and to whip up Armenian nationalism. Instead of focusing on improving their own political and economic conditions within Azerbaijan, these new ethnic

Armenian entrepreneurs chose to secede from Azerbaijan to become important political players in Armenia.

There are several competing approaches to explaining the Armenian separatist movement. In one approach, it is claimed that Turks and Armenians are ancient enemies; Armenians suffered at the hand of the Ottoman Turks; and that these two distinctive cultures—one Christian; the other, Islamic—are incompatible (which is also something that the second president of Armenia, Robert Kocharian, has regularly argued).[5] Those who take this "ancient hatred" approach to explaining the conflict find it natural for Armenians to demand separation from Azerbaijani Turks, owing to their negative history and their fear of being dominated by the latter. Edward Said has argued that societies tend to internalize identities for themselves in opposition to others.[6] Armenian nationalism also was articulated as the opposition to Turkish identity. As contributors to this articulation, emotive Armenian nationalists tend to dehumanize and demonize Turks as "enemy" and genocidal people. The "ancient hatred" approach has two key shortcomings: It lacks an explanation for what transforms dormant ethnic and cultural differences into an ethnic conflict; it overlooks the phases of peaceful coexistence of communities that sometimes conflict.

The second approach seeks to explain the Armenian separatist movement as the outcome of ethnic manipulation by regional elites for the sake of self-serving political mobilization. Armenian political leaders were willing to use force to unify Karabakh with Armenia—a course of action that they also viewed as an opportunity to magnify their status in Armenia. Karabakh's Armenian leaders would use the conflict to jump into Armenian politics as national leaders of Armenia. The two most recent presidents of Armenia were born in Karabakh and had been active in its secessionist movement. The factors of willingness and opportunity were there for the Armenian leadership to start the war.

The adherents of this approach argue that an emergent elite utilizes ethnic identity as an instrument to advance its own interest and gain access to political power.[7] Support for this approach can be found, for instance, in the following claims made by Kocharian in a public lecture he gave in Moscow:

> The Armenian pogroms in Sumgait and Baku, and the attempts at mass military deportation of Armenians from Karabakh in 1991-92 indicate the

impossibility for Armenians to live in Azerbaijan in general. We are talking about some sort of ethnic incompatibility."[8]

As one could see, instead of treating the political incidents he mentions above as a reaction to the separatist activities in Karabakh, Kocharian uses them as a justification for his own separatist claims. In the same lecture, he went on to say that "a nation [Armenians] that has survived genocide cannot allow it to repeat."[9] What Kocharian has expressed is a hatred rooted in an imagined historical grievance—given that Azerbaijanis had nothing to do with the events of 1915.

In making claims such as the above, Kocharian and others overlook historical diversity and nuance in that they equate Ottoman Turks to Azerbaijanis while referencing "genocide" (against Armenians). For Kocharian, this historical distortion is part of the ploy to justify the Armenian deportations of one million Azerbaijanis. Here, it should also be kept in mind that Kocharian and some Armenian historians tend to demonize Azerbaijanis as Turks, Muslims, and/or Orientals. Likewise, ethnic Armenian entrepreneurs seeking to control Armenia's politics tend to exaggerate the suffering of Armenians at the hand of Turks and subsequently perpetuate the conflict between the two republics. For instance, the Armenian elite of Karabakh used the nationalist card to bolster their own popularity and control of power in Yerevan as well as to delegitimize moderates within the Republic of Azerbaijan. Consider, for example, how Levon Ter-Petrosyan was sidelined and attacked as a weak nationalist and even accused of being a "Turcophile."

The third approach stresses the role of insecurity felt by Armenians in fueling the fires of their separatist nationalism. The adherents of this approach argue that the fear of being dominated by Azerbaijani Turks and an anxiety about being outnumbered by them (owing to their higher birthrate as well as Armenian out-migration) has contributed to intensifying Armenian separatism. Armenian nationalists also saw the turmoil in Moscow as an opportunity to carve away Azerbaijani territories to create their own independent state. As Armenians sought to increase their security by removing, even destroying, Azerbaijani communities from Armenia and Karabakh, they made Azerbaijanis insecure and anxious in their regard. Azerbaijani nationalism was mobilized by what they saw as Armenian atrocities. This action-reaction spiral, however, radicalized the situation, resulting in the destruction of Azerbaijani communities in their own ancient lands.[10] Altogether, Armenian militias—with the help of Armenian military forces—would end up occupying around 20 percent of Azerbaijani territories. Armenians thus enhanced their own security at the expense of that of the Azerbaijanis.[11]

The fourth approach identifies the social, economic, and political gap between the two groups as the cause of Armenians' ethnic mobilization in Karabakh.[12] Also known as "deprivation theory," this approach claims that when ethnic minorities experience sociopolitical marginalization and economic injustice, they become politically radicalized and mobilized against the majority.[13] Inside the framework of this approach, some Armenian as well as Russian scholars claim that Karabakh's Armenians have been culturally marginalized and economically deprived within (and by) Azerbaijan. But, empirical research surveys had always indicated that the Nagorno-Karabakh Autonomous Oblast's (NKAO's) Armenians enjoyed far higher living standards than the rest of Azerbaijan's citizens. Moreover, inside the Karabakh region, the Armenians had been in full control of their own education; free to perpetuate their culture; and in charge of their own local economy.

In reality, the critical factor in the formation of the Armenian separatist movement was the role of ethnic Armenian entrepreneurs and the instrumentalization of history by irredentist Armenian nationalism. Politically ambitious Armenian nationalist entrepreneurs—by cooperating with the new political elite in Yerevan—successfully promoted discontent and justified violence among Karabakh's ordinary Armenians, who believed that they were being marginalized by the Azerbaijanis.

Most publications on the Karabakh conflict promote the Armenian perspective by focusing on the conflict's historical origins. They do so presumably because Armenians themselves seek a historical justification for their claims. The Azerbaijani perspective has been reactive—as well as thin in intellectual substance—because Azerbaijanis are not part of a well-established academic diaspora. Moreover, the Azerbaijani perspective is usually expressed in Azerbaijan's native Turkish-language publications. Very few English-language publications let through Azerbaijani counter claims about the origins of the Karabakh conflict.[14]

The Armenian perspective is that the Karabakh region had been inhabited and controlled by Armenians until Stalin handed it over to Azerbaijan and the Soviet Union's close ties with Mustafa Kemal had set favorable ground for the Azerbaijani demands. Other grievances from the Armenian perspective include the following; Azerbaijan has neglected the NKAO's economic development; there has existed cultural discrimination historically against the region's Armenians; and, Azerbaijan has engaged in demographic manipulation to increase the Turkic makeup of the population.

Many Armenian politicians and scholars believe that it was Mustafa Kemal's friendship with Lenin—or Turkey's pressure on the Soviet Union—that compelled the Soviet Union to hand over Nakhchivan and Karabakh to Azerbaijan, and declare autonomy for Ajaria. Even some Armenian historians conclude, without any evidence, that it was its relationship with Turkey that led the Soviet Union "to give" Karabakh to Azerbaijan.[15] These historians argue that Karabakh's Armenians had never accepted that Soviet decision and have always struggled to join Armenia. In reality, though, the Soviet nationality policy determined administrative borders along ethnic lines—which it also set in place and sustained via ethnic identification. The NKAO's autonomy and its institutional framework both contributed to the formation and perpetuation of ethnic political consciousness—whereby "the Armenians" were made to feel different and retain a desire to unify with the Republic of Armenia.

A group of scholars—including Kaufmann—regard national narratives and symbolic myth complexes as the drivers of ethnic-focused conflicts.[16] In this theoretical framework, national narratives and symbolic elements are claimed to be mobilized to foment ethnic-focused conflicts. Jan Asmann usefully defines a national narrative as one that "tells us who 'we' are by telling the story of 'our' development, our past and our becoming."[17] This chapter draws on this framework in arguing that the Armenian national narrative is the main force behind the Karabakh conflict.

Armenia's national narrative is based on suffering and an expectation that the major world powers will help Armenians realize their national goals. Armenian identify themselves as the first Christian nation; they view themselves as a separate ethnicity with a distinctive language; and they claim to have a collective historical memory of genocide perpetrated against their ancestors by the Ottoman Turks. The Armenian Church has helped perpetuate this emotional-religious feeling of victimization. After the Second Karabakh War, Libaridian criticized this victim's identity and said:

After all, is not our history full of heroes and martyrs? Especially martyrs? Are we not blessed with the memory of the Vartanank Battle, when over a thousand fighters died and became martyrs? Did not our history and our Church tell us that it was acceptable to have young men killed, even though a thousand self-sacrifices do not amount to victory?[18]

The Armenian diaspora, too, appears to care less about the well-being of Armenia—say, its economic and social development—than the recognition of Armenian suffering at the hands of the Ottoman Turks as genocide. The Armenian diaspora has spent more money in the United States and Europe on rewriting Armenia's past rather than on writing its future.

By tying Armenian identity to "genocide"—and framing Azerbaijanis as the Ottoman Turks who caused that "genocide"—the Armenian national narrative has articulated its justification for rectifying that historical injustice against Armenians. Therefore, most Armenian nationalists reject Azerbaijani sovereignty over Karabakh and aim to absorb it into Armenia with the help of Russia.

"Azerbaijanis as Turks": The Karabakh Conflict as Continuing the 1915 "Genocide"

Razmik Panossian, a leading historian of modern Armenia, aptly sums up Karabakh's history:

> Administratively, NK had never been part of Armenia in modern history. Under the Tsarist empire it had been part of Baku province. The enclave was fought over by Armenia and Azerbaijan in the late 1910s and the early 1920s before the Sovietization of the two republics. In 1923, it was formally declared an autonomous oblast' within the Azerbaijani SSR. Armenians never fully accepted this decision, and repeatedly questioned the enclave's status, demanding its transfer to the Armenian SSR in 1929, 1935, 1963, 1966, 1977, and 1987.[19]

The current formulation of Armenian nationalism has had two goals: absorb Karabakh into Armenia, and recognize the events of 1915 as genocide.[20] Throughout the Soviet era, Karabakh's Armenians demanded that the region be united into Armenia on the grounds that they were being economically neglected, culturally discriminated against, and politically subdued by Azerbaijani leaders.[21] But when we take a look at the official website of Karabakh's Armenians, we come across an interesting factor in a claim made there: that Mikhail Gorbachev's perestroika was perceived by the people of Nagorno-Karabakh as "an opportunity to correct mistakes of the past."[22]

What could be these "mistakes of the past" that may have driven this conflict? A closer examination of archival documents and secondary literature shows that Armenian nationalism turned Karabakh into a "historic land of Armenians"—as if it were a part of Greater Armenia or *Miats'eal Hayastan*.[23] This nationalist emphasis on a Greater Armenia involves the notion of expanding Armenia's territories to those places where Armenians used to live or are currently living as a compact community; underpinned by the Armenian intellectualist ideal of *Hai Dat* or the Armenian Cause, this nationalist emphasis drives the Karabakh conflict.[24] *Hai Dat* stresses Armenians' suffering *qua* Christians and at the hands of Muslim Turks.[25] *Hai Dat* was incorporated into Armenia's Declaration of Independence in 1991[26]; the preamble to the Armenian constitution reiterates it. It is under the shadow of *Hai Dat* that Karabakh would also shape Armenia's foreign policy as well as domestic politics. When Armenia's Foreign Minister Vardan Oskanian announced the primacy of *Hai Dat*, he identified its three pillars as follows: recognizing the events of 1915 as genocide; restoring to Armenia those territories that were once inhabited by Armenians but are now in Turkey and Azerbaijan; and unifying Karabakh into Armenia on the grounds of self-determination given that Karabakh had always been populated and ruled by Armenians. Within this policy framework, Armenia, however, was required to act as "the strategic extension of Russia."[27] One could summarize it succinctly: Armenia cannot survive without Russia and therefore it must become the outpost of Russia against its eternal enemies (the Turks).

Marina Kurkchiyan adds some nuance to the above context about the Armenian–Russian relationship:

> The Armenian populations tended to regard the Russians as safer for them, whereas the local Muslims felt more secure when the laws were made by their co-religionists…In each territory conquered by the Tsarist army [in the Caucasus], Armenians would move in as the Muslims moved out, and vise-versa.[28]

Armenians became the guide for and a major supporter of Russian imperialist expansion into the Caucasus. In turn, they came to be viewed by anti-Russian locals as the fifth column of the Russian military.

On July 23, 2011, Serzh Sarkisian, then-president of Armenia, said the following in response to an Armenian student's question about the eventual return of Mount Ararat and Western Armenia, which are part of Turkey:

> It all depends on you and your generation. I believe my generation fulfilled its task when it was necessary in the early 1990s to defend a part of our homeland—Karabagh—from enemies. We were able to do that. Your generation should struggle to free western Armenia.[29]

Although some scholars have argued that perestroika allowed Karabakh's Armenians to publicly share their heretofore suppressed grievances, a close examination of relevant material and events indicates that the main goal was unification. This is supported by the fact that the Armenians refused Soviet offers of greater autonomy and development aid to Karabakh as a way out of secession.

Although they framed their desire to unify with Armenia by arguing that economic and political conditions of the NKAO were worse than those of Armenia, they were incorrect—because the NKAO had far higher living standards than Armenia. So, the nationalist goal of creating a Greater Armenia rather than the NKAO's uplift was the real driving force behind this secessionist movement—which goes back to the 1920s as reinforcing Armenian nationalism.

Suffering and Identity

According to Ronald Suny, the most prominent American-Armenian historian, Armenians consolidated themselves as a "unique, identifiable, ethno-religious community when they adopted an exclusive form of Monophysite Christianity and a common language in the fourth century A.D."[30] Following that historical experience, Armenians have tended to operate under the belief that they are an ancient people—the first Christian nation—who formed a series of independent states, and were at the gates to protect Christianity. They believe that they have suffered like Christ—and that, as Christians, they have been made to suffer at the hands of the Zoroastrian, the Arab Muslim, and the Mongol, followed by the Turk. This constructed national narrative "has encouraged Armenians to develop habits of emplotment, or narrative templates that lead them to interpret many events in a similar way—namely as suffering at the hands of external enemies."[31]

Rather than treating Azerbaijanis as a separate ethnic group, Armenians usually treat them as Turks—as if they were the progeny of the Young Turks—whom they blame for the "genocide" of 1915. So long as Armenian nationalism was polarized against Turkey, the Soviet Union did not hesitate to bolster Armenian nationalism. For instance, the Soviet authorities encouraged it when over 20,000 Armenians marched through Yerevan on April 24, 1965 to mark the 50th anniversary of the 1915 events.[32] This Soviet-nourished anti-Turkey nationalism would gradually penetrate the Armenian education system as well—whereby the "genocide" of 1915 would be transformed from an international crime to the essence of Armenian identity. That this "genocide" would become the most important cultural marker of Armenian identity is reflected in how the works of creative writing by Paruyr Sevak, Hovhannes Shiraz, and Silva Kaputikyan, among others, would come to construct a shared, somewhat homogenous memory of that tragedy. During the 1965–1990 period, Armenian intellectuals have reconstructed more than 500 years of relationship between the Ottomans and Armenians almost entirely around the allegations of genocide against the Ottomans. As an anchoring motif, genocide ties the Armenian people to the past while feeding into the image of a genocidal Turk. Such a self-image, I contend, stands to cripple the future of Armenia—which is liable to be left depopulated, poorer, and regionally isolated.

Post-Cold War Armenian nationalism is nested within the anti-Communist Karabakh Committee, which became the Armenian National Movement (ANM), and the Karabakh Committee entered the 1989 elections (as the ANM) and formed Soviet Armenia's government.[33]

From the perspective of Azerbaijanis, Armenians were brought to Karabakh by the Russian empire.[34] In the 1805 population census, only 8% of the population of Karabakh and the surrounding regions was Armenian.[35] As Tsarist Russia expanded into the Caucasus, it relied on Armenians—who were brought over from Persia. Always favoring Armenians as an instrument for their colonization, Russians empowered them, politically and economically.

Tracing the Events of the Conflict

Although our purpose is to understand the impact of the conflict on the state–society relations of Azerbaijan and Armenia, it is useful to divide the conflict into three major stages: (a) the Armenian political struggle to incorporate Karabakh into Armenia (1987–1991); (b) the war between Armenia and Azerbaijan, and the ethnic cleansing of Azerbaijanis (1991–1994); and (c) the formation of the official political positions. In this chapter, we will focus on the first two periods.

The conflict between the region's Armenians and Azerbaijanis was not driven by any inherent insecurity—but owing to the fear generated among Azerbaijanis by aggressive Armenian secessionists. A series of communal conflicts thus erupted in Askeran, Sumgait, and other Azerbaijani towns. Being much better organized than their Azerbaijani counterparts, and fully supported by Armenia, the Armenian leaders of Karabakh were well positioned to take on the risk of the war. This situation is captured with great clarity in the following description by Cornell:

> From a very early stage in the conflict, the Nagorno-Karabakh Armenians—who already had a strong willingness to act given the salience of cultural differences and the remembrance of past conflict—were equipped with three crucial factors: the autonomous status of the province, which had been helpful in sustaining Armenian identity, but more importantly carried with it the political institutions to channel secessionist sentiments; secondly, external support from the republic of Armenia which effectively obliterated the problem of demographic weakness (no more than 150,000 Armenians lived in Nagorno-Karabakh) and any possible problems of economic viability; and thirdly, radical leadership which entailed an uncompromising course of action. In fact, faced with a refusal from both the Azerbaijani SSR and the USSR leadership to acquiesce to its demands and later Soviet military intervention in 1991, the Nagorno-Karabakh leadership continued its uncompromising course of action. These three factors seem to have had a decisive impact on the development of the conflict.[36]

As mentioned earlier, Mikhail Gorbachev's perestroika let Armenians push their case for secession publicly; some scholars go on to insist that a war was unavoidable because there was no previous mechanism to address this type of dissent. Why did the Armenians trust Gorbachev's sympathies for them while viewing perestroika as a political opening for their nationalistic separatism? Moscow was against making any changes to the borders and responded by referring to Articles 73 and 78 of the 1977 USSR Constitution. These articles stipulate that the consent of concerned republics is a prerequisite to any demand for changing their borders—and that any such change must also be approved by the Supreme Soviet and the Congress of the People's Deputies in Moscow.

There is no straightforward, rational explanation for how the Armenians of Armenia as well as the NKAO came to expect Gorbachev to grant their demand for unification. On what grounds did they all conclude that Gorbachev would subordinate the Soviet national interest to their nationalistic demands? While Vichen Ceterian has simply blamed the naivety of Armenian political leaders for their unrealistic expectations from Gorbachev, I tend to think that they were motivated by their intensely nationalistic self-identity.[37] Blinded by their nationalistic, homogeneous self-identify, Armenian political leaders failed to grasp that their course of action defied the Soviet Union; they "believed that the Centre, in the spirit of Perestroika, would easily decide in their favor."

The Armenians I interviewed gave the following three basic reasons for why they or their leaders had taken the course of action on Karabakh that they had:

1. Armenians believe that Russia favors them as it recognizes their positive contributions to promoting Russian interests—and because Armenia comprises the main obstacle against pan-Turkism.
2. Armenians believe that the killings of 27 Armenians during the Sumgait riots exposed Azerbaijani chauvinism to Russia, which would have persuaded it to appreciate their position on the Karabakh dispute.
3. As Russia finds Armenians more dependable than Azerbaijanis regarding the protection of Russian interests regionally, it would prefer a bigger and more powerful Armenia.

I also heard remarks that Armenians believed that the Russian leadership had realized that handing over the Armenian-majority Karabakh area to Azerbaijan "was a clear case of historical injustice," which Russia was now willing to undo. One interviewee also claimed that the Armenian side had been misled by Abel Aganbegyan, who was Gorbachev's close advisor and an ethnic Armenian. Aganbegyan had told the Armenian leadership that Gorbachev would give the NKAO to Armenia.[38]

But, it was the Armenians who wanted to test the limits of Gorbachev's *glasnost* policy by demanding NKAO unification. While some Armenians claim that the conflict originated in the wake of the Sumgait riots that killed many Armenians, there also are scholars who trace the origins to the radical nationalistic Armenian leadership in Armenia as well as Karabakh at the time of the Soviet Union collapse. In reality, the war occurred because Karabakh's Armenian political elite was willing and capable of controlling the region with Russian help. The Karabakh Armenian elite's prejudice against Azerbaijanis and Azerbaijani fears of losing Shusha—the cultural center of Azerbaijan—and Nagorno-Karabakh, as a whole, added fuel to the fire. Armenians were able to assert themselves because Azerbaijan had a weak government and state apparatus. Meanwhile, the Soviet Union remained confused in its policy regarding Armenian nationalists, who were encouraged by this state of affairs. According to Christopher Zurcher, "state weakness emerges as the single most important factor" in the conflict between the two sides.[39]

The First Stage (1987–1991)

In October 1987, the Armenian Academy of Sciences became the first institution to call for unifying Karabakh and Nakhichevan with Armenia and argue for secessionist nationalism.[40] Radical idealism had been a characteristic feature of the Armenian intelligentsia even earlier. Soviet leaders were always aware of Armenian secessionist tendencies and had rejected the Armenian demands, because agreeing to them could have jeopardized the entire Soviet system. As the NKAO's Armenians became more assertive, the local Azerbaijanis also mobilized and there were clashes between the two communities in 1987. Subsequently, the Armenian leaders took several steps to provoke the public; for instance, in late 1987, they expelled Azerbaijanis from the districts of Megri and Kafan in Armenia. The immediate goal of these provocations was to intimidate the Azerbaijanis in Armenia and the NKAO to leave the region.

By the end of 1987, the Azerbaijanis had no option but to leave their ancestral homes in Armenia as well as the NKAO. This led to a refugee crisis—with over 700,000 Azerbaijanis expelled and displaced from their ancestral homes. The evicted, dispossessed Azerbaijanis wanted revenge against Armenians and their trauma became the basis for a new, victim-oriented Azerbaijani nationalism.

In 1987, NKAO floated a petition for unification. Around 80,000 Karabakh Armenians would end up signing that petition, which would be sent to authorities in Moscow and Baku. Armenian nationalists would organize mass demonstrations to support NKAO's unification, most prominently on February 11, 1988 in Stepanakert in Karabakh. The protests would spread to Yerevan, with the message of "one nation, one republic."

On February 20, 1988 in Yerevan, hundreds of Armenians demonstrated, while an Armenian delegation flew to Moscow to meet with Gorbachev. When the delegation returned to Yerevan on February 27, it asked Armenians to halt demonstrations and wait for the decision of the Supreme Soviet of the USSR. The protests, however, would continue in Karabakh. Meanwhile, Gorbachev dispatched troops signaling his determination to prevent any changes in territorial borders. Meanwhile, Armenian militias—known as *borodachi*, or "the bearded ones"—systematically eliminated the Azerbaijanis, both in Armenia and the NKAO. As Azerbaijani refugees reached Shusha and other Azerbaijani cities, their stories of victimization at the hands of Armenians incited Azerbaijanis to rise up against Armenians. Unsurprisingly, some refugees would end up leading some anti-Armenian riots in Sumgait and other cities, which widened the gap between them and Armenians.[41]

The Sumgait Riots

Built in 1949 near the Caspian Sea, Sumgait is Azerbaijan's second-largest city that also was once its most cosmopolitan and ethnically intermixed urban center. The majority of Azerbaijanis coexisted peacefully with ethnic Armenians and many other groups in Sumgait—whose sport clubs, schools, and other social institutions practiced no ethnic segregation or discrimination. The city's population hovered between 300,000 and 350,000 during the Soviet era—and jumped to 500,000 in the wake of the First Karabakh War, as Azerbaijani refugees from Armenia as well as Karabakh were drawn to it in search of jobs. Displaced Azerbaijanis from the districts of Gubadli, Zangilan, and Lachin settled in Sumgait. Even today, one comes across poor Azerbaijanis in Sumgait, who dream of returning to their homes in Karabakh.

While Sumgait had economic prospects and social diversity, these factors failed against external pressures—especially the flood of refugees from Armenia and Karabakh. Directly linked to the conflict in Karabakh, these external pressures destroyed the city's social fabric. When Armenia instigated and openly supported separatism in Karabakh, it also planted the seeds for a long-term conflict between Azerbaijanis and Armenians as communities. During the Armenian mobilization in Yerevan in 1987, the Armenian nationalist rallying cry was that Karabakh be "united" with Armenia. By November of that year, radical Armenian nationalists were attacking Azerbaijanis, starting with those who had been living in Kapan (from where around 2,000 Azerbaijanis had to flee to Azerbaijan, mainly to Sumgait).

On February 20, 1988, the (all-Armenian) Nagorno-Karabakh Supreme Council decided to unite Karabakh with Armenia, destroying any prospects of the Armenians' peaceful coexistence with the Azerbaijanis in Karabakh. Relations between the two communities in Karabakh became tense in the wake of the above decision. On February 21, there were arson attacks on the Demirbulag Mosque and an Azerbaijani secondary school (named after Azerbaijani author Mirza Fatali Akhundov) in Yerevan. A day later (February 22), the Armenian militias killed two Azerbaijanis in Karabakh: Bakhtiyar Uliyev, 16, and Ali Hajiyev, 23. These were the first fatalities of the conflict, which led to inter-communal confrontations in the Aghdam region and the town of Askaran on the Stepanakert (Khankendi)-Aghdam road, where 19 people were injured.

On February 28, 1988, the Sumgait riots took place, killing 26 Armenians and 6 Azerbaijanis.[42] According to the reports, many Azerbaijani refugees from Armenia took part in the riots, which a weak Azerbaijani state failed to prevent.[43] The Armenian elite used the Sumgait riots to advance their argument that Armenians were insecure in Azerbaijan and had no choice but to unify with Armenia; the Armenian nationalists, on their part, exploited the riots to stress their demand to carve away Karabakh from Azerbaijan and to integrate it into Armenia.

The Soviet Union's Prosecutor General's Office appointed Vladimir Sergeyevich Galkin to investigate the Sumgait riots.[44] Galkin issued an indictment—leading to several arrests, and capital punishment for seven individuals. Some Armenians were also among the instigators of the riots. One of the ring leaders was Armenian Eduard Robertovich Grigoryan (b. 1959), who was sentenced to 12 years in prison. Grigoryan was sent to Armenia to serve his sentence, where authorities released him upon his arrival.

As neither state had yet become independent, Armenian nationalists preferred to accuse Azerbaijan and its people rather than the Soviet Union and its authorities. The Armenian nationalists used these riots to mobilize the grassroots and to radicalize their rhetoric suggesting that the option of peaceful coexistence was impossible. For instance, Igor Muradyan—one of the original members of the Karabakh Committee—formed his own *Miatsum* (unification) movement and rejected any compromise with Soviet authorities. He led an armed movement that instigated and lured young people in Armenia to join the fight for the NKAO's secession. These nationalists would eventually hijack Armenian politics and influence its future course. The clashes in Sumgait along with Armenian casualties would galvanize the secessionists.[45]

Following the Sumgait riots, fear spread across the border areas, leading to forced deportations from both sides. Azerbaijanis were systematically attacked in the Armenian cities of Gugark, and Spitak. Azerbaijanis belonging to the Gugark region were targeted for Armenian attacks. The properties of Azerbaijanis were either set on fire or taken by other Armenians. Ostensibly to address this communal divide, the Communist Party Committee of the NKAO voted on March 18 to unify with Armenia. The foregoing decision was not supported by the Communist Party of Azerbaijan; on March 23, 1988, the Presidium of the Supreme Soviet of the USSR rejected the Armenian demands. On March 24, 1988, the Central Committee of the Soviet Communist Party as well as the Council of Ministers adopted a resolution to invest in, and improve the economic conditions, of the Karabakh, for the next seven years.

Meanwhile, there were small anti-Armenian demonstrations in Baku and other cities. Then, in September 1989, larger riots broke out in the cities of Stepanakert and Shusha targeting Azerbaijanis. Hundreds of residences were burned and a systematic attempt was made to rid these cities of its ethnic Azerbaijanis. Kocharian—who later became Armenia's president—justified this response to the riots in Sumgait.[46]

According to the International Crisis Group (ICG), during the first wave of ethnic tensions, all ethnic Azerbaijanis—approximately 250,000 people—had to leave their homes in Armenia and flee to Azerbaijan.[47] The second wave of ethnic tensions started in late 1992 and continued until the end of 1994, resulting in the deaths of 25,000 civilians. According to the Azerbaijani State Committee for Refugees and IDPs, 586,013 Azerbaijanis were forced out of their homes[48]; the US Committee for Refugees (USCR) claimed that 568,000 people from the Karabakh and the occupied regions were deported. While 42,072 refugees were from Nagorno-Karabakh, the rest were from the other occupied regions—as follows: Fizuli (133,725); Agdam (128,584); Lachin (63,007); Kelbadjar (59,274); Jabrayil (58,834); Gubadli (31,276); Zangilan (34,797); Terter (5,171); and Adjabedi (3,358).[49]

Armenians expanded their protests in Yerevan, supporting the NKAO's Armenians' decision. This angered Moscow, which dismissed the first secretaries of the Community party units in Azerbaijan and Armenia on the charge of incompetence. The Soviet move did not deter Armenian nationalists and the Azerbaijani Supreme Soviet rejected Armenia's demands.

In March 1988, Moscow proposed two options to address the concerns of Armenians: an economic investment program, and a political upgrading of the NKAO's Armenians. The proposed Soviet investment—intended for an overall renovation of Karabakh—was worth 400 million rubles ($668 million). As for the political proposal, it offered to upgrade Karabakh from its status as an autonomous region to that of an autonomous republic. (The political offer was made in June 1988 by Egor Ligachev, a leading member of the CPSU Politburo, as a way to appease the Armenian community). The Armenians, however, rejected both proposals and insisted on merging Karabakh into Armenia as the only way to address their concerns. As for the economic incentives dangled by the Soviet Union, they failed to bridge the gap between the Azerbaijanis and the Armenians because of Karabakh's place in the identity of each ethnic group.

The political stalemate worsened in July 1988. In a July 12 meeting held at Stepanakert and attended by 101 deputies (out of a total of 150), the Nagorno-Karabakh Soviet People announced three decisions: (1) secession of Nagorno-Karabakh from Azerbaijan, (2) the renaming of Nagorno-Karabakh to Artsakh Armenian autonomous region, and (3) the call to end a general strike and order employees back to work. The same evening, the presidium of the Azerbaijan Supreme Soviet met in Baku and declared the decisions of the Nagorno-Karabakh's Soviet of People's Deputies null and void on the basis of Article 87 of the USSR constitution. On July 18, the Presidium of the All-Union Supreme Soviet, after listening to the arguments on both sides, decided that Karabakh must remain within Soviet Azerbaijan and proposed a major development project for the region.

3 THE CAUSES OF THE FIRST NAGORNO-KARABAKH WAR   51

The decision of the Presidium of the All-Union Supreme Soviet did not demoralize the Armenian nationalists but made them more aggressive—and they decided to use force to realize their goal of unification. In Karabakh, Armenian militias targeted unarmed Azerbaijanis and burned their homes to provoke them. In September 1988, they killed many Azerbaijanis and burnt their homes in Stepanakert. Through late November, attacks in the Armenian cities of Gugark, Spitak, and Stepanavan led to the deaths of 33 Azerbaijanis. By December 1988, the Armenian militias had removed entire Azerbaijani communities from the NKAO. Rafael Kazaryan, a member of the Karabakh Committee, accepted the fact that he had led the ethnic cleansing of Azerbaijanis in Armenia.[50] The goal of the Armenian nationalists was to create "ethnically pure Great Armenia"—and they achieved it not only in the NKAO but also in seven regions around the enclave.[51]

Realizing that it had lost control of the NKAO, Moscow decided on January 12, 1989 to begin to administer it directly. The Soviet intention was to restore communal peace and carry out a major development project. Moscow appointed Arkady Volsky to the NKAO's governorship but this Soviet attempt at "buying the consent of Karabakh's Armenians" failed since the Armenian nationalists continued to insist on its demand for unification. Inasmuch as the Soviet move failed to stabilize the situation, some Armenians welcomed the Soviet intervention as a first step toward peeling away Azerbaijan's juridical control of the NKAO.

Azerbaijan's reaction to its intervention as well as the inelasticity of the Armenian nationalists prompted Moscow to end its direct rule over the NKAO and to restore Azerbaijani jurisdiction there on November 28, 1988, which angered Karabakh's Armenians. The regional situation became even more complicated in December as the joint session of the Supreme Soviet of Armenia and the National Soviet of NKAO voted to unify Karabakh with Armenia. This Armenian joint decision angered Azerbaijanis, who doubted the effectiveness of their national institutions in countering the Armenian demands.

Consequently, the Azerbaijani public targeted minority Armenians in Baku, for retribution. A major riot against Armenians started on January 13, 1990 and lasted for a few days, prompting Moscow to declare a State of Emergency in Karabakh and some regions of Azerbaijan. When the Azerbaijani government failed to control the situation, around 26,000 Soviet troops entered Baku on January 19–20, 1990—and killed around 300 Azerbaijani civilians who resisted their presence. What would come to be called "Black January," this event was a major carnage against the rise of Azerbaijani nationalism spearheaded by the Azerbaijani Popular Front (APF). A new Azerbaijani nationalist consciousness would thus come to take shape in the wake of Black January.

The Soviet troops installed Ayaz Mutalibov as the First Secretary of the Communist Party and as the new president of the Republic of Azerbaijan. Mutalibov, however, was weak and ineffective as a leader. He tried to disarm the paramilitaries of the Azerbaijani nationalist opposition while relying on Moscow to thwart Armenian expansionism. The Soviet Union tried to crush Armenian militias by cooperating with the Azerbaijani special police. Moscow deployed the 23rd Motorized Rifle Division along the border between Armenia and Azerbaijan in April 1991. These troops coordinated with the Internal Troops of the Ministry for Internal Affairs (or the MVD troops of the Soviet Union)—as part of Operation Ring—in an attempt at ending illegal guerrilla formations among the Armenian communities. These military actions forced the Armenian leadership to negotiate with Moscow whereby Levon Ter-Petrosyan agreed to the new Soviet initiative of Moscow—and there was renewed hope for negotiations between Armenia and Azerbaijan.

On July 20, 1991, an Armenian delegation was sent from Stepanakert to Baku to meet with Mutalibov. Under Soviet pressure, the NKAO's Armenians agreed to relinquish the dream of unification, and to negotiate within the constitutional framework of the Republic of Azerbaijan. However, their more radical factions (which included Kocharian and Sarkisian) rejected this, and insisted on unification. These radical factions—which had undergone militarization and gained prominence among Armenians—rejected any form of compromise with Baku.

The radical factions—most of them members of the Dashnak Party—tried to halt negotiations by killing seven Azerbaijani policemen in Karabakh on August 9, 1991. The next day, they killed Valerii Grigoriyan, an Armenian delegate who was scheduled to meet with Mutalibov in Stepanakert later that month.[52] Throughout the conflict, elite individuals from both Armenian and Azerbaijani sides vied for power—constantly influencing the outcomes of the unfolding events. Armenian entrepreneurs who used nationalism as an instrument to carve a bigger political space for themselves became too radicalized to compromise. Nevertheless, the radicals generally retained a hope that some third force would somehow emerge to help them realize their dreams.

For all that, the modern history of Armenia would remain—all the way through the 1990s and to the present—a story of seeking to realize nationalist dreams through radical organizing. The national Armenian groups tend to exaggerate their own significance while also expecting support from Russia and European powers. At any rate, the Armenian nationalist dream has ignored the option of moderation; in this dream, moderates are perceived as internal enemies. Marked by an ingrained hatred for Turks, Armenian nationalism leaves no room for compromise while aspiring for political goals that are frequently unrealistic.

Competition over the leadership of Armenian nationalism and the divisions within Azerbaijani institutions provided opportunities for the nationalist Armenians. Karabakh's Armenians thus voted for the Proclamation of the Nagorno-Karabakh Republic (NKR) in September 1991. In November 1991, Azerbaijan reacted to this secessionist move by abolishing the legal status of the Nagorno-Karabakh Autonomous Oblast. The Armenian nationalists reacted to this decision by calling and organizing a referendum on NKR's independence.

The Second Stage (1991–1994)

With the formal disintegration of the Soviet Union in August 1991, the conflict between Armenia and Azerbaijan escalated to its bloodiest stage. The Russian Federation, under the leadership of Boris Yeltsin, openly sided with Armenia, and tried to resolve the conflict militarily. Vehemently opposed to Abulfaz Elchibey—the leader of the Azerbaijan Popular Front (which had pan-Turkish inclinations)—Russia supplied "arms, fuels and logistical support" to Armenia, as the worst fight broke out in 1992.[53]

Far better armed and prepared than their Azeri counterparts, the Armenian forces were also the readier to fight. The Armenians were passionate to fight for Greater Armenia. Azerbaijan did not have a regular army; its population was less nationalistic; and it lacked a shared sense of identity as well as a vision for its future. Moreover, the political leaders of Azerbaijan were divided, weak, and ineffective.

Khojaly as the Nanjing of Azerbaijan

When Japan attacked to subdue and colonize China in 1937, it carried out one of the worst massacres in Nanjing—an ancient city and the then capital of China. Murder, rape, looting, and arson were altogether dubbed the "Rape of Nanjing," which saw the killings of between 50,000 and 300,000 people. The massacre of Khojaly can be considered the Nanjing of Azerbaijan—whose natives remember that massacre as the darkest, most humiliating page of their national history.

Through the course of the Khojaly massacre, the Armenian leaders Kocarian and Sarkissian—not unlike the Japanese Generals Iwane Matsui and Hisao Tani—abandoned the standards of humanity in the name of nationalism. The difference between the two massacres might simply be that while the Japanese generals were executed by hanging for their war crimes, the Armenian warlords ended up being rewarded by being elected to Armenia's presidency. These Armenian generals-turned-presidents would go on to pillage their own country's resources and to ruin its future.

On the night of February 26, 1992, the Armenian military, under the command of Serzh Sarkissian, carried out its first massacre of innocent Azerbaijani civilians in Khojaly—a strategically located town of 7000.[54] Sarkissian was assisted by Major Oganyan Seyran Mushegovich, who headed up the 366th Motor Rifle Regiment of the Russian Army.[55] In this military operation, a total of 613 innocent Azerbaijani civilians (106 women, 83 children, and 70 elderly men) were massacred—and some 487 people (including 76 children) were left critically injured; the Armenian forces also captured 1,275 Azerbaijanis, out of whom 150 still remain missing. A Human Rights Watch (HRW) report on this Armenian operation called it "the largest massacre to date in the conflict."[56] But aside from these mass killings, captures, and injuries, Khojaly also saw, on that night, rapes and deportations of hundreds of Azerbaijani civilians. Based upon expert statements on the incident and the testimonies of 2,000 survivors, Azerbaijan's government concluded that Armenian forces tortured the captives through scalping, (sexual) mutilation, blinding, and by burning them alive.[57]

In addition to its immediate casualties (including the targeted deportations), this horrific military operation caused many Azerbaijanis to leave the area in fear. None of this was outside the purview of the Armenian political leadership. Consider, for example, the following statement that Sarkissian gave to Thomas De Waal, the author of *Black Garden: Armenia and Azerbaijan Through Peace and War* (2003):

Before Khojaly, the Azerbaijanis thought that they were joking with us, they thought that the Armenians were people who could not raise their hand against the civilian population. We were able to break that [stereotype]. And that's what happened. And we should also take into account that amongst those boys were people who had fled from Baku and Sumgait.[58]

Consider, also, the following testimony by Markar Melkonian, presented in his book *My Brother's Road* (2005):

> At about 11:00 p.m. the night before, some 2,000 Armenian fighters had advanced through the high grass on three sides of Khojaly, forcing the residents out through the open side to the east. By the morning of February 26, the refugees had made it to the eastern cusp of Mountainous Karabakh and had begun working their way downhill, toward safety in the Azeri city of Agdam, about six miles away. There, in the hillocks and within sight of safety, Mountainous Karabakh soldiers had chased them down. "They just shot and shot," a refugee woman, Raisa Aslanova, testified to a human. Rights Watch investigator. The fighters had then unsheathed the knives they had carried on their hips for so long, and began stabbing... Now, the only sound was the wind whistling through dry grass, a wind that was too early yet to blow away the stench of corpses.[59]

Markar Melkonian, incidentally, had dedicated his book to his brother, Monte Melkonian—the international terrorist who is also known as "Commander Avo."

The Armenian attack on Khojaly constitutes the main story of the Karabakh conflict from the Azerbaijani standpoint. Moreover, Azerbaijan's government has succeeded in building a national narrative around the brutal suffering the Khojaly attack caused its citizens. The upshot of this new Azerbaijani nationalistic narrative is that in Khojaly, the Armenians mercilessly killed, tortured, and humiliated Azerbaijanis, whose children, women, and elderly were also not spared. Khojaly has come to signify the humiliation of Azerbaijan; the inhumanity of Armenian militias; and a historical moment at which Azerbaijani identity would begin to play into a securitization discourse of nationalism.[60]

In as much as Azerbaijanis had to pull themselves together as a nation-state in response to the Armenian attack on Khojaly, their resultant patriotism would owe less to their own positive values than to their bitter memories of how Armenia had occupied and pillaged their lands and destroyed their civilization. The humiliation that the Azerbaijanis felt through this attack would constitute the metanarrative of the Karabakh conflict in the school textbooks of Azerbaijan.[61]

Azerbaijani textbooks are vocal and explicit about how Armenia occupied, raped, tortured, and massacred Azerbaijani civilians when it attacked Khojaly—and how that attack left Azerbaijan humiliated.[62] The attack had left the cultural capital of Azerbaijani civilization, Shusha, in shambles as its mosques, museums, and homes had been destroyed. Shusha's residents had to flee; those who failed to flee were killed.

The Khojaly massacre has served as what Nora calls a "memory site" that has multiple meanings. It is a reminder of the "unmastered past" of the Karabakh conflict[63]; of the inhumanity of one group against another; of an attempt to erase Azerbaijanis from a part of their own ancient land; of the power of racist nationalism and the failure of the international community in its face. But Khojaly also represents resistance—for neither Heydar Aliyev nor Ilham Aliyev passively accepted the humiliation of Azerbaijanis. Indeed, in the wake of this attack, a new Azerbaijan was born on the ashes of its former self that had unsuccessfully waited for three decades for peace and normality. (The post-Khojaly Azerbaijan was led by Aliyev to a recapture of Shusha on November 8, 2020 from the Armenian forces—a victory that helped Azerbaijan move beyond its three decades of humiliation).

Shocked by the Khojaly attack, Mutalibov fled to Russia; and an inexperienced, populist party called the Azerbaijan Popular Front took over in Baku. Azerbaijan was in chaos and demoralized. Despite the Mutalibov's government's attempts to deny these massacres, the average Azerbaijani learned of them by word of mouth—generated by eyewitnesses who had fled Khojaly—and this created a major backlash against the government. Mutalibov had to resign—and the Azerbaijani Parliament chose Yaqub Mammadov as his successor. A professor and practitioner of medicine, Mammadov was infamous for his corruption and love of the American dollar currency. He was widely referred to by the nickname "Dollar Yaqub." Mammadov's appointment was temporary in that the Azerbaijani Constitution mandated a new election within three months of Mutalibov's resignation. During the chaos, on May 8, 1992, Armenian forces occupied Shusha and emptied it of its indigenous Azerbaijani inhabitants. Armenian troops extended their control over the Lachin corridor that links Karabakh and Armenia; they expelled all civilians from the area.

The public was shocked. Now discredited, Mutallibov tried to come back to power ostensibly to save the country, but the nationalist APF-controlled militias launched a countercoup and thwarted him. The parliament then elected Isa Gamber as Azerbaijan's interim president and dissolved itself in preparation for the new elections. The APF, which controlled the capital, rallied around Elchibey as the next president.[64] Elchibey was an honest, clean politician with a romanticized Turkish nationalist ideology but he was ill-prepared to deal with either domestic or external political challenges. While he and his party correctly concluded that Russian imperialism—with its policy of "divide and rule"—was at the heart of the turmoil in the Caucasus, they did not know how to unify Azerbaijan or to address the Karabakh issue. Elchibey took an anti-Russian and anti-Iran stance, which angered both countries.

Russia, in turn, used Surat Huseynov—its "asset" in Azerbaijan—to ruin Elchibey's stature, and extended a helping hand to the Armenian forces. Elchibey accused Huseynov of being a Russian agent; blamed him for Azerbaijan's recent military defeats (especially the fall of Kalbajar); discharged him from his military duties; and stripped him of his title of "Plenipotentiary Presidential Representative." Huseynov refused to obey, with Russia's support, and when the Russian 104th Airborne Regiment left Ganja, it gave weapons to Huseynov. He marched to Baku to remove Elchibey and his government; while he was on his way, numerous military commanders rebelled and tried to form their own fiefdoms. For instance, Alikram Humbatov declared the formation of a Talysh-Mughan Republic. Azerbaijan had failed as a state.

Realizing his weaknesses, Elchibey invited Heydar Aliyev from Nakhichevan to take control of the deteriorating situation. On June 15, 1993, Aliyev was elected speaker of the parliament and when Elchibey realized that Huseynov was about to enter Baku, he fled to his native Nakhichevan. Aliyev then became Azerbaijan's interim president, and appointed Huseynov as his prime minister. On October 3, 1993, a new round of presidential elections was held—leading to Aliyev's election as the third president of Azerbaijan.

Aliyev's main goal was to form a National Army; he started out by disbanding 33 battalions that lacked training and had become a major security issue. Huseynov tried to use his position to empower himself and rebelled against Aliyev in October 1994. His coup failed, however, and he ended up fleeing to Moscow even as his men were removed from Azerbaijan's government positions. Then, on March 13, 1995, Aliyev faced a second coup, staged by the Deputy Minister of the Interior, Rovshan Javadov, and the paramilitary group—the Special Purpose Police Detachment of Azerbaijan (OPON)—that he headed. This coup, too, failed, resulting in the death of Rovshan and the disbanding of the OPON.

Aliyev's main tasks were to unify Azerbaijan and restore law and order; to accomplish the above, he needed a truce with Armenia. Thus, in May 1994, he arranged a meeting in Bishkek, Kyrgyzstan, among the parliamentary heads of Azerbaijan, the NKAO, and Armenia. These leaders signed the cease-fire agreement known as the "Bishkek Protocol." Meanwhile, the position of the international community had been based on four United Nations Security Council (UNSC) resolutions—822, 853, 874, and 884—that were adopted in 1993 in response to Armenia's occupation of Kalbajar, Aghdam, Fuzuli, Jabrayil, Gubadli, and Zangilan. The UN resolutions had recognized Nagorno-Karabakh and the surrounding regions as part of the Republic of Azerbaijan and called for an immediate and unconditional withdrawal of the Armenian armed forces from the occupied territories. Similar statements had since been issued by many other international institutions—including the UN General Assembly. But, the UNSC resolutions have never been implemented, and negotiations between Armenia and Azerbaijan have not had any breakthroughs. Against this backdrop, tensions have only tended to intensify, leading to the existing stalemate.

Truce Agreement and the Composition of the Official Claims (1994–1995)

Aliyev defined the conflict as an interstate territorial conflict between Azerbaijan and Armenia. In a September 29, 1994 speech to UN General Assembly, he had rejected the Armenian argument for self-determination:

> The Republic of Armenia, under the pretext of realization of the right to self-determination of an ethnic group of Armenians living in Nagorno-Karabakh region of Azerbaijan, is openly carrying out plans on annexation of the territories of our state, forcibly changing our state borders and expelling the Azerbaijani population from their homes. All this is cloaked in an arbitrary interpretation of the "rights of people for self-determination" as the right of any ethnic community to self-proclaim its independence and join another state. Such interpretation of the right for self-determination blatantly contradicts the principles of sovereignty and territorial integrity of

a state/.../ I think there is no need to prove that here we are not dealing with the "realization of the right for self-determination" but with a gross violation of international law in the aggression against the sovereignty, territorial integrity and political independence of a UN member state.[65]

Aliyev had presented a nuanced argument rooted in international law. The Armenians, however, had insisted that the conflict was not territorial but it had to do with the people's dignity and their right to self-determination. The Armenian argument was presented at several international fora by Vartan Oskanian, Armenia's minister of foreign affairs. In a statement at the 9th OSCE Ministerial meeting in Bucharest on December 4, 2001, Oskanian said:

> Mr. Chairman, no amount of ambiguous diplomatic language can mask the fact that men, women and children of Nagorno-Karabakh have earned the right to live peacefully on their historic lands, free of alien domination and foreign occupation. Nagorno Karabagh's secession from Soviet Azerbaijan was both legal, peaceful and just... Just as Azerbaijan was no longer willing to accept the Soviet legacy, and withdrew from the Union, Nagorno-Karabakh was no longer willing to live under conditions imposed arbitrarily by Stalin decades earlier... Azerbaijan's claim on Nagorno-Karabakh has been legally invalid. Its absolute and blind adherence to the principle of territorial integrity will do it no good, since Nagorno-Karabakh has never been a part of independent Azerbaijan. The League of Nations did not accept Azerbaijan's territorial claims then, we do not accept them now.[66]

Very few observers anticipated the full costs of the Armenian aspiration to merge Karabakh with Armenia. The influential Armenian diaspora wanted Karabakh to be either unified with Armenia or be recognized as an independent state.[67] Ter-Petrosyan called for some sort of a compromise with Azerbaijan; he supported establishing relations with Turkey. However, the Armenian diaspora refused. Ter-Petrosyan was forced to resign in 1998 and he was replaced by Karabakh's nationalist leader Kocharian, who rejected any compromise with Azerbaijan. Ter-Petrosyan had told Armenians the following:

> It happened in Bosnia. The Serbs lost everything. I don't think that the maintenance of the status quo is a real option. ... I do not think that Karabakh is capable of forcing Azerbaijan to its knees, because it will have to seize Baku.[68]

His prudent, visionary understanding of the region's sociopolitical history had guided him to call for compromise and peaceful coexistence in Karabakh. However, irredentist Armenians rejected his input, and he was sidelined.[69] The maximalist demands blocked alternative pathways to productive negotiations.

Later, at the opening session of a negotiation round in Florida in April 2001, Heydar Aliyev, then-Azerbaijani president, stated the following:

> It is known that this conflict stemmed from the territorial claims toward Azerbaijan by Armenia, which tried to seize and annex Nagorno-Karabakh, an indigenous part of Azerbaijan. It happened in 1988, when Armenia and Azerbaijan still were sister republics within the Soviet Union.... Armenia, striving to realize its territorial claims against the neighboring country of Azerbaijan, has provoked separatist and terrorist forces in Nagorno-Karabakh to an armed confrontation. Later Armenia itself started a military aggression against Azerbaijan.[70]

Conclusion

Following the 1987 conflict, both Azerbaijanis and Armenians rewrote their historical narratives against each other—with each side blaming the other for its past and present disasters. The destruction and occupation of major cities around Karabakh alerted Azerbaijanis to Armenians' capacity for destruction. From the Armenian side, any politician who proposed reconciliation with Azerbaijan was stamped as a traitor, including Ter-Petrosyan. After 1987, the respective memories and identities of each nation evolved in opposition to the other: A sense of "us" as a peaceful group versus "they" who seek to destroy us and deny the existence has overwhelmed the debate between Armenians and Azerbaijanis.

While Armenians continually used tropes of sacrifice, suffering, and victimhood to articulate themselves politically, Azerbaijanis did not have a well-articulated nationalism or a clear sense of "enemy" prior to the Karabakh conflict. The conflict reconstituted and politicized Azerbaijani identity—and its impact on it was greater than on its Armenian counterpart. The most radicalizing feature of the conflict for Azerbaijani identity was "the deportation of the Azeri population from Armenia in 1987 and subsequent anti-Armenian riots in Azeri populated towns."[71]

In the wake of the Karabakh conflict, Azerbaijani leaders remained loyal to Moscow and expected it to confront Armenian nationalists. These leaders believed that the Soviet Union would not give in to Armenian nationalistic demands as that would undermine the union. Moreover, the Azerbaijanis knew that Moscow was fully aware of Karabakh's economic and transportation integral historical significance to Azerbaijan. For example, the repository of water for irrigation was located in upper Karabakh, which was inhabited predominantly by Azerbaijanis.

Gorbachev reacted to Armenian secessionism by making it clear that the boundaries of the republic were to be kept intact. He did not want to destabilize the union by giving in to the secessionist demands. Nevertheless, he hesitated to use force against the Armenian nationalists. Meanwhile, the determination and activism of Armenian leaders deepened anxieties and fears of the Azerbaijani community in and around Karabakh. The Azerbaijani government's weakness and the region's Azerbaijanis' disorganization made the latter an easy target for their Armenian counterparts.

Notes

1. Interview with Araz Aslanli, May 12, 2022.
2. Interview with Cemail Hasanli, March 10, 2021.
3. Tadeusz Swietochowski, "Azerbaijan: A Borderland at the Crossroads of History' in Starr," in Frederick S. Starr, ed., *The Legacy of History in Russia and the New States of Eurasia* (New York: S. Starr, 1994), pp. 277–299.
4. Peter Rutland, "Armenian Nationalism and Democracy," *Europe-Asia Studies"* 46:5 (1994), pp. 839–861.
5. Artur Terian, "Kocharian Says Armenians, Azeris are Ethnically Incompatible" https://www.azatutyun.am/a/1570666.html. Accessed July 10, 2022.
6. Edward Said, *Orientalism: Western Conception of the Orient* (London: Penguin Books, 1978), p. 43.
7. Irina Ghaplanyan, *Post-Soviet Armenia: The New National Elite and the New National Narrative* (New York: Routledge, 2018).
8. Artur Terian, "Kocharian Says Armenians, Azeris 'Ethnically Incompatible,'" January 16, 2003. https://www.azatutyun.am/a/1570666.html. Accessed March 11, 2022.
9. Terian, Artur, "Kocharian Says Armenians".
10. Shiping Tang, "The Security dilemma and ethnic conflict: towards a dynamic and integrative theory of ethnic conflict," *Review of International Studies* 37:2 (2011), pp. 511–536; Michael Brown, "The Causes of Internal Conflict: An Overview" in Michael Brown et al. *Nationalism*

and *Ethnic Conflict* (Cambridge, Massachusetts: The MIT Press, 1997), pp. 3–25.
11. Stuart J. Kaufman, "Spiraling to Ethnic War: Elites, Masses, and Moscow in Moldova's Civil War," *International Security* 21:2 (1996), pp. 108–138.
12. A. N. Yamskov, "Ethnic Conflict in the Transcaucasus: The Case of Nagorno-Karabakh," *Theory and Society* 20:5 (1991), pp. 631–660.
13. Ted Gurr, *Why Men Rebel*, (New Jersey: Princeton University Press, 1971); Ted Gurr, "People Against States: Ethnopolitical Conflict and the Changing World System," *International Studies Quarterly* 38:3 (1994), pp. 344–377.
14. The major works that provide a relatively balanced view of the conflict that includes Azerbaijani perspectives are as follows: Audrey L. Altstadt, "Nagorno-Karabagh- 'Apple of Discord' in the Azerbaijan SSR," *Central Asian Survey* 7:4 (1988), pp. 63–78; Svante Cornell, *Small Nations and Great Powers: A Study of Ethno Political Conflict in the Caucasus* (Richmond: Curzon Press, 2001); Svante Cornell, *Azerbaijan Since Independence* (New York: M. E Sharpe, 2011); Farid Shafiyev, *Resettling the Borderlands: State Relocations and Ethnic Conflict in the South Caucasus* (McGill-Quinn University Press, 2018); Jamil Hasanli, *The Sovietization of Azerbaijan: The South Caucasus in the Triangle of Russia, Turkey, and Iran, 1920–1922* (Salt Lake City: University of Utah Press, 2018).
15. Maria Kurkhiyan, "The Karabagh Conflict: From Soviet Past to Post-Soviet Uncertainty," in Edmund Herzig and Marina Kurkchiyan, eds. *The Armenians: Past and Present in the Making of National Identity* (New York: Routledge, 2004), p. 149.
16. Stuart J. Kaufman, "Ethnicity as a generator of conflict," in Karl Cordell and Stefan Wolff, eds., *Routledge Handbook of Ethnic Conflict* (London: Routledge, 2011), pp. 91–102.
17. Quoted in James V. Wertsch, "Deep Memory and Narrative Templates: Conservative Forces in Collective Memory," in Aleida Assmann and Linda Shortt, eds., *Memory and Political Change* (New York: Palgrave Macmillan, 2012), p. 181.
18. Jirair Libaridian, "What Happened and Why: Six Theses," *Armenian Mirror Spectator*, November 4, 2020. https://mirrorspectator.com/2020/11/24/what-happened-and-why-six-theses/, accessed July 16, 2022.
19. Razmik Panossian, "The Irony of Nagorno-Karabakh: Formal Institutions versus Informal Politics," *Regional and Federal Studies* 11:3 (2010), p. 144.
20. The background information provided here is based on the following works: Svante Cornell, *Small Nations and Great Powers* (Richmond: Curzon Press, 1999); Mark Malkasian, *"Gha-Ra-Bagh!" The Emergence*

of the National Democratic Movement in Armenia (Detroit: Wayne State University Press, 1996). The following accounts are relatively sympathetic to Armenians: Levon Chorbajian et.al. *The Caucasian Knot: The History and Geo-politics of Nagorno-Krabagh* (London: Zed Books, 1994); Christopher Walker, *Armenia and Karabagh: The Struggle for Unity* (London: Minority Rights, 1991).

21. For the social and economic causes of the conflict, see Yamskov, "Ethnic Conflict in the Transcausasus," pp. 631–660. Armenians pursued the policy of unifying Karabakh with the Republic of Armenia. In 1964, for instance, 2,500 Karabakh Armenians petitioned Khrushchev to unify the NKAO with the Armenian SSR; the petition detailed the discrimination they claimed to face at the hands of the Azerbaijani government.
22. More information, see http://www.nkr.am/en/karabakh-national-liberation-movement, accessed June 12, 2022.
23. This Greater or United Armenia consists of Eastern Turkey, Karabakh, Nakhichevan, and the Javakheti in Georgia.
24. Stephen Van Evera, "Hypotheses on Nationalism and War," *International Security* 18:4 (1994), pp. 5–39.
25. Levon Ter-Petrosian, *Armenia's Future, Relations with Turkey, and the Karabagh Conflict* (New York: Palgrave, 2017), p. 3.
26. Armenia's Declaration of Independence, which was published in 1991, rejected the 1921 Treaty of Moscow and the Treaty of Kars between the Soviet Union and Turkey by claiming they surrendered Armenian territories to Turkey. Thus, the Declaration rejects the boundaries between Turkey and Armenia, and it contained a clause clarifying the Armenian state's effort for recognition of the Armenian genocide.
27. Arman Grigoryan, "The Karabakh conflict and Armenia's failed transition," *Nationalities Papers*, 46:5 (1998), p. 854.
28. Kurkchiyan, "The Karabagh conflict," p. 148.
29. The Turkish media covered the whole exchange between Sarkissian and the student, and the Turkish Prime Minister asked Sarkissian to apologize for his response to the student. See "Erdogan Urges Sarkisian to Apologize for Western Armenia Remarks," https://asbarez.com/erdogan-asks-sarkisian-to-apologize-for-western-armenia-remarks/ Accessed July 10, 2022.
30. Ronald Suny, *Looking Toward Ararat: Armenia in Modern History* (Bloomington: Indiana University Press, 1993), p. 7.
31. Rauf R. Garagozov, "Collective Memory and Narrative Toolkit in Turkish-Armenian Mnemonic Standoff over the Past," *Review of Armenian Studies* 30 (2014), p. 87.
32. Eldar Abbasov, "Armenian Irredentist Nationalism and Its Transformation into the Mass Karabakh Movement, "MIATSUM" (1965–1988)," in M. Hakan Yavuz and Michael Gunter, eds., *The Nagorno-Karabakh Conflict:*

Historical and Political Perspectives (New York: Routledge, 2022), pp. 59–88.
33. Peter Rutland, "Democracy and Nationalism in Armenia," *Europe-Asia Studies* 46:5 (1994), pp. 839–861.
34. Shafiyev, *Resettling the Borderlands*, 85.
35. Heiko Kruger, *The Nagorno-Karabakh: A Legal Analysis* (New York: Springer Press, 2010), p. 8.
36. Cornell, *Small Nations*, p. 41.
37. Vichen Cheterian, "Is the Political Status of the Nagorno-Karabakh That Important?" https://bakuresearchinstitute.org/en/is-the-political-status-of-nagorno-karabakh-that-important/#_edn2 Accessed April 12, 2022.
38. Ali Askerov and T. Matyok, "The Upper Karabakh predicament from the UN resolutions to the mediated negotiations: Resolutions or hibernation?" *European Journal of Interdisciplinary Studies* 2:1 (2015), pp. 154–164.
39. Christopher Zurcher, *The Post-Soviet Wars: Rebellion, Ethnic Conflict, and Nationhood in the Caucasus* (New York: New York University Press, 2007), p. 8.
40. Ali Askerov, "The Nagorno Karabakh Conflict - The Beginning of the Soviet End," in Ali Askerov, et al., *Post-Soviet Conflict* (Rowman and Littlefield, 2020), p. 57.
41. Mustafa Mirzeler, "Narrating the Memories of *Ermeni Mezalimi*," *Middle East Critique*, 23:2 (2014), pp. 225–240.
42. For one of the most comprehensive reports on the Sumgait Riot, see Aslan Ismayilov, *Sumgayit-Beginning of the Collapse of the USSR* (Baku: Casioglu, 2011).
43. Ismayilov, *Sumgayit*, pp. 35–45.
44. Ismaylov, *Sumgayit*, pp. 120–135.
45. Libaridian, "The Question of Karabagh," pp. 11–13.
46. James Coyle, *Russia's Border Wars and Frozen Conflicts* (New York: Palgrave, 2018), p. 17.
47. International Crisis Group (2012). Tackling Azerbaijan's IDP Burden. *Crisis Group Europe Briefing*, p. 2.
48. Azerbaijan: After Some 20 years, IDPs Still Face Barriers to Self-Reliance (2010). *Internal Displacement Monitoring Center*, p. 3.
49. USAN Factsheet on the Nagorno-Karabakh region of Azerbaijan (2012, November 9). *USAN*.
    Retrieved from http://karabakh.usazeris.org/.
50. Erik Melander's interview with Kazaryan, see, "The Nagorno-Karabakh Conflict Revisited," *Journal of Cold War Studies* 3:2 (2001), p. 64.
51. Melander, "The Nagorno-Karabakh," p. 65.

52. David Remnick, "Ethnic Conflict overwhelms Caucasus Enclave," *The Washington Post*, September 15, 1991. https://www.washingtonpost.com/archive/politics/1991/09/15/ethnic-conflict-overwhelms-caucasus-enclave/c30e5465-3f2e-4004-9a85-d29759612768/.
53. R. Panossian, "The Irony," p. 145.
54. Thomas T. Goltz, T. (2012). The Successes of the Spin Doctors: Western Media Reporting on the Nagorno-Karabakh Conflict. *Journal of Muslim Minority Affairs*, 32:2 (2012), pp. 186–195; A. Vaserman and R. Ginat, "National, territorial or religious conflict? The case of Nagorno-Karabakh," *Studies in Conflict & Terrorism* 17:4 (1994), pp. 345–362.
55. Shamkhal Abilov and Ismayil Isayev, "The Consequences of the Nagorno-Karabakh War for Azerbaijan and the Undeniable Reality of Khojaly Massacre: A View from Azerbaijan," *Polish Political Science Year Book*, 45 (2016), pp. 291–303.
56. Human Rights Watch. *Azerbaijan: Seven years of conflict in Nagorno-Karabakh* (New York, 1994), p. 6.
57. Nazila Isqandarova, "Rape as a tool against women in war: The Role of Spiritual Caregivers to Support the Survivors of an Ethnic Violence," *Cross Currents*, 63:2 (2013), pp. 174–184.
58. Thomas De Waal, *Black Garden: Armenia and Azerbaijan Through Peace and War* (New York: New York University Press, 2003), p. 172.
59. Markar Melkonian, *My Brother's Road. An American's Fateful Journey to Armenia* (London & New York: I.B. Tauris, 2005), pp. 213–214.
60. Rauf Garagozov, R. (2010). "The Khojaly Tragedy as a Collective Trauma and Factor of Collective Memory" *Azerbaijan in the World*, 2:20 (2010), Baku: Azerbaijan Diplomatic Academy. http://biweekly.ada.edu.az/vol_3_no_5/The_Khojaly_tragedy_as_a_collective_trauma_and_factor_of_collective_memory.htm. Accessed July 10, 2022.
61. Yasemin Kilit Aklar, "Nation and History in Azerbaijani School Textbooks," *AB Imperio*, 2 (2005), pp. 469–497.
62. Nazila Isqandarova, "Rape as a tool against women in war: The Role of Spiritual Caregivers to Support the Survivors of an Ethnic Violence," *Cross Currents*, 63:2 (2013), pp. 174–184.
63. I adapt this term from Charles S. Maier, *The Unmasterable Past: History, Holocaust, and German National Identity* (Cambridge University Press, 1988). This book focuses on whether or not, in what ways, and to what extents the Nazi Holocaust of the German Jews could be compared to other major crimes.
64. "Azerbaijan Communists Yield to Nationalists," *The New York Times*, May 20, 1992.
65. "Excerpts from Aliyev's UN speech," *Azerbaijan International*, Winter 1994 (2.4), www.azer.com/aiweb/categories/magazine/24_folder/24_articles/24_unspeech.ht…

66. "Statement by H.E. Mr. Vartan Oskanian, Minister of Foreign Affairs of the Republic of Armenia at the 9th Ministerial Meeting of the OSCE Bucharest, Romania, December 4, 2001," www.armeniaforeignministry.com/htms/speeches/OSCE_Bucharest_Dec42001.html.
67. Sergey Minasyan, "The Nagorno-Karabakh conflict in the context of South Caucasus regional security issues: An Armenian perspective," *Nationalities Papers* 45:1 (2017), pp. 131–139.
68. Cited in David D. Laitin and Ronald Grigor Suny, "Armenia and Azerbaijan: Thinking a Way Out of Karabakh," *Middle East Policy*, 7:1 (1999), p. 166.
69. Levon Ter-Petrossian and Arman Grigoryan, *Armenia's Future, Relations with Turkey, and the Karabakh Conflict* (New York: Palgrave, 2017).
70. "Statement: Azerbaijan President Heydar Aliyev in Key West, Florida," *Azerbaijan International*, April 3, 2001 www.azer.com/aiweb/categories/karabkh/karabkh.
71. Anastasia Voronkova, "Understanding the dynamics of ethnonationalist contention: political mobilization, resistance and violence in Nagorno-Karabakh and Northern Ireland," Unpublished PhD Thesis, Queen Mary University, (2011), p. 152. The author argues that Western research on the Karabakh conflict totally ignores the impact of the deportation of the Azeri population from Armenia.

CHAPTER 4

The Consequences of the First War on Armenia and Azerbaijan

Providing a concise summary of the effects of the First Karabakh War, De Waal argues that "in 1991, Armenia and Azerbaijan were both forged as new independent states in the crucible of the Karabakh conflict. The conflict is memorialized as a symbol of victory and survival on the Armenian side and of martyrdom and loss on the Azerbaijani side."[1]

In a holistic manner, the conflict crystallized and shaped the respective political coalitions and leadership in both republics. The Karabakh conflict became the standard for determining when political leaders in both republics would rise to the top echelons of their respective governments and whether or not the conflict would embolden or debilitate their political livelihoods.[2] In Azerbaijan, Heydar Aliyev's two immediate predecessors as president, who lasted one year or less in office, were Ayaz Mutalibov (September 1991–March 1992), a neo-communist, and Abulfez Elchibey (June 1992–June 1993), a pan-Turkic nationalist.[3] Their abrupt departures occurred because of the loss of territories in Karabakh.[4]

In the First Karabakh War, Armenia occupied seven districts of Azerbaijan, adjacent to its Karabakh region. The Armenian occupation resulted in 30,000 deaths and the ethnic cleansing of 700,000 Azerbaijanis from Karabakh and the surrounding region. It was a devastating defeat for the newly independent Azerbaijani state. As a result, Azerbaijan's morale was shattered and a major portion of its population was

Table 4.1 From population census data, in thousands of people[9]

	1926	1939	1959	1970	1979
Entire population	125.3	150.8	130.4	150.3	162.2
Armenians	111.7	132.8	110.1	121.1	123.1
Azerbaijanis	12.6	14.1	18.0	27.2	37.2
Russians	0.6	3.2	1.8	1.3	1.3
Other	0.4	0.7	0.5	0.7	0.6

displaced, emphasizing how the rattled Azerbaijani identity took on a profoundly resentful tone toward Armenians. The loss of the cradle of Azerbaijani culture, the city of Shusha, combined with collective guilt and shame sowed the seeds for a new phase of nation-state building, with the goal of liberating ancient cities and restoring them to Azerbaijan. While Azerbaijani society was paralyzed by defeat, Armenia, emboldened by victory, refused to compromise, and imagined a greater Armenia, what L. Broers' calls "augmented Armenia."[5] This transformed peace negotiations into a means of protecting the status quo and consolidating the occupation. Armenia established a subordinate structure in the occupied territories called the Nagorno-Karabakh Republic (also known as the Republic of Artsakh), with the hope of winning international recognition and thus legitimizing the occupation.[6] To the disappointment of the Karabakh Armenians, this illegal entity was never recognized by any United Nations member, including Armenia itself.[7]

The territories over which the two sides have been unable to come to terms are recognized by the international community as part of the Republic of Azerbaijan. Nagorno-Karabakh never had the mandate to define its own demographic or geographic borders and had always remained part of Azerbaijan. When it became an autonomous region in 1921 under the Soviet system, it was surrounded by seven provinces of Azerbaijan. The NKAO in 1979 had 162,181 inhabitants, which was composed of Armenians (123,076) and Azerbaijanis (37,264), along with Russians, Kurds, and Greeks.[8] In contrast, the population of the seven surrounding provinces remained more than 98% Azerbaijani. Meanwhile, Armenians remained a minority and constituted 1.2% of the population (Table 4.1).

Armenia

In Armenia, the Karabakh conflict's impact was deeper and broader: the dismantling of state institutions and political control as wielded by members and leaders of the Karabakh clan.[10] A major consequence of the First Karabakh War was the transformation of the Armenian national identity from victim to victor. For Armenians, this occurred when they claimed victory in the Nagorno-Karabakh War, thereby occupying the former NKAO and the seven surrounding regions, along with ethnically cleansing one million Azerbaijanis and destroying communities in the path of military advancement. The imagined national map of Armenians expanded to include the occupied territories of Azerbaijan as well.

The trajectory of political activism during the last days of the Soviet Union was influenced and directed by the call for the unification of the Karabakh region with the Armenian republic. The Karabakh Committee was the impetus for fostering the debate over Armenian state institutional reforms, the nature of Armenia's independent statehood, and Armenian national identity. One could argue that the Karabakh conflict also took Armenia hostage, consequently preventing its democratic evolution in a post-Soviet world because of an obsession with nationalism. Armenian nationalism is rooted in fears about security being breached but it also became a movement of unwavering faith in Armenian nationalism, propelled in part by remembering the real and imagined past sufferings of Armenians, who were citizens in the first Caucasus nation to be defined by spiritual practices of Christendom. While there were subsequent cracks within the Karabakh movement, especially between those who insisted on focusing on the liberation of Karabakh with the help of Russia (as epitomized in the views of Igor Muradyan[11]), others stressed the democratization project and accompanying state building initiatives of Armenia, now independent and free from the orbit of having been a Soviet satellite (as epitomized in the views of Levon Ter-Petrosyan). These tensions continue to inform the Armenian political landscape and how political coalitions in the country are formed.

The Karabakh conflict resulted in persistent political fragmentation and instability in Azerbaijan as well as among the nationalist kleptocracy in Armenia. The vocabulary of nationalism constituted the dominant language of politics in Armenia, which eventually led to a popular president being forced to resign because of his handling of the Karabakh issue. Meanwhile, in Azerbaijan, the situation was much worse. The conflict resulted in a quick pair of presidential resignations, along with two coups and the total collapse of state institutions. The situation would be reversed when Heydar Aliyev came to power in 1993. The conflict caused both republics to deplete and waste their resources of armaments, and both nations were compelled to compromise their independence in their respective newfound political culture in lieu of appealing to and appeasing the former imperial power that Russia yearned to recoup.

More specifically, the impacts of the First Karabakh War on the Armenian state and society could be summarized as follows:

1. The Karabakh clan became politically dominant and the interest of entire Armenia was subsumed within the interest of Karabakh's desire to become either unified with Armenia or be established as an independent state;
2. The destruction of the Armenian economy, in which legitimate players were replaced by kleptocrats;
3. The formation of a missionary state ideology (*Hai Dat*); the polarization of the elite and society corresponding to their positions on the sovereign and territorial claims of the Karabakh;
4. The reactivation of the "genocide" memory, along with a transformation of the Armenian national identity;
5. The sociopolitical dependence on the Armenian diaspora and Russia, both portrayed separately and collectively as a savior of Armenia. As a result of the Karabakh conflict, Armenia became more dependent on Russia and compromised its sovereignty.

The Rise of the Karabakh Clan

The Karabakh issue did not only direct and inform the origins of the newly formed Armenian state, it also engulfed its most important debates about how to define its national identity, embed a culture of democratization, foster economic development, and articulate a foreign policy as a newly independent state. Every issue was subordinated in varying degrees to the Karabakh cause of either achieving unification with Armenia or gaining independent statehood. Most significantly, Armenia slipped domestic issues and security concerns into the Karabakh envelope and then nested it into another envelope marked "genocide." As a result of the Armenian National Movement's (ANM) myopic vision and ineffective leadership, especially during the tenure of Ter-Petrosyan, the spectrum of Armenia's state and society interests was condensed to the Karabakh cause.

When Ter-Petrosyan belatedly realized his mistake and sought to reverse the course, the window of political opportunity had closed and he was subsequently accused of betrayal and portrayed as an enemy of the Armenian nationalist cause. The mutual communal pogroms of both Azerbaijanis and Armenians already had hardened the security concerns of both parties in the Karabakh conflict, but the deleterious results in Armenia seemed to be more acute, because of the unending fervor among members of the Karabakh Committee. Taline Papazian argues that the Karabakh issue was politicized and radicalized by the Armenian political elite who challenged the legitimacy of their communist counterparts and desired to grab the reins of government.[12]

James J. Coyle explains that the Armenian nationalist elite "turned the Karabakh issue into an instrument of nation building."[13] The ANM, which evolved out of the Karabakh Committee, "legally ran the Republic for a decade, and laid the foundations of the Armenian state," while planting the seeds for negative policy dynamics.[14] It was Ter-Petrosyan who opened the door for the Karabakh Clan to infuse its radical nationalist ideology in the corridors of power.[15] Petrosyan appointed Vazgen Sargsyan, the most successful Armenian military commander who carried out mass ethnic cleansing campaigns, as the minister of defense.[16] By controlling the military and other security institutions, he became the principal strongman of Armenia. In 1995, Ter-Petrosyan reappointed Sargsyan as his minister of defense and added the title of special representative for negotiating the ceasefire. He also appointed Serzh Sargsyan, a leading Karabakh politician and military commander, as the minister of interior, who was the commander of the Armenian forces during the Khojaly massacre. To overcome charges of vote rigging in the 1996 presidential elections and criticism of his government, Ter-Petrosyan appointed Robert Kocharyan as prime minister in March 1997.[17] These two appointments would be disastrous for the health and welfare of the Armenian state, as the Karabakh clan propelled forward at the expense of the rule of law and the larger interests of the Armenian state. When Ter-Petrosyan indicated his will to sign a peace agreement with Azerbaijan, the Karabakh clan, which included then Prime Minister Kocharyan and the Minister of Interior Sargsyan, accused him of capitulation and treason, thereby forcing Ter-Petrosyan to resign in February 1998. However, the

Karabakh clan also would eventually turn against Vazgen Sargsyan, then the prime minister. On October 27, 1999, pro-Kocharyan forces attacked the Armenian parliament and killed Sargsyan, along with other popular politicians.[18]

The Tension Between the Hayastanti and the Karabakhsis

The Armenian transition from a Soviet communist satellite to an independent democratic republic following capitalist economic principles was facilitated by a group of intellectuals from Ter-Petrosyan's ANM, which had evolved from the Karabakh Committee. The ANM also planted seeds for growing a radicalized form of nationalism and mobilized the masses by prioritizing nationalism over stabilizing a democratic state and improving the country's economic infrastructure. In the process, it worked to portray Azerbaijan as an enemy. The elite deployed tactics of nationalism to delegitimize the communist elite and advocate for independence from the Kremlin. In the process, a nationalist monster of sorts was created.

The ANM intellectuals organized themselves soon after Armenia gained its independence in December 1991, believing they could simultaneously manage the formidable objectives of transitioning to a market economy and democracy while pursuing unification with Karabakh. Due to the Armenian occupation of Karabakh and seven surrounding regions, Turkey and Azerbaijan closed their respective borders, which forced Armenia into relying on an informal economy and became the arena for various gangs to fight for control. At the same time, another member of the Karabakh Committee, Vano Siradeghian, who was appointed as minister of interior by Ter-Petrosyan, became a powerful politician who usurped the legal means and legitimate enforcement authority to bring gangs under his control, effectively becoming a criminal syndicate don of the underworld network in Armenia. The corrupt elite and brutal political competition among the post-Soviet Armenian elite manipulated the Karabakh diplomatic crisis to cover up their shortcomings. But, Ter-Petrosyan was a more pragmatic and long-term thinker than anyone, supporting Karabakh Armenians but also refusing to recognize an independent Republic of Nagorno-Karabakh. His reasons were trifold: (a) a higher degree of autonomy for the Karabakh Armenians; (b) support for a resolution of the Karabakh issue while acknowledging the territorial integrity of Azerbaijan; (c) good relations with Turkey and other neighbors. His modest compromise was rejected by those who were fervent nationalists and who criticized him for not being sufficiently adamant on the matter of Karabakh independence while being seen as acting too softly in pressuring Turkey.

There were several long- and short-term consequences of the Karabakh victory for the Armenian state and society. The victory bolstered Armenian self-confidence in believing that the broader Armenian cause was achievable. The military victory consolidated and delineated two camps of Armenian political thought. One camp comprised those who demanded the state honor the principles of the rule of law and fulfill the basic needs of its citizens by developing good and friendly relations with its neighbors to improve the economic and security conditions of its citizens. This camp reiterated its belief that Armenia should become a normal, functioning state without wasting its resources or its own existence to realize history-driven dreams that were no longer as pragmatic as they might have seemed in earlier times. The second camp, led by Vazgen Manoukyan and Armenia's two most recent presidents, advocated for a state with a clear mission to achieve the goals of the Armenian Cause. They insisted that the Armenian state must be "bound by 'national ideology'" of correcting historical injustices as a prelude to manifesting the Armenian Cause.[19] Simply, Karabakh predominantly defined Armenia's foreign policy and domestic politics—the ideal put forth by Armenian intellectuals as *Hai Dat*, the Armenian Cause, which was incorporated into the declaration of Armenia's independence in 1991.[20] Likewise, the preamble to the Armenian constitution puts forth the ideal in similar language.[21]

These two philosophical camps still compete to see their respective vision prevail in the Armenian political landscape. Unfortunately, the first camp, which recommends not committing the state's resources to achieve the Armenian Cause, has very little support among the public inside the country as well as among the global Armenian diaspora.

A major impact of the Karabakh War on Armenia is the intense mobilization toward nationalism and ultimately authoritarianism, which has distorted the vision and compromised the ongoing process of Armenian efforts to become a functioning democratic republic.[22] For instance, when Ter-Petrosyan indicated his will to seek a peaceful solution to the conflict, he was charged with treason and capitulation and forced to resign in 1998. Ter-Petrosyan argued that resolving the Karabakh conflict is embedded within the ongoing normalization process of the Armenian state. He emphasized that time is on the side of Azerbaijan because they could build a new army with investments from their oil wealth. In less than a decade since it had become an independent republic in the post-Soviet era, the Armenian society could not extricate itself from the shackles of nationalism. As a result, the state and society became more militarized while domestic issues were addressed through violence—notably, the October 27, 1999 raid on the Armenian parliament and the assassination of prominent politicians. The militarization of the state and the political elite ruined any chance for the sort of compromise that Ter-Petrosyan sought.

An impact of the war was the Karabakhization of Armenia and the conflict, which arose between the politicians from Armenia (*Hayastanti*) and their counterparts from Karabakh (*Karabakhsis*).[23] Kocharyan was elected president of the Nagorno-Karabakh Republic (NKR), thereby becoming the leader of the pan-Armenian nationalist movement. After ousting the moderate Ter-Petrosyan from office, Kocharyan became president of the Republic of Armenia in 1998, cementing the place of the Karabakh clan in the country's politics. The political goal of unification prevailed over all other concerns of Armenia, which remains to this day as a single issue-based country, absorbed wholly by the tasks of preserving and integrating the occupied territories in and around Karabakh. As Panosian sums up: "In this sense Karabakh has 'taken over' the political agenda of Armenia, and the 'regional' periphery is controlling the national political centre."[24] In the rise of the Karabakh clan to power, Ter-Petrosyan's policies ironically played a critical role. It was Ter-Petrosyan who was in the forefront of the unification movement, and he came to power on the basis of the Karabakh-focused Armenian mobilization. He was the head of the Karabakh Committee to build momentum for Armenian nationalism. In August 1990, in the elections to the Supreme Soviet of the Armenian SSR, the Armenian National Movement (ANM), led by Ter-Petrosyan, received 36% of the vote. He was elected chair of the Supreme Soviet of the Armenian SSR, and in October 1991, with the collapse of the Soviet Union, he became president of Armenia.

The ANM was in power for seven years until Ter-Petrosyan's ouster in 1998. The ANM failed to address Armenia's economic problems, and widespread government corruption. When Ter-Petrosyan rigged the 1996 elections, his popularity declined precipitously. When he confronted angry protestors, who attacked the parliament and used all means to unseat him, Ter-Petrosyan appointed Kocharyan, a popular figure, as prime minister to protect himself from the political fallout of protests. He hoped that Kocharyan would sell the merits of peace with Azerbaijan to the public and especially to Karabakh Armenians. But Kocharyan's presence instead accelerated the process of the Karabakhization of Armenia, and its embrace of holistic nationalism.

At the time, the principal issues were the withdrawal of the Armenian forces around the Karabakh region, the determination of Karabakh's geopolitical status, and the safe return of refugees. During the occupation, two different strands of negotiations emerged. One involved a wholesale package deal to address the problems while the other outlined a step-by-step solution. Ter-Petrosyan favored a step-by-step approach that not only addressed the central conflict but also provided economic relief to Armenia. He had hoped to end the Turkish-Azerbaijani blockade on Armenia and integrate the country into regional development projects. Meanwhile, the opposition, led by the Karabakh clan, carried out a campaign against Ter-Petrosyan indicating that he had sold out Karabakh and undermined national security by advocating for reconciliation with Turkey and Azerbaijan. Kocharyan and Serzh Sargsyan, another politician from Karabakh, forced Ter-Petrosyan to resign. According to the Armenian constitution, if the president resigns or dies, the speaker of the parliament is first in line and then the prime minister. After Ter-Petrosyan resigned, Babgen Ararktsian, the speaker of the parliament, immediately resigned and Kocharyan became acting president. In March 1998, Kocharyan was elected to a full presidential term. The previous Armenian political establishment had opposed Kocharyan and the consolidation of power of the Karabakh clan.

The October 27, 1999 assassinations left nine people dead, including prime minister Vazgen Sargsyan and National Assembly Speaker Karen Demirchian, the popular former first secretary of the Communist Party.[25] Many people claimed that the assassinations occurred because Kocharyan, with total political control in the country, could freely engage in corruption while using the Karabakh issue as a national distraction. Kocharyan's foreign policy comprised unification of Karabakh with Armenia and a campaign to persuade the international community to formally recognize the events of 1915 as genocide and to name and shame Turkey in such declarations. He alienated Turkey and pushed Ankara to be closer to Azerbaijan. Kocharyan also removed Karabakh Armenians from the negotiations, thereby making Armenia the main interlocutor in the diplomatic process. Gerard Libaridian, a leading modern historian of Armenia and political advisor to Ter-Petrosyan, describes post-war Armenia as a country dominated by Karabakh. He argues that Armenia has been dominated and governed entirely by the 'Party of Karabakh!' adding that "[i]n most matters, the Party of Karabakh, whether in Karabakh or Armenia, is nonideological. Karabakh is at the top of the hierarchy of concerns; all else is subject to its logic."[26]

Perpetual War Economy, Regional Exclusion, and Migration

The Karabakh war ruined the economy of Armenia. It has been excluded from major regional economic integration projects. For example, Azerbaijan excluded and rerouted the oil and gas pipeline over Georgia in order to bypass Armenia. Moreover, the Baku-Tbilisi-Kars railroad network excluded Armenia and new lines with destinations leading to Turkey, Azerbaijan, and Georgia bypassed Armenia. The country is mired in poverty and lacks opportunities for independent economic mobility so it has become progressively more dependent upon Russia. Armenia's young and educated population have little or no option but to migrate to Russia, Europe, or the U.S. An even more negative development is Armenia's heavy dependence upon a diaspora that is politically activated by its long-standing grievance to acknowledge the events of 1915 as genocide, which has been reinforced by the tightly knit nationalist Dashnak party. Panossian analyzes the impact of the Karabakh clan on the Armenian economy and he concludes that:

> the strength of the Karabakh 'clan' is also reflected in its control of certain economic sectors in Armenia, especially fuel supply, and to a lesser extent wheat imports. The Armenian economy, as is the case with other former Soviet republics, is divided into sectors which have a monopoly in certain economic domains. The so-called 'mafia' networks are linked to the political elite, and therefore the NK 'mafia' benefits immensely from the political power of the Karabakh 'clan' in governing structures.[27]

A disturbing statistic underscores the problem: since the independence of Armenia, its population has decreased by "roughly 600,000, or about 15 percent."[28]

Changes in Armenian National Identity and the Genocide Rhetoric

In order to justify the conquest and massive ethnic cleansing against Azerbaijanis, Armenians activated and circulated the genocide narrative by reframing Azerbaijanis as Turks. The groundwork for Armenia's victory in the First Karabakh War came at a heavy cost where few considered the long-term consequences of such drastic risk taking. The victory and the rise of the Karabakh clan in Yerevan quieted the public debate over essential national issues, including negotiations considering the fate of the Karabakh territories and the occupied seven Azerbaijani regional areas.[29] The last open debate about a peace plan, which accounted for Armenian public opinion, was in 1997. The victory eventually cemented a deep fault line between those who allied with "the Party of Karabakh" (as Libaridian describes) and those who defended the national interest and well-being of Armenia outside of the Karabakh conflict. In this sociopolitical environment, hating the Turks and blaming them as the primary source of Armenia's problems became the norm. The post-war political culture welcomed proponents of the ideal of Greater Armenia, which lengthened the distance between realities and illusions for the Armenian political elite. Perhaps because he no longer accepted such illusions as tenable, Ter-Petrosyan was removed from office and pegged as a traitor, because he believed that the only pragmatic path for Armenia to position itself for economic prosperity was to find peace with Azerbaijan and Turkey regarding the Karabakh conflict.

The litmus test of nationalism was the only one that mattered for the political elite, which not only was used to quelch the political opposition but also to distract the public from the graft and corruption being carried out in the government. Armenia's political elite acted as entrepreneurs of memories, reactivating and reconfiguring Armenian recollections about the events of 1915 as rallying points to expand public existential fears of the Turks. As a result, the Karabakh victory and goal of not compromising and maintaining the policy of "no war, no peace" isolated Armenia from practically the entire international community, save for Russia. Its dependence on Russia has resulted in Armenia becoming a garrison state of the former Soviet power. Ter-Petrosyan had finally realized that it would be in the ANM's best interests to establish good relations with Turkey and Azerbaijan, but other nationalist groups, led by the Dashnak Party and the Karabakh clan, steeled their unconditional posturing. They relied on confrontation and external forces, namely Russia, to protect Armenia against imaginary enemies, such as Turkey and Azerbaijan. An Armenian student told the author, "we also owe our unity against the Turkish threat. We need it and, if necessary, exaggerate it to create unity."

The Armenian military was heavily influenced by the power of the Karabakh clan. Oleg Kuznetsov sums up the situation:

> The generals of the Armenian army made their career during the rule of the so-called Karabakh clan in the country – a junta of field commanders of the illegal armed formations of the Armenian separatists of Nagorno-Karabakh during the war between Armenia and Azerbaijan in 1990-1994 which includes former presidents of Armenia Robert Kocharyan and Serzh Sargsyan. As we know, the 'Karabakh clan' was expelled from power in Armenia as a result of the peaceful people's revolution in the spring of 2018, after which the current head of Armenia, Nikol Pashinyan, came to power.[30]

The Impact on Foreign Policy: Russia as Chief Patron

Rafael Ishkhanian wrote a comprehensive treatise distilling the trend of Armenia's obsessive fear of the Turks, along with suggested frames of analysis to understand the entire scope of Armenia's modern history on the basis of genocide discourse. He criticized Armenian political thinking, which has relied on the participation of the great powers to secure the Armenian nation's destiny. Ishkhanian concluded that historically the strategy of reliance on outside governments had failed to resolve any aspect of the Armenian Question. On the contrary, such a strategy had brought fateful consequences. The lesson, therefore, was to adopt a strategy relying on Armenians' own strengths and resources, not those of other powers (what Ishkhanyan called "The Third Force"). In a seminal 1989 article titled, *The Law of Excluding the Third Force*, he expanded on the problems of Russophile thinking in Armenia:

> Who told you that Russia is the savior of the Armenian people? Russia itself has never said that. This, my fellow citizens, is your invention. It is you who have placed your hopes on those powers and are now disillusioned.... The Russians are refusing to accept your definition of their interests, but you insist on teaching them. It also does not make sense to be enemies with Russia. Not to rely on Russia, not to make plans based on its power does not at all mean to be enemies with Russia. Let us be friends, but let us not rely on them, be fully devoted to them, believe so much that

they are our saviors. Let us re-Armenianize Armenia, let us be our own nation.[31]

Armenia's liberation plans, according to Ishkhanian, have been based on the ideal of a "third force." That is, some external power(s)—either Russia or a European nation—would augment Armenia's efforts to survive and/or expand its territories to strengthen a buffer against the Turkish threat. Ishkhanian contends that Armenia's dependence on foreign powers has resulted in more suffering affecting the entire nation than in alleviating it through the process of liberation. Thus, the dominant problematic view can be stated concisely as: "The patriotism of Armenians is the love of Russians and hatred of Turks." Ishkhanian dismisses this dominant view, instead calling upon Armenia to "cut its umbilical cord from Russia" as the first step to real independence.[32] He contends that Armenia's survival does not depend on Russia but rather on having good relations with its neighbors, especially Turkey.

One persistent pillar of Armenian nationalism in and outside the country is the belief that Armenia cannot survive against the Turks without Russia's support.[33] This thinking is widespread among the Armenian political and diplomatic establishment. For instance, Ruben Shugarian, Armenia's first ambassador to the U.S., after the republic gained independence in 1991, explains,

> Our ties with Russia are something innate and natural for all Armenians, particularly those residing on the territory of the Republic and the CIS. Its components are common cultural-spiritual values and the traditional perception of Russia as the most significant regional ally and protector of Armenia's security.[34]

This dominant narrative, which Ishkhanian criticized as early as just before the collapse of the Soviet empire in the early 1990s, still informs the majority of Armenians' thinking well into the twenty-first century. Ishkhanian argues, as summarized by Grigoryan, that "the worst calamities visited upon the Armenian people were the result of chasing unrealistic goals vis-à-vis the neighbors' and relying on third parties to achieve them."[35] Ishkhanian, who does not view modern Turkey as an existential threat, has called upon Armenians to protect and preserve their nation's independence by not becoming dependent on Russia. Ter-Petrosyan, as the first president of independent Armenia, rejected the ideological lines of Hai Dat, calling instead for a civic-minded Armenian state maintaining good relations with its neighbors.[36] Only when Pashinyan came to power in 2018 did any semblance of such a vision return to the political discourse.

Victory in the First Karabakh War enhanced the belief that Russia is "the only savior of Armenia," which, in turn, thwarted any hopes of finding a constructive diplomatic path with Turkey and Azerbaijan.[37] Yet, the same Armenia, due to its aspirations to unify with the Karabakh region, also became Russia's outpost in the Caucasus. Russia and Armenia formalized the military alliance they initially established on an ad hoc basis during the First Karabakh War. On March 16, 1995, Boris Yeltsin and Ter-Petrosyan, respectively, signed a bilateral defense treaty that allowed the former Soviet Red Army 261st Rifle Division to remain on Armenian soil. The 5,000-soldier unit was renamed the 102nd Military Base of the Russian Forces in Transcaucasia. located in Gyumri, about 75 miles north of Yerevan. Russia had three bases in Armenia: the 102nd base in Gyumri facing Turkey, the 426th base in Erebuni whose inhabitants participated in the second Chechen war, and Meghri, with 5,000 soldiers, of which 2,000 were border guards.[38]

With Russia now formally established as Armenia's key security benefactor, Armenian intellectuals and politicians agreed nearly unanimously that "not even an inch" of territory would be returned to the Azerbaijani Turks after the war.[39] This uncompromising position was predicated on a narrative of an invincible army that could march unimpeded to Baku. This narrative drove the Armenian political stance for the next quarter century, as Armenians embraced the misinformed stereotype of the Azerbaijani Turk as lazy, cowardly, and uncivilized. Such portrayals that masked Armenia's own unresolved problems appealed to the larger community of Armenians who rallied around the ideal of Armenian nationalism of victorious conquests. The First Karabakh War signified for its people the rebirth of Armenia as an aspiring hegemon in the Caucasus with hopes of crushing its neighbors. This view spread to the global diaspora of Armenians who added their own voice and resources to achieve Armenia's vision of victorious nationalism. Armenia's military victory in the 1990s gave Armenians a sufficient context to reimagine themselves as instrumental pieces of the mythologized Armenian body as an all-powerful geopolitical entity. This strengthened the cognitive processing of Azerbaijanis as lackadaisical, backward Turks, incapable of meeting Armenia's supposed military muscle. The enmity toward Azerbaijanis carried dehumanizing consequences and effectively blocked any political compromise or even sincere acknowledgment of the sufferings of Azerbaijani refugees. The Armenian elite never imagined the possibility (or shocking probabilities) that Azerbaijan could fight and regain these territories far more swiftly than Armenia had claimed them initially. As events in 2020 demonstrated, Armenian stubbornness would prove costly on an enormous scale, effectively eradicating the contention of Armenian military superiority.

The Armenian victory in the First Karabakh War split the country in two over defining the proper functions and objectives of the Armenian governing state, as described earlier. Meanwhile, the more pragmatic school, as Ter-Petrosyan represented, argued that the Armenian state should act and function just like any other geopolitical state in meeting the needs of its citizens and improving the country's economic well-being.[40] The ongoing debate in the pages of *The Armenian Weekly* among Armenian contributors is elucidating in demonstrating the extent to which Armenians appear to trust and have more faith in Russia than in their own capabilities to govern themselves, as one example indicates[41]:

> Russia is the alpha and the omega of Armenian statehood. For the past two hundred years Armenia has lived not because of Armenians and Diasporans but because of Russia and Russians. Without the Russian factor in the South Caucasus, Armenians would still be herding animals in eastern Turkey and making carpets in northern Iran as second-class minorities. Without Russian support, Armenia today won't even last a week in a nasty Turkic-Islamic place like the South Caucasus. In a nutshell: Russia is the fundamental reason why we have a homeland in the South Caucasus. What I just said is difficult to accept/admit, especially for an arrogant/proud people like us Armenians, but what I said is truth and reality. It's best to embrace truth and admit reality than continue lying to yourself which inevitably leads to disaster, as it has so many times in the past.
>
> David, Russians have excellent intelligence agencies, geopolitical institutions and diplomatic corps. Capability wise, these are actually second to none. Their military capabilities are actually also second to none. All this, not to mention, they control one-fourth of all natural resources on earth. Russia is actually the ONLY [emphasis in the original] independent nation-state on earth today. So, taking all this in account, do you seriously think they need advice from someone like you? Do you seriously think the Kremlin does not properly understand what's going on in the South

Caucasus? Do you seriously think that Russia needs Armenia as much as Armenia needs Russia?

One would have expected military victory to be the impetus for self-confidence in Armenia's capacity to develop and function as an independent state, rather than depending more on the graces and support of the Armenian diaspora for rationalizing its refusal to seek a compromise with Turkey and Azerbaijan. To wit:

> At the end of the day, our Russophobes have to be stopped from lying to our people. Whether they realize it or not, our Russophobes are systematically destroying Armenia from within. The danger here is that Armenians are by nature (i.e. genetic makeup) an emotional, shortsighted and politically naive/ignorant people. By filling Armenian heads with misleading information, empty pride and false hope (hope that Western powers will come to Armenia's aid in times of trouble, or that Russia needs Armenia just as much as Armenia needs Russia, or that united Armenians don't need anyone), Armenians will surely destroy their homeland, like they have done so many other times during the past 2,000 years. This process, incidentally, is also how we ended up getting Western financed globalist activists in power in Yerevan today.

Although those who consider Russia the main friend of Armenia declined from 83% in 2013 to 57% in 2019, Russia still remains the most trusted country.[42] Yet, the number of Armenian intellectuals, who criticize Armenia's dependence on Russia, is increasing and becoming more vocal. They argue that it has been too risky and costly for Armenia to put all its foreign policy decisions into the hands of just one power, instead of a multilateral regional coalition.

Azerbaijan

The Consequences of the War on Azerbaijan

In an interview with the author, Rauf Garagozova explains that, for Azerbaijan, the "Armenian failure to recognize the crimes of the past does not destroy the memories of the past. It was this past which prepared us for the Second Karabakh War and is making our present. The scars of Khojaly and massive ethnic cleansing of Azerbaijanis have their own life. They are part of who we are today and their shadow will be on our future."[43]

In the short term, the Armenian defeat of Azerbaijan in Karabakh shattered the nationalist legitimacy of the Azerbaijani state and replaced it with morose anxiety about whether or not Azerbaijan would be able to survive in its recognizable form as a nation. In the longer term, there were four major sociopolitical consequences of the defeat for Azerbaijan:

1. Securitization of Azerbaijani society and the formation of victim nationalism
2. Reconfiguration of national identity as Azerbaijanism and redefinition of independence with Karabakh
3. Consolidation of state power and the strengthening of the military
4. New foreign policy that focused on the liberation of Azerbaijani territories.

Ilham Aliyev had a clearer understanding of the sources of the conflict than any other leader, including Heydar Aliyev. Aliyev also had become disenchanted with the international community because of its indifference to the destruction of Azerbaijani towns. He was just as disappointed with the U.S. and France, which had been engaged in the diplomatic process and had usually supported the Armenian position. Ilham Aliyev lost his faith in the international community, realizing the concrete realities that the only way he could restore the territorial integrity of Azerbaijan is to fortify the state institutions, especially the military. He rejected a package approach for resolving the Karabakh conflict. Rather, he preferred a step-by-step approach by addressing specific problems of the conflict. He decided to leave the question of political status of the Karabakh region to the final stage.

Securitization

Azerbaijan's society and state were enveloped by an existential sense of insecurity after the devastating defeat in the First Karabakh War. Not only its physical security (such as its territory) was seen as compromised, but also its cultural and political identities were paralyzed by a startling lack of confidence. According to ontological security theory, actors do not only seek physical security but also the security of their national and sociocultural identities. Many Azerbaijanis worried about the stability and continuity of their state and their Azerbaijani identity at the same time.[44] As a result of this sense of ontological insecurity, the state viewed nearly all opposition movements/discourses as security threats destined to destroy the Azerbaijani state as traditionally known. This fueled the ruling party's goals of liberating Azerbaijani territories.

With the opposition treated as a crisis of national security, I would argue that Aliyev and his government found their legitimate ground for extraordinary measures of oppression, which included imprisoning leaders of the political opposition and effectively banning any challenge to the government authority. According to Ole Weaver,[45] securitization is not about whether threats are real or not but rather threats are equally dangerous as a mere act of speech.[46] For example, a specific issue such as troop movements, migration (immigration), or environmental degradation (climate change) can be socially constructed as a threat. Therefore, the Armenian occupation of the contested Karabakh territories framed the anxiety-laden and insecurity-driven rhetoric of the existential threat Azerbaijanis were experiencing in the public and the governing state.

With securitization as the holistic priority of the governing agenda, the opportunities for normal relationship dynamics between the state and society hampered the prospects for real democratic reforms. Azerbaijan's delayed development as a democratic state in the post-Soviet era was entirely due to the emergency of securitization policies which usurped the prior focus on developing a mature democratizing process. Through securitization, the Azerbaijani political elite set the agenda, which ultimately would lead to Azerbaijan's victory in the Second Karabakh War, thereby completing the country's project of reclaiming a positive self-confident sense of its national identity.

Victimhood

As Armenia had articulated its agenda for the purposes of addressing its national sense of victimhood in the wake of its earlier defeats, Azerbaijan developed its own national sense of victimhood, which would drive the country's rebuilding project on a comparatively more expansive scale. Thus, the suffering in the hands of Armenians framed the Azeri national identity and this, in turn, legitimized for many Azerbaijanis the moral position of *hating* the enemies who had caused Azerbaijanis to suffer. A near-total resentment toward Armenia constituted Azerbaijan's post-war national identity. By imagining itself as victimized, Azerbaijan projected itself as the innocent party and its enemy as the guilty perpetrator. Just as Armenia had experienced its victimhood on a holistic scale, the parallel occurred in Azerbaijan. During the Karabakh negotiations, the main goal of Azerbaijani diplomats was to persuade the international community to recognize their suffering as victims of Armenian aggression. After establishing this claim, there was an effort to make political claims on the status of being a victim. Thus, the Azerbaijani negotiators insisted on justice and reparations for restoring Azerbaijan's territorial integrity, as historical facts already had confirmed it.

The discussion continues by examining the new sociopolitical force: Azerbaijani victimhood, followed by its impact on nationalism and on state-building. Although Armenian identity, just like the Jewish identity, was predicated on the matter of genocide, the Azerbaijanis framed their victimhood status as a result of the First Karabakh War. Thus, in the case of Azerbaijanis, a sense of victimhood has less probability to become embedded as a transmitted memory and subconscious dynamic from generation to generation.

There are very few systematic studies on the impact of the defeat on Azerbaijani national identity. Charles van der Leeuw's *Azerbaijan: A Question for Identity* is an important study that examines the origins and the evolution of Azerbaijani identity. Another study deals with the war and its societal impact of weakening and destroying the feelings of pride in Azerbaijani society: Thomas Goltz's *Azerbaijani Diary*, a first-hand account of the impact on the Azerbaijani sense of national identity and the ensuing loss of faith in state institutions. Finally, Joshua Kucera's journalistic account also offers a constructive perspective on recent fluctuations in Azerbaijani identity, by stressing the role of the political elite in reconfiguring and radicalizing national identities.[47] Both Heydar and Ilham Aliyev successfully imbued the defeat and a sense of victimization in the public consciousness. With the state institutions, education, media, and visual arts aiding the message positioning, both leaders turned the sense of victim identity into a new political bond for advocating for the national goal of liberating the territories. Being a victim and having a victim identity prepared the next generation of Azerbaijanis to embrace the singular goal of national existence: the liberation of the occupied territories and the restoration of Azerbaijani dignity.

Therefore, the Khojaly massacre became a significant, instructive moment of shame and innocence for anchoring the post-war victim identity. It also clarified the calamity for Azerbaijanis because they "lacked wise leadership; society was fragmented; and had no sense of national purpose." A professor in Baku said, "Imagine how snow covers the mountains with that white and innocent color. We have been also covered by shame and defeat and yet a deep sense of innocence remains." In the words of Vamik Volkan, there was the "chosen trauma" of Azerbaijani society which played a decisive role. The unsuccessful rounds of peace negotiations, which were marked by perceptions of Armenian arrogance and the indifferent attitude of the international community toward doing anything other than maintaining the status quo reinforced the sense of victimhood among Azerbaijanis.

Azerbaijan's humiliating defeat facilitated the rise of the Azerbaijani Nationalist Front (ANF) in July 1988. This reactive movement of nationalism was led by Abulfaz Elchibey, a pan-Turkish nationalist who romanticized the historical chronicle to less than accurate effect. This was not only based on a sense of pain and suffering, it was anti-Russian, anti-Armenian, and anti-Persian, in nature. Elchibey's exaggerated reading of nationalism terrified everyone, including the leadership in the Republic of Turkey. A Turkish diplomat said, "He was engulfed in a romanticized reading of geopolitics and had no sense of Realpolitik. Demirel, [the Prime Minister and President of Turkey], and many politicians strived to avoid him."[48] Yet, Azerbaijani victimhood-focused nationalism had three goals: restoring the territorial integrity of the Azerbaijani homeland (*vatan*) by freeing the occupied territories from Armenia; enhancing the sovereignty of Azerbaijan; and establishing closer ties with Turkey and other Western powers to balance against Russia's regional presence. The "loss" of the center of Azerbaijani culture, namely the city of Shusha, also was prominent.

A New Sense of Nationalism

Armenian actions, including secession, mobilized the Azerbaijani public to accept a sense of nationalism built around the effects of victimhood. Armenian irredentism, in the long run, undermined the sovereignty of Azerbaijan as well as Armenia and instead served more for Russian interests. Today, Armenia has become a Russian protectorate but Azerbaijan's sovereignty is also constrained by the presence of Russian troops in the country. Both sides became dependent on Russia. An Azerbaijani diplomat summarized the situation:

> For us the Karabakh issue became our collective trauma. Modern Azeri identity is constituted by this trauma. The Armenians expelled us, killed us, humiliated us, and denied us a space to develop our democratic identity and build a healthy national identity. Yet, in the process they also turned themselves into a Russian protectorate, wasted their limited resources and sent their best and brightest men to war to be killed. They helped us to become just like them! A nation with deep wounds. The worst outcome of the conflict is because of Armenian secessionism and because of the wars we have the Russian troops in our country today. Just like them we also became more dependent on Russia. In fact, Armenian nationalism denied us to become a healthy nation and sovereign state. During four decades of conflict, we resembled the Armenians and we should overcome this victim identity.[49]

Another Azerbaijani historian added:

> We won the war. Thanks to the leadership of Ilham Aliyev who prepared our army and built a good network of a coalition around Azerbaijan. However, we have Russia back in Azerbaijan. Armenia wasted our time and energy. They provided all the tools for Russia to remain in the Caucasus.[50]

In Jan Assman's words, a "national narrative tells us who 'we' are by telling the story of 'our' development, our past, our becoming."[51] I do not argue that the Karabakh defeat solely constitutes the narrative template for Azerbaijani society but it also resurrected a once-familiar narrative in a revised version that offered a new cognitive map and framework for understanding the meaning and goals of Azerbaijani society and the state as well. This also became a victimhood narrative, which accounted for the instances where Azerbaijanis were expelled, murdered, and raped by Armenian militias.[52] The memories of killing, deportation, and occupation acted to codify a sense of victim identity and this, in turn, had a dramatic impact on how Azerbaijan designed its foreign policy.[53] Azerbaijan's main strategy during negotiations was to convince the international community to recognize its victimhood status.[54] As the Armenians rejected the notion of recognizing, much less sharing victim status with Azerbaijanis, this. more or less, steeled Azerbaijan's moves to resist proposals as well as compromises during negotiations.

Few seemed to comprehend just how strong Azerbaijani's victimhood was based not on long-ago historical memories but more on the brutally acute awareness of events that occurred in the just concluded

First Karabakh War. The emotional dynamics operated swiftly, making an imprint not only on the survivors of the First Karabakh War but also on the generation immediately following the events, which represented Azerbaijanis who had not experienced the war. The Azerbaijani government institutionalized commemoration of the war, dedicating resources to making the war experiences, defeat, mass killings, and the loss of major cultural centers part of the social fabric for the country's citizens. The process of remembering sustained the deep feeling of revenge and determination to prepare for the next war, adding to its propagandistic effects. The public approved of the government's efforts to make events of remembrance part of the formal process for the state and society. In Baku, the government authorized several memorials and encouraged documentaries and publications devoted to recollections of the war. There was an elite honor guard and an eternal flame memorial in the *sehidlik* (Martyrs' Mosque). Azerbaijani school textbooks devoted chapters documenting the atrocities of Armenia and framing the Azerbaijanis as victims of the aggression, thereby sustaining the post-traumatic effects of the devastating war in the minds of the generation of Azeri youth who would be recruited as adults to rectify the grievances of the war. The Karabakh story was integral to every aspect of Azerbaijan's civic livelihood, public opinion, politics, and the functions of the state institutions.

The public willingly accepted and endured hardship for the cause of correcting the humiliations of the historical injustice that had been inflicted on the country. The joint cause of victimhood and nationalism also gave Azerbaijani officials the cover they needed to sweep away the corrupt and ineffective leadership during the First Karabakh War. Muttalibov and Elcibey failed because they had been detached from grassroots politics. With the leadership of Heydar and Ilham Aliyev, they succeeded at galvanizing the government and the society in "coming to terms with the past humiliation" by stressing their innocence and the egregious effects of aggression, ethnic cleansing and mass murder carried out by the Armenians. Thus, the manifestation of the modern Azerbaijani nation-state has been crafted by Heydar Aliyev and carried through its full incorporation by Ilham Aliyev. Every annual commemoration started with the premise of the Khojaly massacre, which eventually was recognized by the Azerbaijanis as the gravest crime of humanity, genocide. Ernest Renan astutely observes that "shared suffering unites people more than common joy, and mourning is better than victory for the national memory."[55]

The government of Ilham Aliyev did not miss a beat in the mission that his father had set forth, ensuring that the Karabakh defeat would never retreat from the country's central political stage. The government's budget lines were authorized to allocate monies for statues, museums, photographic exhibitions, books, and publications, all for marking the anniversary of the Khojaly massacre. As noted elsewhere in the book, Khojaly became the Nanjing historical parallel for Azerbaijan: rape, killing, and inhumane torture and detention were inflicted on the bodies of innocent Azerbaijanis, who were called Turks by Armenian militias. As presidents, both Heydar and Ilham Aliyevs ensured the public comprehended the scale and scope of the Armenian occupation and acts of ethnic cleansing and mass killings. They acknowledged that national identity is essential but also not all interests of the state and society can be wholly defined by identity. But, identity is often used as a filter to legitimize the governing interests. Ultimately, this guaranteed that there would be a Second Karabakh War, particularly in lieu of the long dormant diplomatic process. Meanwhile, in Azerbaijan, the sociopolitical and sociocultural project of sustaining and magnifying the memories of the First Karabakh War had achieved the intended effect. The youngest Azerbaijanis who had fled their homes in Karabakh in the 1990s would now return in 2020 on top of Azerbaijani tanks to reclaim their lands.

The Azerbaijani View of Russia

As the author conducted 85 interviews in Azerbaijan, a majority of Azerbaijanis who agreed to respond (63) said they blamed Russia more than Armenia for the Karabakh conflict. Many of those same respondents regard Armenians as weak and lacking the agency to determine their own destiny. They see the Armenians as tools easily manipulated in the hands of Russia. Yet, a small number of Azerbaijanis also characterize Armenians as a shrewd nation that keenly uses Russia, and other major European powers, to realize their national goals. However, both groups of Azerbaijani respondents agree broadly that Armenian foreign policy is subordinated to Russia and that the Armenian national interest is to serve Russia. Notably, this view was not commonly or publicly shared among Azerbaijani government officials. Meanwhile, the Azerbaijani citizen in the street is most likely to cite the longer historical record for their opinion about Russia's negative role in the Karabakh matter, including riots in Baku in 1905 as well as clashes between 1918 and 1922. Nevertheless, in 2017, there seemed to be near unanimity in the corridors of the Azerbaijani state and society about a collective sense of humiliation and victimhood, as based on the commonly expressed grievances of loss of territories that rightly belonged to their country and incidents of massive ethnic cleansing.

Some Azerbaijanis believe that they have long been victims of Russia, their own government and Armenians who became easily manipulated pawns in Russian hands. For example, a male respondent identified as Galib Aliyev, said, "We Azerbaijanis and Armenians suffer and became enemies because of Russia. Russia wants to dominate the Caucasus and they use Armenians as their agent to control us. It was the Russian Empire that brought Armenians from Iran and from the Ottoman Empire and settled then in Karabakh and other regions of Azerbaijan. In fact, Armenians created and became the destructive elements in the Ottoman Empire and Persia."[56] Another respondent, who gave his name as Mahmud Ceyhunlu, said, "Armenia is not independent. Their borders are protected by Russia. Their entire gas and electrical infrastructure is owned by Russia. Thus, they exist to keep Russia present in the Caucasus."[57] Rasul added, "We lost the Karabakh because of Russia. We are fighting not against Armenia but Russia and their servant Armenians. They serve Russian interests. Russia's 366th division in Shusha gave all of them weapons and led the war."[58]

Farid echoed his fellow citizens, explaining, "We all know that Armenia depends on Russia. Georgians and Azerbaijanis are aware of this fact. As they serve the interests of Russia, the people of the region do not like Armenians. You can't trust them. Armenia fully depends on Russia. Yet, the same Russia tries to portray us as the enemy of Armenians. They never will give up their tactic of divide-and-rule!".[59]

Mehriban added some nuance, saying, "Armenian and Azerbaijanis are close. Russians are different. Russia does not want these two people to live together. Russia killed over hundreds of people in January 1990 in Baku. You can't trust them. Armenians trust them and I never understand them."[60] Javad likewise laid blame on Russia, noting, "the negotiations failed because Russia did not want to resolve the issue. Russia wanted to place its troops on the ground. They are in Armenia but neither Georgia nor us allowed them. You can't trust Russians."[61]

In 2004, early in his presidency, the younger Aliyev summarized the dominant narrative of events in a speech to a Council of Europe session in

Strasbourg. He said, "This occupation started with aggressive separatism by Armenia against Azerbaijan. This policy resulted in the occupation of the former Nagorno Karabakh Autonomous Oblast (NKAO) and our seven regions outside the administrative borders of the oblast. Armenians never lived in these seven regions of Azerbaijan. They are areas settled only by Azerbaijanis." He continued, "As a result of the aggression and the policy of ethnic cleansing of Armenia against Azerbaijan, more than a million of our compatriots found themselves in the position of refugees and settlers. Today everything was destroyed in the occupied Azerbaijani lands. All buildings, schools, hospitals, museums are plundered, our national values are destroyed or looted. Armenians razed our sacred centers, mosques, to the ground."[62] In the lead-up to the Second Karabakh War in 2020, it was evident that a super majority of Azerbaijani citizens had inculcated Aliyev's words in their views and support for the campaign to rectify historical injustices and national humiliation suffered in the First Karabakh War.

Azerbaijanism as Identity

After the First Karabakh War, the Azerbaijan national identity was wholly transformed in the name of fortifying and justifying the Azerbaijani claims over the lost territories.[63] The war brought to the fore more than circumstances in the recent period. Now, the entirety of the history behind the borders, the definition of homeland, the ancestral origins of groups, the role of historical chronicles, and long patterns of population migrations in and around Karabakh were encompassed in the discourse. Both Armenians and Azerbaijanis trace their roots to Caucasian Albanians (note the difference from the Albanians associated with the Balkans).[64] By utilizing Russian and other sources, the discourse of the Azerbaijani historiography indicates that the ancient kingdom of Caucasian Albanians was the predecessor to the modern Azerbaijani people and identity.[65] For instance, this kingdom ruled Karabakh and Nakhichevan.[66] Alstadt sums up this argument as Azerbaijanis claim that they "are heirs to the Albanian state and territory."[67]

The Karabakh conflict forced Azerbaijan and Armenia to rally the dynamics of history to advance their respective political arguments. Azerbaijani historians insist that the Azerbaijani people originated from the blending of Caucasian Albanians and Turks. This point countered the Armenian argument, which claims that Azerbaijanis as Turks have no historical link to the Caucasus, as they came from Central Asia. Reacting to this attempt of denying Azerbaijani presence in the region, Azerbaijanis have backed up their connection to ancient Caucasian Albanians through archeological studies indicating that the indigenous inhabitants of the Karabakh were Albanian Christians and some of them were Islamized and some came under the influence of the Armenian Christian Orthodox Church. In addition, the historical records also show that many Armenians were settled in Karabakh and they moved from Persia and the Ottoman Empire. As a result of these historical exegeses, Azerbaijanis reject the Armenian territorial claims over the region.[68]

Armenian historiography reacted to the Azerbaijani argument by suppressing the older argument that prevailed during the Soviet Era that the Armenians moved to the Caucasus, indicating they were not an indigenous population of the region. This is also known as the Armenian migration theory. With the Karabakh issue moving into active conflict status, this once dominant paradigm now was suppressed and replaced by a revisionist thesis, which claimed instead that Armenians were not migrants but, in fact, they were descended from aboriginal inhabitants who lived in the Armenian plateau for at least 6,000 years. Astourian summarizes these two conflicting Armenian theses and indicates how the revisionist formulation ascended as the preferred explanation for Armenians due to their political assertions and the rising temperature in the Karabakh conflict.[69] To advance their claim on Karabakh, the post-Soviet era historians advocating for Armenians accepted the revisionist argument that Armenians were aboriginal inhabitants in the Karabakh region.

Meanwhile, a new Azerbaijani view has developed, which is summarized by Altay Goyus, a leading intellectual in Baku. Goyus explains:

> The Azerbaijani language is Turkish. However, we should not reduce language to the ethnogenesis of Azerbaijani people. By language, we speak Turkish but by ethnogenesis we are a blended people of Albanians, Turks, Persians, Georgians, and other ethnicities who lived in the territories of Azerbaijan. Our ethnicity does not clearly coalesce with our language (Turkish). As far as the past is concerned, Albanian ethnogenesis is a very important aspect of who we were. As far as today's identity is concerned, the Turkish language is an important component of our Azerbaijani identity, along with the amalgamation of out ethnic origins.

There are two reasons for the emphasis on the Albanian ethnogenesis of the Azerbaijani identity. First, it provides a common memory and history for the people of Azerbaijan. Second, the argument of the Albanian origins explains the importance of continuity and permanent presence to the Azerbaijanis regarding these territories, including Karabakh. By developing this argument, "Azerbaijanis do not treat Armenians as non-indigenous but rather indicate that indigenous Armenians are Armenized Albanians."[70] Smith argues that during the Russian period, "Nagorno-Karabakh became an area of refuge for many Armenians fleeing from Persia and the Ottoman Empire."[71]

The Popular Front Government (PFG) of Elchibey, which came to power in 1992 during the First Karabakh War, reframed the nationalist identity as Turkism and identified the language as Turkish rather than Azerbaijani. Moreover, the PFG advanced the argument about the Turkish origins of the Azerbaijani nation while rejecting the Soviet thesis concerning Azerbaijani identity. However, when Heydar Aliyev came to power in 1993, he used all necessary means to make the Azerbaijani identity the new bond to keep diverse ethnic and religious groups together.

His nation-building project was based on a cosmopolitan, tolerant understanding of *Azerbaijani citizenship identity* without privileging any single ethnic identity or religion. Aliyev had three goals: strengthen the national sovereignty and political stability of Azerbaijan; modernize Azerbaijan along the lines of the European secular model; and articulate an independent foreign policy to secure the liberation of the Karabakh region. Aliyev's conception of nationhood was not based on ethnicity or a narrow historical past but rather rooted in the much longer historical timeline of Azerbaijani territory and the cultures that survived on the land. The emphasis was on territory, coexistence, and pride in Azerbaijani institutions rather than a celebration of a particular ethnicity.[72] The First Karabakh War facilitated the process of reframing territorial identity given that the main argument had been the territorial unity and sovereignty of Azerbaijan. During the Aliyev era, the lost part of this territory was treated as a metaphorical loss of an essential part of the national body, which must be restored in order to have any normal life-sustaining function as a nation. Those who live in the territory of Azerbaijan are all Azerbaijanis, regardless of their ethnicity or religion. In this sense, Armenians are also Azerbaijani.[73]

Turkey's indifference to the defeat and humiliation of Azerbaijani 'Turks" had a major impact not only on Azerbaijan's perception of Turkey but also on how its reconstituted identity placed less emphasis on its Turkish characteristics.[74] There have always been two competing and sometimes overlapping discourses of identity in Azerbaijan: Turkism (*Türkçülük*) and Azerbaijanism (*Azerbaycancılığ*).[75] Although during the Soviet era, especially after 1937, the Azerbaijani identity was predicated on the territory and the state framework of the country's existence, there was also an outpouring of Turkish nationalism during the collapse of the Soviet Union.[76] In particular, Elchibey and his inner circle emphasized Turkish nationalism as part of defining the future of Azerbaijani identity. Turkey's role during the First Karabakh War and its indifference to Elchibey had a major impact on sentiments of Turkism in Azerbaijan. While Azerbaijan was losing territories and expelled from its own lands, Elchibey asked for help from Turkey, including humanitarian aid. Demirel, however, remained indifferent because he never trusted Elchibey and regarded him as a liability. Demirel, however, had "great respect for Heydar Aliyev as a pragmatic and rational statesman." He said, "Aliyev is aware of the limits of his power as well as our capacity to know what we can and cannot do."[77]

State-Building and the Military

Heydar Aliyev's political project was a nation-building mission because he realized the fact that there was neither an adequately functioning state nor a nation to liberate Karabakh. As Charles Tilly argues, the nation-state building processes always entailed two simultaneous processes of (a) building a shared history and memory about the origins of the nation as a homogenized entity; and (b) the construction of state institutions and bridging the state with this newly conceptualized nation.[78] Aliyev was conscious of the problems of Azerbaijan and he insisted on *Azerbaijani* identity over Turkism. On the basis of my own study on Azerbaijan, I would conclude that the nation-building process became the indispensable aspect of turning around the outcome of the conflict over Karabakh. His stress on Azerbaijanism was not motivated by his anger at Turkey or reaction to Turkey's indifference to the defeat of Azerbaijan, but rather he stressed the cosmopolitan nature of the Azerbaijani identity. He echoed the claim that Azerbaijanis were indigenous as much as Armenians and Georgians were, by stressing that the Azerbaijani nation is an amalgam of diverse ethnic groups and cultures who had survived in the territories of Azerbaijan. He also redefined the national aims as the liberation of Karabakh, while strengthening independence through alternative energy routes, and modernizing Azerbaijan. At the core was the spread of the new Azerbaijani nationalism through the mass education system. The legitimacy of his reforms was cemented by a newfound sense of political stability, which rectified the failed state conditions which plagued the country before 1993. Regardless of the impact of the reforms, the Azerbaijani public always measured the strength of their state in terms of preparing for the eventual liberation of the Karabakh region. Thus, reforms and the state legitimacy were finally cemented by the military victory in the Second Karabakh War in 2020.

From the earliest days of his presidency, Heydar Aliyev realized that to achieve anything in Azerbaijan, the most important condition was political stability with a functioning acknowledgment of law and order. He took advantage of Azerbaijan's natural resources as much as possible and boosted the Azerbaijani oil industry. He gained independence for his country's oil industry by creating an alternative pipeline through Georgia and Turkey. Aliyev signed the "Contract of the Century" in 1994 which aimed to improve the oil industry through foreign companies. The deal proved incredibly lucrative for the Azerbaijani economy and the revenue was allocated to build a stronger military force to free Azerbaijani territories. Later, he agreed to allow the flow of oil to Turkey.

Giving the rebellions and fragmented political situation in Azerbaijan in the 1990s, Aliyev was the right person to overcome these challenges. He knew the country better than any other leader, as he had a comprehensive grasp of the old Soviet political culture as well as that of his native country. He had two goals: the political stability of the country and the formation of a new army. He is the true father of the current Azerbaijani state. Aliyev was reelected in October 1998 and he dedicated his second term to completing the project. Aliyev remained the most popular politician in Azerbaijan and when he died in 2003, there was no question that his son Ilham would succeed him. The elder Aliyev's major legacy was to stabilize a chaotic and fragmented nation and build the requisite institutions to enhance the state's capacity for economic development, military and security, and a functional bureaucracy. Today, especially after the Second Karabakh War, the Aliyev legacy is stronger than ever in the hands of the younger Aliyev, serving as a bond as strong for its emotional connections as the Azerbaijani flag or national anthem.

Single-Issue Foreign Policy: Liberation of Karabakh

While the Armenian desire to annex Karabakh and its surroundings removed any workable option for Armenian foreign policy but to rely on Russia, the occupation of Azerbaijani territories encompassed the primary determinant of Azerbaijan's foreign policy. While Azerbaijan expected to receive support from the U.S. and Europe against the Armenian occupation of its territories, this support did not materialize, as Western powers instead supported Armenia. Azerbaijan had to reconfigure its foreign policy and adopt a more neutral, pro-Turkey, and pro-Russian stance. Baku's strategic gravitation toward Russia was an outcome of its desire to preserve its territorial integrity and end the Armenian occupation. Baku painfully witnessed how Russia had fragmented and crippled Georgia and Ukraine before the eyes of the Western powers. One should note that Russian foreign policy in the Caucasus comprises three parts. First, Armenia is the closest military and political ally of Russia, so is without any option but to rely on Russia for its security and economic well-being. The second, the Karabakh conflict became a bargaining chip to prevent an Azerbaijani drift to the Western camp and, as a result, keep the country under Moscow's influence. The third uses the Karabakh conflict to remind everyone in the region to recognize Russia as the hegemon with a still formidable power to (de)stabilize the region.

Azerbaijan is one of the world's most important energy markets. Heydar Aliyev's main goal was to gain full control over the country's oil production and export traffic. He coordinated stakeholder support to build the Baku-Tbilisi-Ceyhan pipeline, an advancement in infrastructure that diversified the Azerbaijani economy and strengthened its sovereignty as a power of oil diplomacy. Moscow had desired to gain full control over the exports of Azerbaijani oil as well as persuade the Aliyev government to bring back Russian military bases to Azerbaijan. When Aliyev came to power he was aware of such Russian demands and opted instead to carefully navigate a complicated path in the government's foreign policy and security affairs so as not to anger Russia to the point of hostile action. Aliyev regarded oil as a strategic weapon to distance Azerbaijan from Russia; enhance its independence; and prepare the country to liberate the occupied territories. Aliyev saw Azerbaijan's ample oil reserves as the ideal path for strengthening relations with the West and a balancing mechanism against Russian desires to muscle into the region. He frequently invited multinational Western oil companies to explore and export Azerbaijani oil. Yet, Aliyev also was extremely cautious not to foment any emotions that might trigger Russia to seek aggressive retribution.

When Aliyev became President, he visited Russia early in his administration and agreed to have Azerbaijan join the Commonwealth of Independent States in September 1993. Moreover, to prevent any possible Russian intervention and trade obstacles, he invited the Russian company Lukoil to join his country's oil exploration and refining projects. The Azerbaijani state oil company (SOCAR) transferred ten percent of its share in the Azeri, Chirag, and Guneshli offshore fields to Lukoil. Again, by acknowledging the potential range of Russian intentions and its capacity to derail Azerbaijani's oil ventures, Aliyev saw the stock transfer as a prudent preventive measure and as an opportunity to obtain Russia's support in the pipeline project traversing Turkey as well as Moscow's diplomatic backing in the Karabakh conflict.[79] Aliyev succeeded in gaining the favorable terms of the "deal of the century" with Western oil companies along with the start of construction of the pipeline crossing into Tbilisi and Turkey.

Aliyev's main foreign policy objectives included consolidating the sovereignty of Azerbaijan, resisting Russian pressure, welcoming Western corporate oil interests as part of his energy diplomacy, and ultimately freeing the territories from Armenian occupation. Kesici said, "According to Suleyman (Demirel) bey, Heydar Aliyev was fully aware that the future of Azerbaijan was based on having good relations both with the West and Russia. He used the oil to develop his country and enhance the sovereignty of Azerbaijan. He realized that Azerbaijan's independence requires Western support against Russia and its expansionist policy. His main concerns were the Russophile elite in Baku and the Russian support for Armenia."[80] Through the multinational oil companies, Aliyev found likely supporters for Azerbaijani foreign and security policies and for its efforts to liberate the Karabakh territories. This position was aptly summed up by Vafa Gulizade, who was Aliyev's top foreign policy adviser and confidante: "Oil is our strategy; it is our defense, and it is our independence. Iran is having envious dreams of Azerbaijan, and if the Russians were strong, they would colonize Azerbaijan. But they can't because Aliyev invited the whole world to watch."[81] Aliyev's policy gamble worked on all counts.

Meanwhile, U.S. foreign policy has persistently been under the influence of ethnic lobbies. Although the broader Armenian lobby is not as powerful as the Jewish or Greek lobbies, it has considerable support to not serve principally the interests of the U.S. as much as it is to serve the objectives of their respective homelands. The Armenian community has lobbied strenuously to push the U.S. government to support Armenia's occupation and ethnic cleansing policies in the Karabakh region.[82] In April 1992, for example, the U.S. Congress passed the Freedom Support Act, which prohibited any economic or military assistance to Azerbaijan. Thus, the U.S. never became a reliable player and missed the opportunity to pull Azerbaijan toward the Western sphere of influence and free the Caucasus from the influence of Russia or decrease its role. Russia still remains the hegemon in the South Caucasus because of the Karabakh conflict and the anti-Azerbaijani activities of the Armenian ethnic lobby in the U.S.

Conclusion

It is striking to see the impact of victimhood, as expressed in Armenia, which persisted in anchoring its perceptions even after its decisive military victory in the First Karabakh War, and then in Azerbaijan, which used victimhood following its humiliating defeat to become the all-encompassing motivation to prepare for its own decisive victory in the Second Karabakh War. Both nations faced similar circumstances as newly independent states in the challenge of stabilizing and building the institutional infrastructure to carry out domestic and foreign policies. The major difference is the amount and extent of effective political change. Despite its victory in the 1990s, Armenia appeared to retreat deeper into a defensive geopolitical posture, as the frozen status of the territorial conflict produced no tangible progress in resolving the issues. Meanwhile. The Karabakh conflict "galvanized Azerbaijani national consciousness" but it also became the most consequential catalyst of political change in Baku.[83] From all dimensions—political, economic, social, cultural, educational, military and security—Azerbaijan and its citizens accepted the singular focus on gaining a second opportunity to rectify and reverse the effects of its humiliation in the first war. It was at this point where both former Soviet republics diverged, as Armenia gradually stepped closer to its old imperial superior for economic and military support while Azerbaijan managed a strategic distance to assert its economic independence and self-determination in matters of foreign policy and national security. The events of January 1990 became a critical pivot for policymakers, when Soviet troops entered Baku and killed Azerbaijanis. It set in motion the resolve of Azerbaijanis to reject the Soviet Union, which was in its final months, and to make legitimate their own formulation of a nationalist movement, which thrived in particular after the defeat in the First Karabakh War.

Notes

1. Tomas de Wall, *Black Garden: Armenia and Azerbaijan Through Peace and War* (New York: New York University Press, 2003), p. 129.
2. Michael P. Croissant, *The Armenian-Azerbaijani Conflict: Causes and Implications* (Westport, CT: Praeger, 1998).
3. Yaqub Mammadov, known as the "Dollar Yaqub" due to his corruption, was the president of the Republic of Azerbaijan between March and May 1992. His successor Isa Gambar held the post between May and June 1992 as an acting president, followed by Adulfaz Elchibey who was elected and stayed in the office from June 1992 until October 1993. Heydar Aliyev was elected on the 3rd October 1993 and stayed in the office until October 2003.
4. Audrey Altstadt, *Frustrated Democracy in Post-Soviet Azerbaijan* (Columbia University Press, 2017).
5. By "augmented Armenia," Broers means the common map of Armenia which includes all those occupied territories as a part of Armenia. Those who promoted "augmented Armenia" were those who stressed security, rejected any compromise with Azerbaijan, and were involved in the informal economy and informal politics of Armenia and had close ties with Armenian oligarchs.
6. Levon Chorbajian, *The Making of Nagorno-Karabakh: From Secession to Republic* (New York: Palgrave, 2001).
7. Farhad Mirzayev, "The Nagorno-Karabakh Conflict: International Law Appraisal," in M. Hakan Yavuz and Michael Gunter, eds., *Nagorno-Karabakh Conflict: Historical and Political Perspectives* (New York: Routledge, 2023), pp. 168–202; Kamal Maliki-Aliyev, "International Law and the Changes in the Status Quo of the Nagorno-Karabakh Conflict in 2020," in M. Hakan Yavuz and Michael Gunter, eds., *Nagorno-Karabakh Conflict: Historical and Political Perspectives* (New York: Routledge, 2023), pp. 203–220.
8. According to the 1979 population census, the total population of Nagorno-Karabakh was 162,181. Out of this population, 123,076 Armenians; 37,264 Azerbaijani; 1265 Russian, and 140 Ukrainians.
9. Narodnoe khoziaistvo Azerbaidzhanskoi SSR za 60 let, iub. stat. sbornik (hereafter, NKhA za 60 let) (Baku, 1980), p. 350.

10. More on the meaning and evolution of the Karabakh Clan, see "Armenia: Internal Instability Ahead," 18 October 2004 (International Crisis Group, 2004), especially pp. 9–11; https://d2071andvip0wj.cloudfront.net/158-armenia-internal-instability-ahead.pdf.
11. Igor Muradyan (1957–2018), an Armenian political activist, who spearheaded the idea of unifying Karabakh with Armenia. He shaped the early debate on the Karabakh movement, along with Zori Balayan, Silva Kaputikyan, and Victor Hambardzumyan.
12. Taline Papazian, "State at War, State in War: The Nagorno-Karabakh Conflict and State-Making in Armenia, 1991–1995," *The Journal of Power Institutions in Post-Soviet Republics* 8 (2008). Web. Accessed 31 March 2022. https://journals.openedition.org/pipss/1623.
13. James J. Coyle, *Russia's Interventions in Ethnic Conflict: The Case of Armenia and Azerbaijan* (Palgrave, 2021), p. 66.
14. Taline Papazian, "State at War, State in War."
15. Vazgen Manukian, who challenged Levon Ter-Petrosyan, had a charismatic personality and recreated himself in the battlefields of Karabakh in 1992–1993. He was a product of the Karabakh conflict and never hesitated to reject reasonable compromise on the Karabakh issue.
16. De Waal, *Black Garden*, p. 257.
17. Vano Siradeghian, Ter-Petrosyan's interior minister at the time of the election, accepted the fact that the 1996 elections were rigged. For more on the debate, see Emil Danielyan, "Armenia: 1996 Presidential Election Was Rigged, Aide Suggests" (9 January 1999), Radio Free Europe/Radio Liberty. 9 January 1999. https://www.rferl.org/a/1090270.html; Emil Danielyan, "Armenia: Ter-Petrossian Criticizes Charges Against Old Ally," RadioFreeEurope/RadioLiberty (9 January 1999), https://www.rferl.org/a/1090434.html (Retrieved July 7, 2022).
18. More on the killings, see.
19. Grigorian, "Forward," in Levon Ter-Petrossian, *Armenia's Future, the Relations with Turkey, and the Karabagh Conflict*, ed. Arman Grigoryan (New York, NY: Palgrave Macmillan, 2018), pp. 8–9. For more on the consequences of the Karabakh conflict on Armenia's domestic politics, see Grigorian, "The Karabagh Conflict and Armenia's Failed Transition to Democracy," *Nationalities Papers* 46:5 (April 2018), pp. 844–860.
20. More on Hai Dat, see https://jamestown.org/program/irredentism-enters-armenias-foreign-policy/; Armenia's Declaration of Independence, which was published in 1991, rejected the 1921 Treaty of Moscow and the Treaty of Kars between the Soviet Union and Turkey by claiming that it surrendered Armenian territories to Turkey. Thus, the Declaration rejects the boundaries between Turkey and Armenia, and contained a clause on the task of the Armenian state to work toward the recognition of the Armenian genocide.

21. Instead of acting pragmatically, the newly independent Armenia was obsessed by Hai Dat, with the notable exception being the administration of Levon Ter-Petrossian, as the essential condition for pursuing its nationalistic dreams. When Armenian foreign minister Vardan Oskanian announced the primacy of *Hai Dat*, he identified three pillars supporting this policy theme. They included recognizing the events of 1915 as genocide; restoring territories in present-day Turkey and Azerbaijan that were once inhabited by Armenians, and unifying Karabakh with Armenia because it always had been populated and ruled by Armenians and consequently the principle of self-determination legitimized such a policy.
22. There are very few articles which deal with the consequences of the Karabakh conflict on Armenian and Azerbaijani societies. For a thoughtful article, see Tigran Mkrtchyan, "Democratization and the Conflict of Nagorno-Karabakh," *Turkish Policy Quarterly* 6:3 (2007), pp. 79–92.
23. Brian Whitmore, "Armenia Spotlights 'Karabakh Clan,'" March 5, 2008, Radio Free Europe, https://www.rferl.org/a/1079586.html.
24. Panossian, "The Irony," p. 152.
25. Stephan Asturian, "Killings in the Armenian Parliament: Coup d'Etat, Political Conspiracy, or Destructive Rage?" *Contemporary Caucasus Newsletter in Soviet and Post-Soviet Studies* 9 (Spring 2000), UC-Berkeley, pp. 1–6.
26. Gerard Libaridian, *The Challenge of Statehood: Armenian Political Thinking Since Independence* (Watertown, MA: Blue Crane Books, 1999), p. 94.
27. Razmik Panossian, "The Irony of Nagorno-Karabakh: Formal Institutions versus Informal Politics," *Regional & Federal Studies* 11:3 (2001), p. 156.
28. https://eurasianet.org/migration-out-of-armenia-spikes#:~:text=In%20the%20three%20quarters%20of,loss%20represented%20almost%2064%2C000%20people. For the changing of the population, see https://worldpopulationreview.com/countries/armenia-population.
29. Oleg Kuznetsov, "The Coup That Never Happened and 'the Karabakh Clan' in the Armenian Army," March 2, 2021, https://politicstoday.org/the-coup-that-never-happened-and-the-karabakh-clan-in-the-armenian-army/.
30. Kuznetsov, "The Coup That Never Happened."
31. Ishkhanian, 1999, pp. 31–33.
32. Ishkhanian, 1999, p. 22.
33. Gaidz Minassian, *Armenia, a Russian Outpost in the Caucasus?* Paris: Ifri Russie. Nei.Visions 27, IFRI Russia/NIS Center, February 2008, p. 11. https://www.ifri.org/sites/default/files/atoms/files/ifri_RNV_minassian_Armenie_Russie_ANG_fevr2008.pdf, accessed March 23, 2022.

34. As quoted in Alla Mirzoyan, *Armenia, the Regional Powers, and the West: Between History and Geopolitics* (New York: Palgrave, 2010), p. 22.
35. Grigorian, ""The Karabagh Conflict and Armenia's Failed Transition to Democracy," p. 846.
36. Ter-Petrosyan, *Armenia's Future*.
37. Mirzoyan, *Armenia, the Regional Powers*; Taline Papazian, "From Ter-Petrossian to Kocharian: Explaining Continuity in Armenian Foreign Policy, 1991–2003," *Demokratizatsiya* 14:2 (2006), pp. 235–251; A. Aram Terzyan, "The Evolution of Armenia's Foreign Policy Identity: The Conception of Identity Driven Paths. Friends and Foes in Armenian Foreign Policy Discourse," in K. Kakachia and A. Markarov, eds., *Values and Identity as Sources of Foreign Policy in Armenia and Georgia* (Tibilisi: Publishing House Universal, 2006), pp. 145–183.
38. Gaidz Minassian, "Armenia, a Russian Outpost in the Caucasus?" IFRI Russie.Nei.Visions 27, IFRI Russia/NIS Center, February 2008, p. 11. Web. Retrieved 23 March 2022. https://www.ifri.org/sites/default/files/atoms/files/ifri_RNV_minassian_Armenie_Russie_ANG_fevr2008.pdf.
39. Ohannes Geukjian, *Ethnicity, Nationalism and Conflict in the South Caucasus: Nagorno-Karabakh and the Legacy of Soviet Nationalities Policy* (Farnham, UK and Burlington, VT: Ashgate, 2012).
40. More on this debate see Libaridian, *The Challenge of Statehood*.
41. David Boyajian, "Why Russia Needs Armenia and Vice Versa," *The Armenian Weekly*, February 5, 2019, https://armenianweekly.com/2019/02/05/why-russia-needs-armenia-and-vice-versa/.
42. Caucasus Research Resource Center, "Main Friend of the Country," Caucasus Barometer time-series dataset Armenia, 2019, https://caucasusbarometer.org/en/cb-am/MAINFRN/.
43. Interview with Rauf Garagozova, February 16, 2022.
44. Anthony Giddens, *The Consequences of Modernity* (London: Stanford University Press, 2021), pp. 261–287.
45. Ole Weaver, "Securitization and Desecuritization,,,,," in Ronnie D. Lipschutz, ed., *On Security* (New York: Columbia University Press, 1995), pp. 46–86.
46. Ralf Emmers, "Securitization," in Alan Collins, ed., *Contemporary Security Studies* (Oxford: Oxford University Press, 2007), pp. 109–125; Jef Huysmans, "Revisiting Copenhagen: Or, on the Creative Development of a Security Studies Agenda in Europe," *European Journal of International Relations* 4:4 (1998), pp. 479–505.
47. Charles van der Leeuw, *Azerbaijan: A Question for Identity* (New York: ST. Martin's Press, 2000); Joshua Kucera, "Between Europe and Asia": Geography and Identity in Post-Soviet Nation-building Narratives," *Central Asian Affairs* 4:4 (2017), pp. 331–357.

48. Interview with Ilhan Kesici, May 12, 2021.
49. Interview with Elin Suleymanov, February 17, 2017.
50. Interview with Eldar Abbasov, May 10, 2022.
51. Quoted in James V. Wertsch, "Deep Memory and Narrative Templates: Conservative Forces in Collective Memory," p. 181.
52. R. Garagozov, "Memory, Emotions, and Behavior of the Masses in an Ethnopolitical Conflict: Nagorno-Karabakh," *The Caucasus & Globalization* 5:3–4 (2011), pp. 77–88.
53. M. Najafizadeh, "Ethnic Conflict and Forced Displacement: Narratives of Azeri IDP and Refugee Women from the Nagorno-Karabakh War" (internally displaced persons) (Report). *Journal of International Women's Studies* 14:1 (2013), pp. 161–183; Najafizadeh, "Poetry, Azeri IDP/Refugee Women, and the Nagorno-Karabakh War," *Journal of Third World Studies* 32:1 (2015), pp. 13–43.
54. Aytan Gahramanova, "Paradigms of Political Mythologies & Perspectives of Reconciliation in the Case of the Nagorno-Karabakh Conflict," *International Negotiation* 15:1 (2010), pp. 133–152.
55. Renan, "What is a Nation?" reprinted in Geoff Eley and Ronald G. Suny, (eds). *Becoming National: A Reader* (New York: Oxford University Press, 1996), pp. 45–46.
56. Interview with Galib Aliyev, January 15, 2020.
57. Interview with Mahmud Ceyhunlu, May 10, 2021.
58. Interview with Rasul Haciyev, May 9, 2021.
59. Interview with Farid Agayev, May 9, 2021.
60. Interview with Mehriban Valiyev, May 9, 2021.
61. Interview with Javad Eltur, May 9, 2021.
62. OIK vystupila protiv sepratizma i sotrudnichestva s armeniei *Echo of Baku*, 2009.
63. Ceylan Tokluoglu, "The Political Discourse of the Azerbaijani Elite on the Nagorno-Karabakh Conflict (1991–2009)," *Europe-Asia Studies* 63:7 (2011), pp. 1223–1252.
64. S.H. Astourian, "In Search of Their Forefathers: National Identity and the Historiography and Politics of Armenian and Azerbaijani Ethnogeneses," in D.V. Schwartz and R. Panossian, eds., *Nationalism and History: The Politics of Nation- Building in Post-Soviet Armenia, Azerbaijan and Georgia* (Toronto: University of Toronto, Center for Russian and East European Studies, 1994); George A. Bournoutian, *A History of Qarabagh: An Annotated Translation of Mirza Jamal Javanshir Qarabaghi's Tarikh-e Qarabagh* (Costa Mesa, CA: Mazda Publishers, 1994); George A. Bournoutian, "The Ethnic Composition and the Social-Economic Condition of Eastern Armenia in the First Half of the Nineteenth Century," in Ronald G. Suny, ed. (1996b); L. Chorbajian, P. Donabedian, and

C. Mustaflan, *The Caucasian Knot: The History and Geo-politics of Nagorno-Karabagh* (London: Zed Book, 1994).
65. Feride Mammadova (1938–2021)'s PhD dissertation, which examined the Armenian documents, claimed that Armenians migrated from Asia Minor and they are not aboriginal inhabitants of the Caucasus. On the basis of these Armenian documents, she concluded that Armenians Karabakh and Nakhichevan are not part of Armenian lands. By exploring the Soviet and Russian sources on the Albanians, she argued that there was a distinct Albanian ethos and Armenians migrated to the territory of Azerbaijan in the early nineteenth centuries. Her work was criticized by Victor Shnirelmann. See more, Victor Shnirelmann, *The Value of the Past: Myths, Identity and Politics in Transcaucasia*, Senri Ethnological Studies, No. 57 (Osaka: National Museum of Ethnology, 2001).
66. A.L. Altstadt, "O Patria Mia: National Conflict in Mountainous Karabagh," in W.R. Duncan, and G.P. Holman, eds., *Ethnic Nationalism and Regional Conflict: The Former Soviet Union and Yugoslavia* (Boulder, CO: Westview Press, 1994), p. 111.
67. Altstadt, 1992, p. 23.
68. Audrey L. Altstadt, *The Azerbaijani Turks: Power and Identity Under Russian Rule* (Stanford, CA: Hoover Institution Press, 1992), p. 6; Svante Cornel, *Small Nations and Great Powers: A Study of Ethnopolitical Conflict in the Caucasus* (Richmond, VA: Curzon Press, 2001), p. 66.
69. S.H. Astourian, "In Search of their Forefathers: National Identity and the Historiography and Politics of Armenian and Azerbaijani Ethnogeneses," in D.V. Schwartz and R. Panossian, eds., *Nationalism and History: The Politics of Nation-Building in Post-Soviet Armenia, Azerbaijan and Georgia* (Toronto: University of Toronto, Center for Russian and East European Studies, 1994), p. 49.
70. Although Armenian historian H. Tchilingirian insists that the Azerbaijanis seek to reject the Armenian presence in Karabakh and treat then as non-indigenous to the region, this is not true. Azerbaijanis accept the fact that many Albanians were Armenized and also some Armenians from Persia and the Ottoman Empire also moved to the region. H. Tchilingirian, "Nagorno Karabagh: Transition and the Elite," *Central Asian Survey*, 18:4 (1999).
71. G. Smith, V. Law, A. Wilson, A. Bohr, and E. Allworth, *Nation-Building in the Post-Soviet Borderlands: The Politics of National Identities* (Cambridge: Cambridge University, 1998), p. 53.
72. Ceyhan Mahmudlu, "Theorizing Nation Building in Azerbaijan," in Aliaga Mammadli, Adeline Braux, and Ceyhun Mahmudlu, eds., *"Azerbaijan" and Beyond: Perspectives on the Construction of National Identity* (Berlin: Verlag Dr. Köster, 2017), pp. 124–150.

73. See the program of the New Azerbaijani Party of Haydar Aliyev. It says "Azerbaijanism, motherland loving principle: The New Azerbaijan Party considers all Azerbaijan citizens living in the country and outside of it, who obey Azerbaijan State and its Laws, irrespective to their language, ethnic and social origin, as Azerbaijan people and considers Azerbaijan as their common, indivisible motherland and native country." New Azerbaijan Party, "The Program of the New Azerbaijan Party Adopted in the First Congress of the New Azerbaijan Party on December 21, 1999," New Azerbaijan Party, December 21, 1999. http://www.yap.org.az/en/view/pages/9.
74. A.L. Altstadt, *The Azerbaijani Turks, Power and Identity under Russian Rule* (Stanford, CA, 1992), p. 124; Charles van der Leeuw, *Azerbaijan. A Quest for Identity: A Short History* (New York, 2000); T. Swietochowski, "Russia's Transcaucasian Policies and Azerbaijan: Ethnic Conflict and Regional Unity," in Marco Buttino, ed., *In a Collapsing Empire* (Milan, 1993), pp. 191–192.
75. Ayca Ergun, "Citizenship, National Identity, and Nation-Building in Azerbaijan: Between the Legacy of the Past and the Spirit of Independence," *Nationalities Papers* (2021), pp. 1–18.
76. Harun Yilmaz, "The Soviet Union and the Construction of Azerbaijani National Identity in the 1930s," *Iranian Studies* 46:4 (2013), pp. 511–533.
77. Interview with Ilhan Kesici, June 12, 2021. Kesici was very close to Demirel.
78. Charles Tilly, *Stories, Identities, and Political Change* (Lanham, MD: Rowman and Littlefield, 2002), pp. 5–12.
79. Cheterian, "Dialectics of Ethnic Conflicts and Oil Projects in the Caucasus," pp. 11–37, and Kamer Kasim, "The Nagorno-Karabakh Conflict, Caspian Oil and Regional Powers," in Bulent Gokay, ed., *The Politics of Caspian Oil* (New York: Palgrave, 2001), pp. 185–198.
80. Interview with Ilhan Kesici, June 12, 2021.
81. Jeffrey Goldberg, "Getting Crude in Baku: The Crude Face of Global Capitalism," *The New York Times Magazine*, October 4, 1998.
82. F. Wallace Hays, "The US Congress and the Caspian," *Caspian Crossroads* 3:3 (Winter 1998), http://ourworld.compuserve.com/homepage/usazerb/casp.htm.
83. Audrey L. Altstadt, *Frustrated Democracy in Post-Soviet Azerbaijan* (New York: Columbia University Press, 2017), p. 2.

CHAPTER 5

Failed Negotiations

There have been many attempts at negotiations by regional and international actors—both states and organizations—to begin solving the festering and dangerous ethnic, and territorial conflict over Karabakh. Thus, although cease-fires ending bloody fighting were reached in 1994, 2016, and most recently in 2020, it would be naïve to argue that negotiations have been successful. Why? As Thomas de Waal concludes, "both Armenia and Azerbaijan compulsively portray themselves as victims of the other's aggression and their own violence as necessary acts of self-defense."[1] Thus "any just solution to the Nagorny-Karabakh dispute will entail painful compromises on both sides, and it will have to balance radically opposing principles."[2] Even worse, "the biggest problem is not so much lack of a readiness to compromise as lack of readiness to contemplate any future with the other side at all."[3]

Any analysis of this situation quickly becomes entangled with the military struggle. This was true because both sides usually felt that the military option was preferable since both parties received foreign support, mainly from Russia to continue the war. Each side hoped to win and emerge politically dominant. In addition, each side readily acquired or simply confiscated military equipment from the demoralized Soviet military that enabled them to continue their protracted conflict. Subsequently, mainly Russia, but others too, have continued to supply the belligerents. Although many big and middle-sized states such as Russia, Iran, and

© The Author(s), under exclusive license to Springer Nature Switzerland AG 2023
M. H. Yavuz and M. M. Gunter, *The Karabakh Conflict Between Armenia and Azerbaijan*, https://doi.org/10.1007/978-3-031-16262-6_5

Turkey as well as such intergovernmental security organizations as the Organization for Security and Cooperation in Europe (OSCE)'s Minsk Process with its subsequent Madrid Principles as well as UN Security Council resolutions supposedly sought to resolve and end the conflict, many conclude that these outside actors actually helped continue and even facilitate the conflict because they gave first priority to their own interests and stalled the process of negotiation.[4]

For example, in the conflict's early days on September 23, 1991, Russian president Boris Yeltsin and Kazakhstani president Nursultan Nazarbaev tried to negotiate a peace agreement. Yeltsin even flew into Karabakh to proclaim his initiative for a cease-fire, hold new elections, arrange refugee returns, and establish a new constitutional government. At first, Yeltsin's initiative looked promising because this was not the later pathetic, drunken Russian leader, but the hero who had just stood up successfully to the attempted coup against Gorbachev and supposedly saved nascent democracy in Russia. Thus, at the time, Yeltsin was basking in prestige and seemingly willing to use and therefore risk it for peace and democracy.

However, at the first resulting meeting on October 25, 1991, supposedly "fruitful" talks resulted in little more than an appeal to the combatants "to refrain from violence and voluntarism and to compliment the inter-republican talks with diplomacy by the people."[5] Fighting continued. Then on November 4, 1991, Azerbaijan closed a pipeline that had been carrying natural gas from Russia to Yerevan. Soon life in the Armenian capital was paralyzed. The Armenian representatives to the Yeltsin-backed negotiations walked out. Finally, Yeltsin's effort at negotiation was literally shot down on November 20 when Armenian forces apparently downed a helicopter, carrying Russian and Azerbaijani officials, killing the Russian and Kazakhstani observers to the peace talks as well as some Azerbaijani officials. Both combatants had sought to gain an advantage via military victories before the negotiating process began, thus preferring conflict over negotiations.

Moreover, Soviet/Russian military forces along with Azerbaijani Special Function Militia Troops (OMON) already had launched a big offensive to reestablish control in Karabakh. Operation Ring involved Soviet complicity with the Azerbaijani forces and led to many violations of human rights.[6] The Soviet and Azerbaijani forces justified their operation by explaining they were trying to capture illegally obtained Armenian weapons and arrest Armenian militias opposing Gorbachev's decree of 25

July 1990 on disarming such groups and attacking Azerbaijani villages. However, far from restoring order, Operation Ring led to even more militant Armenian determination in Karabakh to protect perceived Armenian rights and life. It also enabled the Armenians to build up their military, while the Azerbaijanis initially foundered by depending on the Russians. This contributed to the Armenian victory in the First Karabakh War. Only later did Azerbaijan successfully construct its military which enabled it to win the Second Karabakh War many years later in 2020. What is more, Armenian president Levon Ter-Petrosyan saw the initial Soviet actions in support of the Azerbaijanis as undeclared war and state terrorism.[7]

Furthermore, these clumsy Russian military efforts that in retrospect were also too late, dampened more promising diplomatic initiatives. In December 1991, for example, Turkish prime minister and shortly to be president Suleyman Demirel congratulated newly elected Armenian president Levon Ter-Petrosyan and even offered Armenia access to the Turkish Black Sea port of Trabzon and support for Armenian membership in the soon-to-be-established Black Sea Economic Cooperation Organization (BSEC) headquartered in Istanbul. In addition, Turkey wanted to build a gas and oil pipeline through Armenia that would connect the oilfields of the newly emerging Turkic republics of Central Asia with Trabzon. Landlocked Armenia desperately needs such economic and diplomatic opportunities, but the false promise of territorial gain soon trumped them. Even more, Russia's economic needs in Transcaucasia conflicted with proffered Turkish economic possibilities in the west. Thus, Russia proved unwilling to countenance an Armenian drift to the west that also involved a Western-financed oil pipeline in its near abroad. Negotiations became entangled with Russian economic, diplomatic, and military needs and thus failed.

In addition, the Armenian leadership of Nagorno-Karabakh and the then-president of Azerbaijan Ayaz Mutalibov both preferred a hardline approach over negotiations. Despite Armenian president Ter-Petrosyan's less belligerent attitude, Karabakh's leaders rejected any peaceful solution that did not provide for the enclave's independence including Shaumian (Geranoi), territory excluded from Karabakh's final borders in 1923.[8] In addition, the influential Armenian diaspora had no interest in seeking equitable peace so long as their kin was winning. Along with what was now Russian military assistance for its traditional Armenian ward, the Armenian diaspora also provided economic and military support.[9] For his part, Azerbaijani president Mutalibov authorized a complete economic blockade of Armenia and Karabakh.[10]

Thus, instead of renewed attempts at negotiations, on February 26, 1992, an Armenian attack on the Azebaijani town of Khojaly just north of Stepanakert in the middle of Nagorno-Karabakh killed more than 600 Azerbaijani civilians. To this day, in an ironic reversal of the usual Armenian claims of genocidal victimhood, the Turkic Azerbaijani term this event, genocide. The Armenians, on the other hand, downplay what occurred while also replying that it was payback for the Azerbaijani pogrom in Sumgait (a northern suburb of Baku on the Caspian Sea) that officially killed 32 ethnic Armenians from February 26–March 1, 1988, but which Armenian sources claim were much higher. In both cases, the Soviet/Russian forces theoretically in charge of developments were missing in action.

Cengiz Candar—a very prominent, leftist Turkish journalist who once enjoyed high-level, official connections, but in recent years has fallen out of favor with Turkish officials so is currently residing in Sweden—recently revealed secret Turkish attempts at negotiations that further illustrate the inherent difficulties.[11] In February 1992, when the current conflict was in its earlier days, visionary Turkish president Turgut Ozal entrusted Candar with a "dual corridor" proposal for Azerbaijani president Ayaz Mutalibov. This proposition would resolve the conflict by swapping connecting territories between Armenia and Azerbaijan which would partially help resolve the problem of their mixed ethnic populations. Ozal's suggestion would grant the Armenians a corridor through Azerbaijani Lachin in the south that would connect Karabakh with Armenia proper. In return, the Azerbaijani exclave Nakhichevan would be connected with Azerbaijan proper by a corridor through the Armenian territory of Zangezur in the south and also known as Meghri. Both proposed corridors lay close to the Iranian border in the south and somewhat further in the west to the Turkish frontier.

In addition to settling the conflict over Karabakh, Ozal was also trying to further Turkish interests by linking it to Azerbaijan proper through its exclave Nakhichevan, which shared a minuscule six-mile border with Turkey between Armenia in the north and Iran to the south, Mt. Ararat of Biblical fame towering spectacularly just to the west. Ozal's gambit would thus connect Turkey with its lengthy Black Sea shore to the Caspian Sea and the newly independent central Asian Turkic states beyond it. This would have opened up potential economic opportunities in the rapidly developing, post-Soviet region to Turkey. Indeed, Ozal told Candar that if the Azerbaijanis agreed, he could get the Armenian to endorse it, possibly based on Demirel's earlier offer to Armenia of access to the Turkish Black Sea port of Trabzon and support for Armenian membership in the soon-to-be-established Black Sea Economic Cooperation Organization (BSEC) referred to above. Unfortunately, Azerbaijani president Mutalibov, "with no hesitation or consideration, turned it down," telling Candar, "Lachin is ours. Zangezur is also ours. It is an Azerbaijani territory. It was seized from Azerbaijan in 1920 unjustly. We must recover it. Why should we concede our Lachin in order to recover our Zangezur?".[12]

At the time, Armenia was in the process of winning its proposed corridor by force, while the then-Azerbaijani president Ayaz Mutalibov and his successor Abulfaz Elchibey feared that Heydar Aliyev, then domiciled in his native Nakhichevan, would use the proposed deal to depose him and assume the Azerbaijani presidency himself, which is exactly what Aliyev did two years later largely due to successfully blaming Mutalibov for Azerbaijani losses in its war against Armenia. Later, one Armenian analyst explained why his state opposed an Azerbaijani corridor through Zangezur (Meghri), by describing it as the "Pan-Turkish Superhighway" that would enable Turkey to forge a pan-Turkic state into central Asia. Artashes Geghamian, the chairman of the nationalist National Unity Party in Armenia, elaborated, "the creation of a landbridge between Turkey and Azerbaijan would result in the formation of a union between those two states within 5–10 years."[13] With such a myopic vision, how could negotiations succeed? The Armenians would have little to do with Turkey outside of its unilateral apology for the massacres in 1915, an apology Turkey felt would ignore all the Muslims who had perished at that time as well as correctly reckoning would segue into further Armenian demands for compensatory Turkish territory where earlier large Armenian minorities had lived.

Interestingly, Ozal earlier had discussed his corridors proposal with U.S. President George H.W. Bush who had queried the Turkish president about what would happen to the Armenians who live in the Zangezur area that would go to Azerbaijan. Ozal replied, "All together, not more than 50,000 people would have to be moved. Otherwise, this war will continue forever."[14] Possibly based on this interchange, the United States' Goble Plan, named for the former U.S. State Department official Paul Goble, envisaged the same corridor swap.[15] Indeed, in 1999, Heydar Aliyev, the new president of Azerbaijan, and Robert Kocharyan, the president of Armenia and originally from Karabakh initially agreed on a corridor that would link Nakhichevan with Azerbaijan proper through southern Armenia. In exchange, Azerbaijan would recognize Nagorno-Karabakh including the Lachin region as Armenian territory. However, in 2001, Aliyev backed away from this plan during a meeting held in Key West, Florida as part of the Minsk Process.[16]

Unfortunately, the Armenians found the Goble Plan "outrageous.... It would have been a blunder of historic proportions for Armenia."[17] However, the reasons for this belief were based on outright errors of fact as well as sheer mistrust of anything dealing with Turkey. For starters, the Armenian critique argued that a corridor connecting Azerbaijan proper with its exclave Nakhichevan would amount to Azerbaijan "absorbing the autonomous Republic of Nakhichevan, a territory historically claimed by Armenia." In addition, "Armenia would lose its borders with Iran, the only reliable country through which Armenia could communicate with the outside world." Finally, the Armenians saw the Goble Plan as "an open door to Pan-Turkic designs of Turkish leaders" to create a "Republic of Western Azerbaijan (Irevan)" that would "return [to Azerbaijan] all historic lands, including Yerevan, Zangebasar, Goichu, Zangezur, Gyumri, Drlayza [Daralageaz?], and all remaining historical lands within the border of Armenia." Turkey had "the clear plan of destroying Armenia." Thus, to counter this reputed Turkish plot, Armenia should establish and then host "a Republic of Western Armenia government-in-exile, coinciding with the centennial of the Sevres Treaty [that had provided for such a greater Armenia]."[18]

A few years later, Goble admitted he had mistaken the economic and psychological value of an Iranian border for Armenia. Accordingly, he suggested a modification in his plan "by calling for Azerbaijan to cede a small portion of western Nakhichevan so that Armenia could have a border with Iran."[19] (However, doing this would eliminate the minuscule common border between Nakhichevan and Turkey, which clearly would have been unacceptable to Turkey and Azerbaijan.) Further illustrating that his plan was not merely a one-sided concession to Turkey and Azerbaijan as Armenia was claiming, Goble also urged "the international community put pressure on Turkey to open its border with Armenia as part of the package deal to end this conflict." Of course, this only became possible after the second war for Karabakh in 2020 returned Azerbaijan's territories between Armenia proper and Karabakh that Armenia had been occupying, the situation that had led to Turkey closing its border with Armenia in the first place. The hodge-podge ethnic mixing in the Caucasus continued to play havoc with any attempt to draw viable border lines that would implement ethnic demands.

Rejected at the time, the Goble Plan in effect rebirthed as part of the cease-fire ending the Second Karabakh War in November 2020 with the added provision of Russian peacekeeping troops securing it.[20] Unfortunately, it took thirty years of failed negotiations to reach this potential agreement adumbrated earlier by the Goble Plan, but of course who can foretell whether it will now be successful even after all the blood and failure that has occurred? True, Matthew Bryza, a former U.S. ambassador to Azerbaijan who had attempted to mediate the Karabakh conflict a decade earlier as the U.S. co-chair of the OSCE's Minsk process, stated the accord ending the second war over Karabakh on November 10, 2020, "has the potential to kick-start economic growth across the Caucasus."[21] One proposal was the restoration of a Soviet-era railway that had connected Yerevan to Russia but had been blocked by the hostilities resulting from the Soviet Union's breakup. However, now it could pass through the Azerbaijan exclave of Nakhichevan, southern Armenia, and then on to Azerbaijan proper. The plan would also give Azerbaijan a direct rail connection to Turkey by branching off from Nakhichevan. Iran too claimed it wanted to establish a rail link through Nakhichevan to Armenia. Thomas de Waal, the author of *Black Garden*, an important, early analysis of the Karabakh conflict referred to above, stated that he believed the OSCE's Minsk Process and other international groups could now help win needed financial backing to restore long-broken transport and border infrastructure. However, de Waal emphasized that this had to be done in a way that benefitted Armenia (and the Armenians in Karabakh) as well as Azerbaijan, Turkey, and Russia.

The World Bank also emphasized the improvement of trading ties and cooperation between local communities on both sides of the stressful borders: "If the blockades are lifted, trade distortions will be alleviated, bringing about positive short-term welfare effects—including more rational trade flows, resumption or a major increase of regional trade in some major commodities such as energy, and lower prices and/or higher profit margins on some important consumption and production goods."[22] Turkey was ready to open its borders with Armenia now that Armenian forces had been removed from the seven Azerbaijani provinces surrounding Karabakh it had been occupying.

However, this would prove difficult for Armenia because it blamed Turkey for its losing the second war against Azerbaijan over Karabakh: "Turkey's open support to Azerbaijan's war of aggression in the form of its top military expertise, consultants, weapons as well as recruitment and transportation of Islamic mercenaries [from Syria] resuscitated century-old held Armenian fears of genocide,"[23] asserted a senior Armenian diplomat speaking on condition that he not be identified by name. Jake Hanrahan, the creator of the independent conflict journalism platform Popular Front and who had recently journeyed to Nagorno-Karabakh, declared that the Armenian people would be "absolutely disgusted" by any deal with Turkey. Hanrahan also claimed that "Armenians had [had] their heads cut off on camera by Turkish-backed Azerbaijani forces" in the recent war. Although Amnesty International said that the video of the supposed atrocity was authentic, it was not certain whose heads had been severed. Indeed, Amnesty International and Human Rights Watch accused both sides of war crimes.[24] Furthermore, there was no valid evidence that Turkey had actually recruited and transported Islamic mercenaries from Syria to fight in the recent war over Karabakh.

IRAN

Neighboring Iran next tried its diplomatic hand, arranging two cease-fires in February 1992 and a meeting among representatives from Armenia, Azerbaijan, and Iran in Tehran from March 14–16. Often forgotten as an interested party, Iran, of course, not only bordered both Armenia and Azerbaijan, but also lay just south of greater Karabakh. Thus, violence could easily spill over into Iran and destabilize its large ethnic Azerbaijani population. However, an Iranian brokered peace proved illusory and fighting resumed by the end of the month. The Iranians blamed the military leadership of the newly formed Commonwealth of Independent States (CIS), that is Russia, although specifics were lacking.[25]

However, almost immediately Iran renewed attempts to restart negotiations. Mahmoud Vaezi began shuttle diplomacy to both Armenia and Azerbaijan, where he held several meetings, which led to a formal meeting of the states' two leaders in Tehran on May 7, 1992. The resulting Tehran Communique was mediated by Iranian president Akbar Hashemi Rafsanjani and signed by Yagub Mammadov, the acting president of Azerbaijan and Levon Ter-Petrosyan, the president of Armenia. It provided that meetings between leading representatives from both combatants including military personnel would be held and that all disputes would be solved by peaceful means on the basis of the principles of the Conference for Security and Cooperation in Europe (CSCE, subsequently OSCE), international law, and the UN Charter. Mahmoud Vaezi, the Iranian envoy was to initiate the process by visiting Baku, Yerevan, and Stepanakert and also involve CSCE observers for the continuation of mediation efforts.

Although the Iranian set process seemed well formulated and Iranian prestige was imbedded, the effort collapsed the very next day, when Armenian troops attacked and captured the Azerbaijani city of Shusha (an important cultural heritage) on May 8, 1992 before acting Azerbaijani president Yagub Mammadov could even return from Tehran. Armenian troops followed this blatant cease-fire violation by attacking and capturing Lachin on May 18. Lachin connected Karabakh with Armenia in the south and thus constituted a great prize for Armenia and a loss for Azerbaijan.

Azerbaijani authorities regarded Iran as morally responsible for the failure of negotiations. Embarrassed, Iran emphasized that it would not accept any border alterations, which implied its disapproval of the Armenian actions. A decade later former Armenian president Robert Kocharian (who came from Nagorno-Karabakh) explained that he thought Azerbaijans and Armenians were "ethnically incompatible"[26] and that it was not possible for the Armenians in Karabakh to live within an Azerbaijani state.[27] Walter Schwimmer, the former secretary-general of the Council of Europe, averred that Kocharian's comments were tantamount to warmongering.[28] Such attitudes testify to why successful negotiations over Karabakh proved unlikely if not impossible. Neither side was serious about negotiations.

In their analysis of why Iran's attempts at furthering negotiations failed, Ceyhan Mahmudlu and Shamkhal Abilov listed the following four points: (1) Memories of the earlier clashes between the combatants that prevented confidence building between them; (2) Armenia's superior military power and resulting unwillingness to mediate because it would inhibit further victories; (3) Iran's lack of powerful status and political leverage decreased its mediation effectiveness; and (4) Russia and other regional powers' desire not to enable Iran by allowing it to be successful in promoting negotiations.[29] In addition, the United States, "which was imposing sanctions over Iran and keeping Iran in isolation, wouldn't allow

Iran active involvement in the regional process even though this process aimed at stabilizing the region."[30]

Fast forward to the Second Karabakh War in 2020. At first glance, one might believe that their shared Shia religion and civilizational background would make Iran and Azerbaijan natural allies, especially since Armenia was Christian. However, Armenia expressed no irredentist claims on Iranian territory, while Turkic Azerbaijan held an attraction for Iran's large Azerbaijani minority bordering Azerbaijan. In addition, secular Azerbaijan had developed a working relationship with the United States, Israel, and Saudi Arabia, Shiite Iran's bitter enemies. Rival Turkey also supported Azerbaijan, while Iran remained isolated in its regional influence. Thus, once again Iran found itself in a difficult position regarding its possible role in promoting negotiations.[31]

UNITED NATIONS

On March 20, 1992, former U.S. secretary of state Cyrus Vance briefly visited Karabakh in an attempt to establish facts and prepare a report for the UN secretary-general. Asked about a solution to the conflict in Karabakh and how it compared to those in the former Yugoslavia, in which he also had played a mediating role, Vance averred that it was "not easy and this is very obvious."[32] Unfortunately, nothing substantive came of Vance's now all-but-forgotten visit on behalf of the United Nations.

UN Security Council Resolutions 822, 853, 874, and 884 adopted in 1993 recognized Nagorno-Karabakh and the seven surrounding Azerbaijani districts occupied by Armenia as part of Azerbaijan and called for the immediate and unconditional withdrawal of Armenian troops. Armenia did not comply, so these UN resolutions became a mere part of the frozen situation. UN-promoted negotiations failed to proceed and the role of the international organization became negligible. Instead, by 1993, the UN tacitly agreed to let a regional organization become much more important in the attempted process of negotiations.

MINSK GROUP/PROCESS

The Helsinki Final Act of 1975 that recognized Europe's existing borders resulting from World War II also established the Conference on Security and Cooperation in Europe (CSCE)—renamed in December 1994 the Organization for Security and Cooperation in Europe (OSCE) to reflect its permanence. Meeting in Helsinki on March 24, 1992, the CSCE established the Minsk Group/Process[33] when it suggested convening a conference in Minsk to negotiate a peaceful settlement of the Karabakh conflict on the basis of the CSCE's principles. Although such a conference was never held, since 1992, this regional organization supposedly has been the main third-party mediator seeking to facilitate negotiations between the two combatants through its Minsk Group/Process. Although most observers consider the Minsk Group process a dismal failure,[34] a brief survey of its actions follows since it has been the main theater in which negotiations, such as they have been, have transpired. Analyzing the process, contributes to understanding the reasons for the failure.

Initially, the West had exhibited a keen interest in solving the conflict in Karabakh. This led to the creation of the Minsk Group and a flurry of activity including the so-called 3 + 1 initiative involving the Italian Minsk Group chair joining private U.S.-Russian-Turkish talks. Subsequently, Armenia and Azerbaijan also joined, creating the so-called 5 + 1. However, preliminary discussions in Rome between June and September 1992 foundered over the official status of Armenian representatives from Karabakh. The Azerbaijani representatives refused to negotiate with the Karabakh Armenians on the grounds that to do so would compromise Azerbaijani sovereignty. Instead, Armenia and Azerbaijan should remain the sole negotiators.[35] The two combatants also failed to agree on the legal status of Karabakh. Armenia maintained that this should be decided after the permanent cessation of combat and the deployment of international peacekeeping forces in Karabakh. However, Azerbaijan argued that any such authorization would diminish its sovereignty over the contested area. Thus, the legal status of Karabakh must first be settled before any further talks with Armenia.[36]

The two combatants did seem to accept a proposal for Armenian forces to pull out of Kelbajar, one of the Azerbaijani provinces Armenia was occupying that lay between Armenia and Karabakh. However, eventually, the Karabakh Armenians rejected the proposal because in their view it failed to guarantee their rights and eliminate the Azerbaijani economic embargo on Karabakh.[37] By that time, the Armenian diaspora in the United States had piled on by successfully lobbying for The Freedom Support Act 907a which denied all forms of U.S. government aid to Azerbaijan unless it lifted its embargo on Armenia and Karabakh.[38] This resulted in Armenia receiving badly needed U.S. aid, while Azerbaijan was left out of the distribution until its Caspian oil exports led the United States to resume aid.

Meeting on December 5–6, 1994—where the CSCE turned itself into the more permanent sounding OSCE—the Budapest Summit of the Heads of State or Government decided to establish a co-chairmanship for the process and also expressed in theory its political will to employ multinational peacekeeping forces as part of an eventual settlement. The actual Minsk Conference was to convene once the armed conflict had ceased and peacekeeping forces deployed. Although the combatants agreed to a cease-fire in 1994, the basic conflict remained unsolved, merely frozen.

At the Lisbon Summit in 1996, all except Armenia accepted the proposal for maintaining territorial integrity, which, of course, was the guiding principle of the original Helsinki Accords in 1975 from which the OSCE had originally sprung. Earlier Sweden and then Finland had served as co-chairs of the Minsk Group, but since 1997, Russia, France, and finally the United States since Azerbaijan preferred it to France. (This tortuous process of choosing co-chairs, at least, explains why there are three, instead of two co-chairs.) Nevertheless, Azerbaijan has always remained somewhat uncomfortable with this arrangement since all three of these co-chairs contained relatively large and politically influential Armenian diasporas potentially able to bias their host state's position toward Karabakh in favor of the Armenians. Several other states including Belarus, Finland, Germany, Italy, Sweden, Turkey, and, of course, Armenia and Azerbaijan also participated in the Group in lesser roles at one time or another.

During the late 1990s, the Minsk Group broached three separate proposals: (1) A complete package plan in June 1997 that Armenia rejected because it did not want to withdraw its troops from the occupied areas until the process had reached a final settlement. (2) A complete step-by-step plan in December 1997 that Armenia again rejected for the same reasons. (3) A common state plan that Azerbaijan rejected because it had no intention to compromise on its territorial integrity.[39] After the failure of these three proposals, the OSCE's Minsk Group altered its negotiating process and began to stress one-on-one meetings between Armenian and Azerbaijani officials. On January 26, 2001, and again on March 4–5, 2001, representatives of Armenia, Azerbaijan, France, Russia, and the United States met twice in Paris and then again on April 3–7 in Key West, Florida.[40] Despite some initial promise, no real progress occurred.

In 2004, the Prague Process consisted of direct bilateral contact between the foreign ministers of the two combatants. However, politicians in both combatant states were wary to compromise on delicate issues for fear of being denounced as a traitor. Therefore, some thought that 2006 might be the "golden year" for negotiations because the absence of elections in both states that year might permit the necessary compromise that otherwise seemed unlikely. However, this scenario failed to materialize.

The Madrid Principles reached in November 2007 were possibly the most notable, but still unsuccessful, achievement: (1) The return of the Armenian-occupied territories surrounding Karabakh to Azerbaijan. (2) An interim autonomous status for Karabakh that would provide guarantees for security and self-governance. (3) A corridor linking Armenia to Karabakh. (4) Future determination of the final legal status of Karabakh through a legally binding expression of popular will. (5) The right of all internally displaced persons (IDPs) and refugees to return to their former places of residence. (6) International security guarantees that would include a peacekeeping operation.[41] Although both combatants agreed to negotiate according to these Madrid Principles, very little real progress ever occurred. Indeed, in August 2016, the influential Armenian lobby in the United States claimed that the Madrid Principles were "reckless" and "undemocratic," and that the United States should reject them.[42]

On March 19, 2016, President Ilham Aliyev of Azerbaijan explicitly accused the Minsk Group co-chairs of provocation against his state and declared that its confidence in their activities had been completely undermined.[43] Nevertheless, the Armenian and Azerbaijani presidents—Serzh Sargsyan and Ilham Aliyev—held summits as part of the Minsk process in Bern, Switzerland on December 19, 2015, and Geneva, Switzerland on October 16, 2017, but again without success. Moreover, in between these two conferences, a four-day war broke in April 2016 that saw some very minor Azerbaijani gains.

The OSCE Minsk Group's "lack of experience with these types of conflicts and reduced solidarity among its member, combined with Russia's regional ambitions and Turkey's advocacy role serve[d] to weaken the intervention,"[44] explained one knowledgeable source. Understandably, Russia felt it had a priority role in its near abroad. Everyone also knew that any settlement without Russian approval would be impossible. However, Russia's unique role tended to undermine the Minsk Group. In addition, the Russian-led Commonwealth of Independent States (CIS), in which both Armenia and Azerbaijan held membership, also began to play a role as a de facto rival of the Minsk Group.

By 1993, Russia began proposing its own cease-fires and sometimes acting independently of the Minsk Group, a situation that fostered confusion. Initially, Russia's support of Operation Ring against Armenian militias had favored Azerbaijan, but by October 1992 Russia returned to its more traditional support of Armenia, which also, as mentioned above, is a member of the Russian-led Collective Security Treaty Organization (CSTO), considered by some as the current Russian-led counterpart to NATO. Thus, an estimated 5,000 Russian troops are permanently stationed in Gyumri (formerly Leninakan/Alexandropol) located in northwestern Armenia close to the Turkish border. Azerbaijan does not belong to the CSTO that supposedly guarantees each one of its six members protection against foreign aggression. Moscow also heavily subsidizes its sale of weapons to Yerevan and is its most important trading partner. On the other hand, Russia is also an important supplier of weapons to Azerbaijan as are Turkey and Israel.

Thus, both combatants have had occasion to blame Russia for failure as an honest broker. Azerbaijan, for example, initially rejected a Russian peacekeeping force that would have patrolled the Russian-brokered Bishkek cease-fire finally reached on May 12, 1994.[45] Instead, along with the Western members of the Minsk Group, Azerbaijan argued that any peacekeeping force should be multinational. However, the CSCE/OSCE's Minsk Group lacked the mechanics to establish such a force. Furthermore, at this time the Western powers were over-taxed with the Bosnian war, and thus unwilling to commit additional peacekeeping troops even further afoot. For its part, the OSCE could be constricted by its large membership, all of whom possessed veto power. Moreover, its own rules prohibited it from using force. Frequent changes in leadership made it difficult to understand the nuances of the conflict. At times it was not clear whether the supposed mediators placed the actual conflict at the head of their concerns or wanted to extract the maximum benefits from the frozen status quo. Caspian oil access motivated all participants.

In addition, the Minsk Group lacked "the instruments to conduct investigations into ceasefire violations, much less establish responsibility."[46] These difficulties reinforced claims that the Minsk Group is a "useless structure" whose co-chairs "do nothing." The Minsk Group's "passive mediator" approach placed its "co-chairs in a weak position, particularly vis-à-vis parties entrenched in maximalist positions." Thus, one might question whether the Minsk Group possessed the necessary attributes of even being a potentially effective mediator.

Accordingly, there have been proposals to move the format for negotiating from the OSCE's Minsk Group to another medium such as the Parliamentary Assembly of the Council of Europe (PACE). Some have suggested that Turkey, Germany, or Kazakhstan become co-chairs of the Minsk Group. Indeed, the latter had successfully avoided post-Soviet minority violence with its own population and had previous experience already as an attempted mediator in Karabakh. However, Matthew Bryza, the former U.S. ambassador to Azerbaijan, replied that the European Union (EU) would make more sense because it would represent all of Europe and had experience mediating similar conflicts in the Balkans.[47] However, it is difficult to see how any such changes would be anything but cosmetic, and thus failing to address the essence of the problem.

At one point in 1994 the Russian mediator, Vladimir Kazimirov, declared that Sweden, acting in its then-role as a co-chair of the Minsk Group, twice scheduled meetings of the Group in Paris and Prague. However, these Minsk Group meetings would have clashed with CIS meetings in Moscow where the Russians intended to hold peace talks. For their part, the other Minsk Group mediators complained that the Russians were holding talks without informing them. Each side seemed to be working against the other, a situation that prompted Armenian president, Levon Ter-Petrosyan, to complain, "the impression is created that the mediating countries and international organizations are not interested so much in settling the conflict, as in setting their own accounts and relationships, which are unconnected with it."[48] Relations among members of the Minsk Group grew poor as both sides accused each other of proposing conflicting initiatives.

Eventually, however, all participants in the Minsk Group began to realize that successful negotiations depended not only on satisfying the demands of the two combatants, but also those of Moscow. However, "given the considerable influence afforded to Russia by its deep links with both Armenia and Azerbaijan, many analysts question Moscow's desire to see a peaceful and comprehensive resolution... to the conflict, and suggest that Moscow may be most interested in maintaining the leverage afforded to it by the uneasy status quo."[49] The International Crisis Group agreed that "neither side views Moscow as disinterested; both view it as using the conflict to advance its position and military presence in the South

Caucasus, an area it considers to be within what Russian officials typically describe as the country's 'sphere of privileged interests.'"[50] Nevertheless, Russia proved the only one able to broker the cease-fires that ended actual wars in 1994, 2016, and 2020.

Renewed Conflict

Given the failure of the Minsk Group to successfully conclude negotiations between the combatants, it was only a matter of time before the frozen conflict again heated up. The aggressive rhetoric of Armenian prime minister Nikol Pashinyan proved to be the immediate instigator. Pashinyan's role was ironic because he had originally come to power on May 8, 2018, calling for the resolution of the conflict. This represented a strong break from the hardline Karabakh Armenians who had mostly dominated Armenia since the first Karabakh war had ended in 1994 and thus found a welcoming reception in Baku.

However, Pashinyan soon altered his approach and called for the unification of Karabakh and Armenia. Disdaining true negotiations, the Armenian prime minister now declared, "Artsakh [Karabakh] is Armenia, and that's it."[51] Just a few months earlier, while attired in a military uniform, Armenian defense minister, Davit Tonoyan, already had told the Armenian diaspora in the United States that if Azerbaijan dared to regain its lost territories by force his state's policy was no longer "land for peace," but "war for new territories"[52] Others even began to speak about Armenian soldiers "drinking tea in Baku."[53]

Adding further fuel to these incendiary boasts, in August 2020, Pashinyan rehashed the long dead Treaty of Sevres—that after World War I had sought to create a greater Armenia in land that today is eastern Turkey—declaring that defunct treaty still a "historical fact" that "remains so to this day."[54] This gratuitous remark was a not-so-subtle threat against the territorial integrity of Turkey. Jirair (Gerard) Libaridian, a leading Armenian scholar and former adviser to Levon Ter-Petrosyan, the first Armenian president after the Soviet Union collapsed, agreed. Libaridian argued that Pashinyan's statements amounted to "at a minimum, a declaration of diplomatic war" against Turkey, reframing the conflict over Karabakh from one of Armenian self-determination into one of Armenian expansionism.[55] Pashinyan had left Azerbaijan no possibility to negotiate anything but capitulation. As Razmik Panossian—writing for an Armenian conference organized by the Zoryan Institute in May 1998 and referring to Armenian diaspora squabbles with independent Armenia, aptly confessed, "arrogant righteousness and intolerance have marked Armenian politics since 1988."[56] This thought Libaridian was a colossal mistake.

Indeed, Pashinyan's aggressive mixture of delusional self-confidence and naïve sentimentality reminded one of the mea culpa and caveat of Hovannes Katchaznouni, the first prime minister of Armenia after World War I, regarding similar Armenian delusions of power that had proven disastrous a century earlier: "We had created a dense atmosphere of illusion in our minds.... We had lost our sense of reality and were carried away with our dreams.... We overestimated the ability of the Armenian people, its political and military power."[57] Reviewing what had now occurred a century later, Jirair Libaridian sadly concluded, "We have lost a war we should have avoided at all cost, a war we could not have won."[58] Libaridian correctly faulted Pashinyan's "unwillingness to act as a statesman and negotiate the return of occupied districts in an orderly and peaceful manner in return for equivalent security guarantees for our people on their land and for peace." He added, "our problem is our political culture that relies on dreams rather than hard facts; the way we strategize, the way we easily set aside what the outside world and our antagonists say and do if these disturb any of our prejudices and predetermined beliefs.... Our problem is the way we insist on overestimating our capabilities."

Libaridian's honest evaluation bore an uncanny resemblance to Katchaznouni's similar post-mortem regarding the reasons for the Armenian catastrophe during World War I. Although in no way justifying the unjustifiable massacres of those earlier times, Libaridian's severe honesty and Azerbaijan's correct evaluation of its own future, should now combine to inform us that in the end, the Minsk Process failed because its ultimate principles for successfully negotiating a solution to the conflict—territorial integrity, self-determination, and protecting minorities through autonomy—proved contradictory. This led the two combatants to disdain compromise upon what each perceived as their existential positions.

Conclusion

Did the latest war in the fall of 2020 alter this situation? There is always hope, of course, but "while the war may be over, a repository of hatred, reinforced by reports of atrocities by both sides, including videos of executions and beheadings of prisoners, promises to linger for generations to come."[59] Although Azerbaijani officials have promised reconciliation and equality to Armenians remaining in Karabakh, few believe this will actually work. Even Gerard Libaridian expressed pessimism concerning the future when he mused: "There is no reason for Armenians to want to live under Azerbaijani rule. It would be a domination. It would not be a governance." Indeed, "many Armenians say they will keep fighting for Nagorno-Karabakh to be recognized as an independent country, despite an international consensus that the territory is part of Azerbaijan." Furthermore, "the deadlock was complicated by Armenian politicians and activists around the world increasingly taking the position—disputed by Azerbaijanis—that all of the captured lands were rightfully Armenian."

In a wide-ranging question-and-answer session held during an international forum on the "South Caucasus: Development and Cooperation" on April 29, 2022, Ilham Aliyev, the president of Azerbaijan, made the following realistic points concerning his country's victory in the Second Karabakh War. 1. Do not accept the occupation of your territory. Continue to maintain your territorial integrity. 2. Do not depend on international organizations. The unanimous UN resolutions supporting the Azerbaijani position alluded to above, did nothing to return occupied Azerbaijani territory. There was no help from the international community. 3. Build and maintain a strong military to regain your lost territory.[60]

President Aliyev went on to make the following additional important points.[61] Nagorno-Karabakh no longer exists; to employ the term disputes Azerbaijani territorial integrity. Rather the proper term to use is simply Karabakh. Azerbaijan will no longer negotiate with Armenia about Azerbaijani territorial integrity. However, Azerbaijan sincerely hopes for meaningful negotiations with Armenia about creating a new, mutually successful economic and political order for the South Caucasus. Azerbaijan intends to be magnanimous toward Armenia in these state-to-state negotiations. However, the Karabakh issue is settled within the bounds of Azerbaijani territorial integrity. The Armenians living in Karabakh will enjoy cultural autonomy regarding their language, schools, etc., but not political autonomy. Apropos to this pronouncement, a recent article in *The American Political Science Review* concluded: "We have found that, on its own, regional autonomy is likely to be 'too little, too late." Too little, "because only full inclusion through power sharing at the central level reduces conflict propensity significantly." On the other hand, "it is too late since regional autonomy could be effective, but only if offered in a timely, preventive fashion before group-government relations turn violent."[62]

For the present, the Russian peacekeepers are keeping the corridors open. However, given the Russian invasion of Ukraine in February 2022, the authors of this book detected a suspicion of ultimate Russian intentions. Specifically, these Russian peacekeepers in Karabakh and the remaining Russian military forces in Armenia, could serve as the Russian key to reintegrate the South Caucasus lost when the Soviet Union collapsed in 1991. Finally, the dysfunctional Minsk Process is dead.

Despite Moscow's inescapable geostrategic influence, the EU has taken an important role as an honest broker. Indeed, shortly after his nearly three-hour q & a session alluded to above, Aliyev met Pashinyan in Brussels in talks mediated by European Council president Charles Michel.[63] The two leaders reached a tentative agreement on the task of delineating their borders and establishing transit routes. Encouragingly, Turkey and Armenia have also begun to make tentative efforts to open their long-closed borders and even restore economic ties. Or course, this is only a cautious beginning. Many more difficulties remain.

Throughout his nearly three-hour-long tour de force to the conference in late April mentioned above, the Azerbaijani president illustrated a very impressive ability to speak, understand, and reply in English. He also manifested a most impressive, broad command of facts upon a great variety of unrehearsed subjects, while occasionally exhibiting a refreshing sense of humor. The two authors of this book came away from the session impressed that Aliyev was a rare leader able to shoulder the tall responsibilities to win the peace.

Based on these observations, two contending models exist for the future of Karabakh. The first model argues for a generous, magnanimous peace that provides for maintaining Azerbaijani territorial integrity while allowing meaningful cultural autonomy for the Armenians living in Karabakh. The Aland Islands model between Finland maintaining its territorial integrity, while the Swedish-speaking Aland Islands exercise considerable autonomy offers a successful example. However, Scandinavia is what Karl Deutsch aptly referred to as a security community where resorting to war to solve problems is unthinkable.[64] The Caucasus remains an insecurity community region where violence and war remain likely for solving problems. Although it is useful to study other attempted solutions, each specific example needs its own particular solution. The ultimate solution to Nagorno-Karabakh will probably be unique to its own specifics.

Landlocked Armenia needs a viable land bridge to the world and diplomatic relations with Turkey. An opening of the border with Azerbaijan and Turkey offers a partial solution to Armenia's economic isolation and resulting poverty. The failed promises of large amounts of economic help from the rich Armenian diaspora that encourages Armenian intransigence has proven not the solution for the Armenians in their homeland. Mutually agreed-upon land bridges between Armenia and Karabakh for Armenia and another land bridge connecting the Nakhichevan exclave with Azerbaijan would benefit both Armenia and Azerbaijan. However, such a land bridge for Azerbaijan would eliminate Armenia's valuable border with Iran.

A mutually agreed-upon term for the Armenian massacres in 1915 should also be found that would satisfy Turkey and Azerbaijan on the one hand and Armenia on the other. Genocide is not the word because it exaggerates the Turkish guilt, assumes the official Ottoman government intent to murder Armenians which was unlikely, and fails to put what specifically happened to the Armenians into the overall context of mutual deportations and killings that had been occurring since the latter part of the nineteenth century, among others. Connected to this is the necessity for Armenia to eliminate its constitutional claims to Turkey's eastern Anatolia, which it claims as Western Armenia. On the other hand, Azerbaijan must make a sincere attempt to implement a generous, magnanimous peace and also search for Armenian interlocutors who agree that lasting peace is now necessary. Unfortunately, this first model will be extremely difficult to implement given Armenian historical interpretations.

Therefore, a second, probably more realistic model for the future of Karabakh must be considered. Most military and political observers feel that Armenia will do all it can to regain its military superiority and then strike when the moment is right in order to regain what it deems its rightful ownership of Karabakh. Thus, Azerbaijan must maintain its present military superiority as a deterrent in peace and a defense in war while offering generous peace. In addition, such military realism directs that Azerbaijan must maintain its successful alliance-like understandings with Turkey and Israel, among others, while also seeking to move Iran closer to the Azerbaijani point of view. Most importantly, Russia must be satisfied with the present situation as it is Armenia's traditional ally and if so decided, could overturn the current peace that is favorable to Azerbaijan.

On this point, it must also be understood that Russia's ultimate goal is most likely to reincorporate the south Caucasus lost when the Soviet Union collapsed in 1991. Russia's wanton invasion of Ukraine in February 2022, aptly demonstrates its intentions to its near abroad and that the supposed new world order ushered in by the United Nations Charter Article 2(4) making the usage of force or even its threat illegal under modern international law is largely utopian. Earlier, of course, the Armenian invasion of Azerbaijan when the Soviet Union collapsed demonstrated this fact up close to Azerbaijan. We continue to live in a brutal dystopian Hobbesian world of war, not a utopian Lockean one of peace. Azerbaijan must not lose sight of this existential fact of reality or suffer the inevitable consequences.

Nevertheless, given this bleak outlook and the abject failure of past negotiations, it is incumbent upon both sides, their supporters, and potential third-party mediators to realize the futility of continued conflict, that there can be a better future, and that it must begin with the victors in the latest war manifesting magnanimity, while the losers accept reality. Otherwise, both sides will be condemned to relive their dismal past of failed negotiations and renewed conflicts. Thus, with this newly achieved understanding, let us renew a determination to negotiate a solution that finally will bring equity and honor to both combatants. The current cease-fire that returns occupied Azerbaijani lands, while allowing the core of Armenian-populated Karabakh to remain, a situation policed by Russian peacekeepers, seems a possible start. We do not need any more parents mourning the deaths of their children.

Notes

1. Thomas de Waal, *Black Garden: Armenia and Azerbaijan through Peace and War* (New York: New York University Press, 2003), p. 274.
2. Ibid., p. 280.
3. Ibid., p. 281. "Even without the war, Armenia and Azerbaijan leaders have cooperated very little over the past hundred years. In Soviet times, they would conduct most of their business in and through Moscow." Ibid., p. 282. However, more optimistically, see Ohannes Geukjian, *Negotiating Armenian-Azerbaijani Peace: Opportunities, Obstacles, Prospects* (Farnham, Surrey, England and Burlington, VT: Ashgate, 2014).

4. This is precisely the argument of Bahar Baser, "Third Party Mediation in Nagorno-Karabakh: Part of the Cure or Part of the Disease?" *OAKA* 3:1 (2008), pp. 86–114.
5. Cited in Michael P. Croissant, *The Armenia-Azerbaijan Conflict: Causes and Implications* (Westport, CT: Praeger, 1998), p. 45.
6. Human Rights Watch/Helsinki, *Azerbaijan, Seven Years of Conflict in Nagorno-Karabakh* (New York: Human Rights Watch, 1994), p. 4.
7. Elizabeth Fuller, "What Lies behind the Current Armenian-Azerbaijani Tensions?" *Report on the USSR*, 3:21 (May 24, 1991), p. 13.
8. Suzanne Goldenberg, *Pride of Small Nations: The Caucasus and Post-Soviet Disorder* (London: Zed Books, 1994), p. 166.
9. Jonathan Aves, *Post-Soviet Transcaucasia* (London: Royal Institute of International Affairs, 1993), p. 36. The Armenian diaspora is particularly influential in the United States and also in France, two of the co-chairs of the Minsk Process that supposedly seeks to mediate the Karabakh conflict. In addition, Russia, the most important co-chair of the Minsk Process and also home to a large Armenian diaspora, is also committed to defend Armenia under the Collective Security Treaty Organization, a regional security grouping of selective post-Soviet states established on February 14, 1992.
10. Croissant, *Armenia-Azerbaijan Conflict*, pp. 45–46.
11. The following narrative is largely based on Cengiz Candar, "South Caucasus Deal Echoes Plan from 30 Years Ago," *Al-Monitor*, November 13, 2020, https://www.al-monitor.com/pulse/originals/2020/11/turkey-russia-nagorno-karabakh-deal-armenia-azerbaijan.html, accessed November 24, 2020.
12. Ibid.
13. Cited in "How the 'Goble Plan' was born and How It Remains a Political Factor," Reliefweb, June 9, 2000, https://reliefweb.int/report/armenia/how-goble-plan-was-born-and-how-it-remains-political-factor, accessed February 3, 2021.
14. Cited in Candar, "South Caucasus Deal Echoes Plan from 30 Years Ago."
15. For background, see Paul Goble, "Coping with the Nagorno-Karabakh Crisis," *The Fletcher Forum* 16:2 (Summer 1992), pp. 18–26.
16. Candar, "South Caucasus Deal Echoes Plan from 30 Years Ago."
17. The following discussion is largely based on Edmond Y. Azadian, "Paul Goble is for Real," *The Armenian Mirror-Spectator*, May 18, 2020, https://mirrorspectator.com/2020/05/18/paul-goble-is-for-real/, accessed February 3, 2021.
18. However, Azadian failed to mention that the Sevres Treaty had never been implemented due to Kemal Ataturk's victories and subsequent creation of modern Turkey out of the ashes of the Ottoman Empire.

19. "How the 'Goble Plan' Was born and How It Remains a Political Factor," Reliefweb, June 9, 2000, https://reliefweb.int/report/armenia/how-goble-plan-was-born-and-how-it-remains-political-factor, accessed February 3, 2021.
20. During the war in 2020, the United States tried to broker a cease-fire on three separate occasions. None of them held. Congressional Research Service, "Azerbaijan and Armenia: The Nagorno-Karabakh Conflict," January 7, 2021, pp. 17–18.
21. The following discussion is largely based on Ron Synovitz and Susan Badalian, "Fear and Loathing vs. Trade across the Armenian-Azerbaijani Border," RadioFreeEurope/Radio Liberty, February 7, 2012, https://www.rferl.org/a/fear-and-loathing-vs-trade-across-the-armenian-azerbiajani-border/31090569.html, accessed February 12, 2021.
22. Ibid.
23. The following discussion is largely based on Amberin Zaman, "Turkey's Talk of Peace with Armenia Rings Hollow," *Al-Monitor*, February 4, 2021, https://www.al-monitor.com/pulse/originals/2021/02/erdogan-turkey-normalize-united-states-azerbakjan.html, accessed February 12, 2021.
24. RFL/RL, "Amnesty Calls for Probe into Civilian Casualties in Nagorno-Karabakh Conflict," RadioFreeEurope/RadioLiberty, January 14, 2012, https://www.rferl.org/a/amnesty-probe-civilian-casualties-nagorno-karabakh/31045850.html, accessed February 12, 2012.
25. Elizabeth Fuller, "Nagorno-Karabakh: Internal Conflict Becomes International," *RFL/RL Research Report*, 1:11 (March 13, 1992), pp. 1–2.
26. "Rferl.org: Nagorno-Karabakh: Timeline of the Long Road to Peace," http://www.rferl.org/content/article/1065626.html. Archived, https://web.archive.org/web/20140329025222/http://www.rferl.org/content/article/1065626.html, from the original, March 29, 2014, accessed January 2, 2020.
27. "Newsline," http://www.rferl.org/content/article/1142847.html. Radio Free Europe/Radio Liberty. February 3, 2003. Archived, https://web.archive.org/web/20141006122039/http://www.rferl.org/content/article/1142847.html, from the original, October 6, 2014, accessed January 31, 2013.
28. Ibid.
29. Ceyhun Mahmudlu and Shamkhal Abilov, "The Peace-Making Process in the Nagorno-Karabakh Conflict: Why Did Iran Fail in Its Mediation Effort?" *Journal of Contemporary Central and Eastern Europe* 26:1 (2018), p. 37.
30. Ibid., p. 47.
31. For further background, see Arvin Khoshnood and Ardavan Khoshnood, "Iran's Quandary on Nagorno-Karabakh," *Middle East Policy* 28

(Spring 2021), https://www.meforum.org/62069/iran-in-quandary-on-nagorno-karabakh, accessed July 21, 2021.
32. Cited in USC Dornsife Institute of Armenian Studies, "From the Archives: Ex-Secretary of State Cyrus Vance in Karabakh," October 23, 2017, https://armenian.usc.edu/from-the-archives-ex-secretary-of-state-cyrus-vance-in-karabakh/, accessed February 22, 2021.
33. Initially, the Minsk Group consisted of 12 members: Armenia, Azerbaijan, Belarus, the Czech Republic, France, Germany, Italy, Russia, Slovakia, Sweden, Turkey, and the United States.
34. For cogent thoughts on how the Minsk Group's "unwieldy and absurdly heavy piece of negotiating machinery," including five interpreting booths, early in its existence inhibited progress, among other difficulties, see John Maresca, "Lost Opportunities in Negotiating the Conflict over Nagorno-Karabakh," *International Negotiation* 1 (December 1996), p. 482. In 1992, Maresca was appointed U.S. Ambassador and Special Representative for mediation of the conflicts in Karabakh and Cyprus. In this role he was responsible for helping to create the Minsk Group. Previously, he had been Ambassador and Chairman of the U.S. delegation to the CSCE.
35. Elizabeth Fuller, "Ethnic Strife Threatens Democratization," *RFL/RL Research Report* 2:1 (January 1993), p. 22; and Elizabeth Fuller, *Azerbaijan at the Crossroads* (London: Royal Institute of International Affairs, 1994), p. 13.
36. Human Rights Watch/Helsinki, *Azerbaijan, Seven Years of Conflict in Nagorno-Karabakh* (New York: Human Rights Watch, 1994), p. 106.
37. For further background, see Wendy Betts, "Third Party Mediation: An Obstacle to Peace in Nagorno Karabakh," *SAIS Review* 19:2 (1999), pp. 161–183; David D. Laitin and Ronald Grigor Suny, "Armenia and Azerbaijan: Thinking a Way Out of Karabakh," *Middle East Policy* 7 (October 1999), pp. 145–176; and Marta-Lisa Magnusson, "Why No Settlement in the Nagorno-Karabakh Conflict?—Which are the Obstacles to a Negotiated Solution?" in Karina Vamling, ed., *Language, History and Cultural Identities in the Caucasus: Papers from the Conference, June 17–19, 2005*, Malmo University, 2010, pp. 114–143, https://www.academia.edu/1265456/M%C3%A4rta_Lisa_Magnusson_Why_No_Settlement_in_the_Nagorno_Karabakh_Conflict_Which_are_the_obstacles_to_a_negotiated_solution, accessed July 12, 2022.
38. Svante E. Cornell, "Undeclared War: The Nagorno-Karabakh Conflict Reconsidered," *Journal of South Asian and Middle Eastern Studies* 20 (Summer 1997), p. 10.
39. For details, see Baser, "Third Party Mediation in Nagorno-Karabakh," p. 95/n. 34.
40. Thomas de Waal has described the five days of talks in Key West as "the most high-profile and intensive negotiations ever on the dispute" as of

2003, of course, when he penned these words. Aliev basically offered to give Karabakh to Armenia in return for a road link across Armenia from Azerbaijan to Nakhichevan that would have been policed by international troops and the right of Azerbaijani refugees to return to the Azerbaijani cultural center of Shusha. Subsequent to the meeting, one of the mediators even averred they had reached agreement on "80 to 90 percent" of the issues. However, the Armenian parliament rejected any compromise, while the Azeri side was even more vehement in its rejection. Thomas de Waal, *Black Garden: Armenia and Azerbaijan through Peace and War* (New York: New York University Press, 2003), pp. 267 and 5.
41. Helsinki Commission Report, "The Nagorno-Karabakh Conflict," June 15, 2017.
42. "Tell President Obama: Reject the Reckless Madrid Principles: Support a Real Karabakh Peace," https://cqrcengage.com/anca/app/onestep-write-a-letter?0&engagementld=236274, accessed December 22, 2016; and "ANCA Launches Campaign Prioritizing Artsakh Freedom, Rejecting Undemocratic 'Madrid Principles': Absbarez.com," http://asbarez.com/153657/anca-launches-campaign-priortizing-artsakh-freedom-rejecting-undemocratic-madrid-principles/, accessed December 22, 2016.
43. "Speech by Ilham Aliyev at the Nationwide Festivities on the Occasion of Novruz Holiday," March 19, 2016, https://en.president.az/articles/19436, accessed October 10, 2017.
44. Baser, "Third Party Mediation in Nagorno-Karabakh," p. 92.
45. The following discussion is largely based on de Waal, *Black Garden*, p. 254.
46. The following discussion is largely based on International Crisis Group, "Nagorno-Karabakh's Gathering War Clouds," June 1, 2017, No. 244, https://www.crisisgroup.org/europe-central-asia/caucasus/nagorno-karabakh-azerbaijan/244-nagorno-karabakhs-gathering-war-clouds, accessed December 3, 2020.
47. "OSCE's Minsk Group's Format Changing on Agenda," February 3, 2015, http://www.azerbaijan/76977.html, accessed April 23, 2018.
48. Cited in Ibid.
49. Helsinki Commission Report, "The Nagorno-Karabakh Conflict," June 15, 2017, p. 4.
50. International Crisis Group, "Nagorno-Karabakh's Gathering War Clouds."
51. Cited in Joshua Kucera, "Pashinyan Calls for Unification between Armenia and Karabakh," Eurasianet, August 6, 2019, https://eurasianet.org/pashinyan-call-for-unificaton-bewteen-armenia-and-karabakh, accessed February 27, 2021. See also Carlotta Gall, "Roots of War: When Armenia Talked Tough, Azerbaijan Took Action," *New York Times*,

October 27, 2020, https://www.nytimes.com/2020/10/27/world/europe/armenia-azerbaijan-nagorno-karabakh.html..., accessed November 3, 2020 and its reference to how "Armenia's populist prime minister declared the area [Karabakh] indisputably Armenian."
52. Cited in "'New Territories in the Event of New War,' Says Defense Minister," *Asbarez*, April 1, 2019, http://asbarez.com/178701/new-territories-in-the-event-of-new-war-says-defense-minister/, accessed February 28, 2021.
53. Cited in Michael A. Reynolds, "Confidence and Catastrophe: Armenia and the Second-Karabagh War," War on the Rocks, January 11, 2021, https://warontherocks.com/2021/01/confidence-and-catastrophe-armenia-and-the-second-nagorno-karabagh-war/, accessed February 28, 2021.
54. Cited in Ibid.
55. Cited in Ibid.
56. Razmik Panossian, "The Diaspora and the Karabagh Movement: Oppositional Politics between the Armenian Revolutionary Federation and the Armenian National Movement," in Levon Chorbajian, ed. *The Making of Nagorno-Karabagh: From Secession to Republic* (New York: Palgrave, 2001), p. 171.
57. Cited in Hovhannes Katchaznouni, *The Armenian Revolutionary Federation (Dashnagtzoutium) Has Nothing To Do Anymore* (Reprint), trans. from the original by Matthew A. Callender and ed. by John Roy Carlson (Arthur A. Derounian) (New York: Armenian Information Service, 1955).
58. This and Libaridian's subsequent citations were taken from Jirair Libaridian, "What Happened and Why: Six Theses," *The Armenian Mirror-Spectator*, November 24, 2020, https://mirrorspectator.com/2020/11/24/what-happened-and-why-six-theses/, accessed February 22, 2021.
59. This and the following citations were taken from the insightful article by Carlotta Gall and Anton Troianovski, "After Nagoro-Karabakh War, Trauma, Tragedy and Devastation," *New York Times*, December 31, 2020, https://www.nytimes.com/2020/12/11/world/europe/nagorno-karabakh-armenia-azerbaijan.html, accessed March 19, 2021.
60. Ilham Aliyev, "Keynote Speech by H. E. Ilham Aliyev, President of the Republic of Azerbaijan, Shusha International Forum, 'South Caucasus: Development and Cooperation,'" Baku and Shusha, Azerbaijan, April 29, 2022.
61. Ibid.
62. Lars-Erik Cederman et al., "Territorial Autonomy in the Shadow of Conflict: Too Little, Too Late?" *The American Political Science Review* 109:2 (May 2015), p. 368.

63. The following information was taken from Emil Avdaliani, "With the EU's Help, Armenia Is Inching Closer to Peace with Azerbaijan," *World Politics Review*, July 15, 2022, https://www.worldpoliticsreview.com/articles/30680/two-years-after-azerbaijan-armenia-war-a-new-hope-for-peace, accessed July 15, 2022. The term "honest broker" was used by Azerbaijani president Ilham Aliyev while he was addressing the conference on April 29, 2022.
64. On this important concept, see Karl W. Deutsch, *Political Community and the North Atlantic Area* (Princeton: Princeton University Press, 1957), p. 5.

CHAPTER 6

Self-Determination or Territorial Integrity? International Legal/Political Doctrines in Opposition & Their Implications for Karabakh

Introduction

The long-running, frozen-unfrozen conflict between Armenia and Azerbaijan over Karabakh (Artsakh)[1] constitutes the most recent example of the continuing clash between the oft-opposed international legal/political doctrines of self-determination and territorial integrity.[2] As explained earlier, the United Nations Charter includes specific references to self-determination in Articles 1(2) and 55, and to territorial integrity in Article 2(4). Put simply, self-determination refers to the right of a people to choose their own form of government (usually independence), while territorial integrity means the right of a state to maintain its existing borders.[3] Thus, in the case of Karabakh, Armenia has supported the doctrine of self-determination because the vast majority of its population is ethnic Armenian. On the other hand, Azerbaijan has maintained the doctrine of territorial integrity because Karabakh is part of Azerbaijan.[4] Illustrating the most recent deadly results of this conflict that suddenly unfroze in September–November 2020, Russian president Vladimir Putin declared "there were more than 4000 killed in both countries… including civilians, 8000 wounded and thousands driven from their homes."[5] The U.S. Congressional Research Service listed higher figures: "Based on official statements and reports, the 2020 war led to more than 6000 combat deaths (about 3360 Armenians and 2820 Azerbaijanis) and more than 150 civilian deaths."[6]

Which doctrine takes precedence? In its famous "Declaration on the Granting of Independence to Colonial Countries and Peoples,"[7] the United Nations gave a definitive answer to this question. While proclaiming in paragraph 2 of this celebrated Resolution that "all peoples have the right of self-determination," the General Assembly warned in paragraph 6 that "any attempt at the partial or total disruption of the national unity and the territorial integrity of a country is incompatible with the purposes and principles of the Charter of the United Nations." This definitive interpretation or "safeguard clause" that territorial integrity supersedes self-determination has been reiterated on several occasions, in particular by the "UN Declaration on Principles of International Law concerning Friendly Relations and Co-operation among States in Accordance with the Charter of the United Nations,"[8] which was adopted by consensus and "is considered to be the authoritative interpretation of the UN Charter."[9] The Helsinki Final Act of 1975 that recognized Europe's existing borders resulting from World War II also prominently recognized this interpretation.[10] In 1993, the United Nations World Conference on Human Rights held in Vienna concurred, when it specifically declared the right of self-determination "shall not be construed as authorizing or encouraging any action which would dismember or impair, totally or in part, the territorial integrity or political unity of sovereign and independent States."[11]

It is true that the two Human Rights Covenants on (1) Civil and Political Rights and (2) Economic, Social, and Cultural Rights which entered into force in 1976 both declared, "All peoples have the right of self-determination: By virtue of that right they freely determine their political status and freely pursue their economic, social and cultural development" without any specific mention of territorial integrity.[12] However, from the drafting history of these two international treaties and a systematic interpretation of their full texts, it is clear that in the sense of secession, self-determination is not a right of minorities in existing states, even when they might have a relatively obvious territorial basis within the existing, larger state. As James Crawford concludes, "Outside the colonial context, the principle of self-determination is not recognized as giving rise to unilateral rights of secession by parts of independent States.... Self-determination for peoples or groups within the State is to be achieved by participation in its constitutional system, and on the basis of respect for its territorial integrity"[13] Joshua Castellino adds, "The law as it stands suggests that *uti possidetis juris* [original] lines may be modified [only] by consent... between sovereign states.... Non-state actors have no explicit right in international law to demand or even raise questions of territorial adjustment, rendering the territorial aspects of self-determination relatively meaningless."[14]

Furthermore, in the territorial dispute between the African states of Burkina Faso and Mali, the International Court of Justice (ICJ) also recognized the obligation to respect existing borders in cases of state succession—which of course aptly describes the dispute between Armenia and Azerbaijan over Karabakh—by declaring, "There is no doubt that the obligation to respect pre-existing international frontiers in the event of a State succession derives from a general rule of international law."[15] Similarly, the Conference on Yugoslavia Arbitration Commission that was established in 1991 by the initiative of the European Community supported by the United States and the former Soviet Union to render opinions on matters arising from the dissolution of Yugoslavia pronounced, "Except where otherwise agreed, the former boundaries become frontiers protected by international law. This conclusion follows from the principle of respect for the territorial status quo."[16]

In addition, the UN General Assembly Declaration on Minorities—while granting certain rights to individual members of ethnic, linguistic, or cultural minorities to have their language and identity respected by the state in which they resided—emphasized the preservation of the existing state's territorial integrity. Thus, Article 8(4) of the Declaration declared, "Nothing in the present Declaration may be construed as permitting any activity contrary to the purposes and principles of the United Nations, including sovereign equality, territorial integrity and political independence of States."[17] Indeed, any right of self-determination or secession is not mentioned in the Declaration on Minorities.

International law gives no justification to a "kin-state" pursuing irredentism to intervene by force under the claim of protecting portions of the population of other states with which they have some type of ethnic affiliation. The UN General Assembly Resolution on the Inadmissibility of Intervention specifically declares, "No State has the right to intervene, directly or indirectly, for any reason whatever, in the internal or external affairs of any State."[18] Understandably, states which create international law and draw up international treaties or declarations in the first place are not in the business of committing suicide. Redrawing internationally recognized borders by force contravenes international law as defined by the UN Charter and the Helsinki Final Act that recognized Europe's existing borders resulting from World War II.

Indeed, the same reasoning has been used by the West to oppose Russia's annexation of Crimea in 2014 and much larger aggression against Ukraine in 2022 as well as Moscow's earlier recognition in 2008 of South Ossetia's and Abkhazia's secession and independence from Georgia, which, of course, borders on Armenia and Azerbaijan. Thus, the doctrine of territorial integrity clearly trumps that of self-determination in the case of Karabakh. Indeed, not a single state in the world recognizes (or recognized) Karabakh as an independent state or part of Armenia, not even Armenia, its progenitor and protector. What Russia's flagrant violation of international law in attacking Ukraine in 2022 will ultimately mean, of course, remains to be seen and is beyond the scope of this present analysis.

Additional Reasoning

The international legal doctrines of sovereignty, state succession, and uti possidetis give further definition to territorial integrity. Jean Bodin originally defined sovereignty in 1576 as a defense for the unlimited power of the French king. Thus, sovereignty means a state's lawful and exclusive control of its territory with the authority to govern, make laws, and enforce laws for all persons, property, and events within its territory. As the eminent Swiss jurist Max Huber noted in the famous Isle of Palmas case in 1928 involving a dispute between the United States and the Netherlands concerning who owned or possessed sovereignty over an island between the Indonesian and Philippine archipelagoes, sovereignty amounts to independence or the right to exercise in a territory the powers of a state to the exclusion of any other state.[19] The UN Charter declares in Article 2(1) that "the Organization is based on the principle of the sovereign equality of all its Members." Related elements of sovereignty such as exclusive territorial jurisdiction, state immunity, and the immunity of diplomatic agents are also strongly upheld by all states and thus reinforce the doctrine.

As already discussed in the case of Burkina Faso and Mali, state succession is another principle of international law that relates to and helps to define the opposing doctrines of self-determination and territorial integrity. Put simply, state succession deals with the legal consequences of a change of sovereignty over territory. The failure of the two draft Vienna conventions (treaties) of 1978 and 1983[20] to codify the existing customary international law on the issue has created no small amount of confusion and controversy. The specific cases of the Soviet Union, Yugoslavia, and Germany resulting from the end of the Cold War in the 1990s added to this uncertainty as different conclusions and resulting precedents emerged. An analysis of these developments, of course, is beyond the scope of this chapter. Suffice it to note, however, that the current miasma of Karabakh is one specific result of the political consequences of the breakup of the Soviet Union and the state succession that occurred. Armenia and Azerbaijan were 2 of the 15 internationally recognized states that emerged from the collapse of the Soviet Union. As such, both of these newly independent Caucasian states assumed all the rights under international law possessed by states, members too of the United Nations. Their territorial integrity was obviously among these rights despite the controversies involving the overall doctrine of state succession.

As noted above, the legal doctrine of uti possidetis (literally in Latin "as you possess under law [so you shall continue to possess]") is closely related to the doctrine of territorial integrity or maybe best understood as an aspect of the latter. Beginning as a specific example of regional or non-universal international law (admittedly a literal contradiction in terms and therefore originally not as solid a principle as other modes of territorial succession and acquisition), the doctrine of uti possidetis arose early in the nineteenth century during the disintegration of the Spanish colonial empire in Latin America in the interests of stability and peace. In civil Roman law, the term referred to a judicial pronouncement to preserve the existing state of possession over immovable property pending further litigation. Thus, the principle began to be used to mean that old administrative colonial boundaries would remain legal international boundaries upon independence.

In the twentieth century, the International Court of Justice also referred to the principle of uti possidetis in cases involving borders during decolonization in Africa. The frontier dispute between Burkina Faso and Mali referred to above is a specific example. In this case, the ICJ referred to "the obligation to respect pre-existing international frontiers in the event of a State succession... whether or not the rule is expressed in the formula of *uti possidetis*," and thus by implication that this principle prevails even over the right of self-determination of peoples.[21] Legal cases based on uti possidetis have also been raised between Asian states. The famous Temple of Preah Vihear Case[22] between Cambodia and Thailand in 1962 and the Rann of Kutch arbitration[23] between India and Pakistan in 1968 are two specific examples. Furthermore, in the matter of state succession regarding the former Yugoslavia, the Conference on Yugoslavia Arbitration Commission noted: "*Uti possidetis*, though initially applied in settling decolonization issues in America and Africa, is today recognized as a general principle, as stated by the International Court of Justice."[24]

On the other hand, Eritrea's secession from Ethiopia in 1993 after a checkered colonial history and 30 years of subsequent civil war, raised questions about the sanctity of African borders and the principle of uti possidetis.[25] However, given the fact that Eritrea was originally a separate Italian colony forcibly attached to Ethiopia after World War II, some have argued that Eritrea's independence actually did not violate the principle of uti possidetis, but rather belatedly reinforced it. Furthermore, Ethiopia finally had agreed to Eritrea's independence.

Nevertheless, the case of Eritrea's secession from Ethiopia obviously has elements contradicting the principle of uti possidetis and territorial integrity that might be applicable to the case of Karabakh. However, one might also argue that when a rule of law works well in most cases but causes a problem in a rare incident like this, the best solution may be to turn a blind eye to violations of the rule. Indeed, in some municipal (domestic) law systems, legal authorities sometimes exercise a certain amount of discretion on whether or not to prosecute. Moreover, as will be analyzed below, there is nothing in international law that prohibits secession. International law eventually will recognize the winner of a civil war as legitimate. Indeed, traditionally in international law and still so today, the formation of a new state was simply a matter of fact, not law.[26] Therefore, in this case, of course, Eritrea won its independence by force of arms, not by any legal right of self-determination. The same basic reasoning applies to Kosovo's successful secession from Serbia.[27] This political fact, of course, shows the ultimate limitation of analyzing such cases as Karabakh solely in terms of the international legal doctrines of self-determination and territorial integrity.

In addition to these weighty limitations on the doctrine of self-determination as applied to Karabakh in light of the superseding doctrine of territorial integrity, the doctrine of self-determination is even more restricted in actual legal practice. For example, who precisely are the selves or peoples who have the right of self-determination and what precisely is it they can determine? As a legal doctrine—with the exceptions of the now only historical case of South Africa under the apartheid regime that ended in the early 1990s[28] and the continuing case of the Palestinians[29]—self-determination in the practice of the United Nations can only be exercised by trust and non-self-governing territories (i.e. colonies) which have not yet achieved independence. In addition, and most importantly for Karabakh by implication, self-determination may be exercised by a territory only within its already existing administrative boundaries inherited from the colonial power, without any breakup of the state's territorial integrity. Accordingly, since Karabakh was legally a part of Azerbaijan which was not a colonial power, Karabakh was not eligible for self-determination on its own. Although some might argue that this amounted to a double standard, it was still the international legal reality.

Indeed, given that the decolonization process has virtually come to an end and barring a newly agreed upon further legal definition not likely to occur, it must be concluded that self-determination has largely become a doctrine of only historical interest. Ironically, given these facts, self-determination as a legal doctrine remains ludicrously applicable only to the few remaining bits and pieces of former colonial empires such as Pitcairn Island's 50 odd inhabitants, while lying beyond the reach of such large, well-defined entities as the Kurds who unfortunately for their rights inhabit various other states whose territorial integrity prohibit them any legal right of self-determination.

Future Possibilities

On the other hand, using the exceptional examples of the Black majority in apartheid era South Africa and the Palestinians in territorial limbo, both referred to above, the United Nations might also theoretically single out Kurds as entitled to self-determination. Similarly, after World War I, the right of self-determination was granted by some treaties to the inhabitants of a few territories in central and eastern Europe. For example, the Treaty of Versailles in 1919 provided for a plebiscite in Upper Silesia to determine whether it should become part of Germany or Poland. However, nobody has ever suggested such special treatment for Karabakh.

Of course, this constraining legal definition does not prohibit secessionist movements claiming the unilateral political right of self-determination as indeed the Armenians have regarding Karabakh. To make such a claim legally valid, however, the secessionist entity must win its civil war or possibly have the existing state countenance the secession peacefully as indeed occurred when Norway seceded from Sweden in 1905. As noted above, Eritrea and Kosovo succeeded in so doing, while Karabakh did not.[30]

Neither does this inhibiting legal definition prevent various proposed distinctions between "internal" self-determination as some sort of right to implement real democracy or autonomy for a group contained within an existing state (see above) and "external" self-determination defined in most cases as independence for the group concerned.[31] However, to equate the right of "internal" self-determination with democracy would seem merely verbal legerdemain and not any real solution to the definitional dilemma. Thus, although a great deal has been written about these possibilities concerning the meaning of self-determination, they do not constitute legal rights that currently would be applicable to Karabakh.

Nevertheless, in recent years, counter trends have suggested a loosening of the strict legal definitions discussed so far. This line of reasoning leads along the path of soft (developing) law or *de lege ferenda*, relating to the law as it ought to be or is to be developed, in contrast to *de lege lata*, i.e. according to the law currently in force. On January 25, 2001, for example, Prince Hans-Adam II of Liechtenstein, speaking before the International Institute for Strategic Studies (IISS), a prominent British think tank, suggested the coming necessity for a more flexible attitude toward the doctrine of territorial integrity.

> Let us accept the fact that states have lifecycles similar to those of human beings who created them. Hardly any Member State of the United Nations has existed within its present borders for longer than five generations. The attempt to freeze human evolution has in the past been a futile responsibility and has probably brought about more violence, rather than if such a process had been controlled peacefully. Restrictions on self-determination threaten not only democracy itself but the state which seeks its legitimation in democracy.[32]

Remedial secession is a proposed principle that if a specific people living in the territory of a larger state is egregiously misrepresented within that larger state and there is no remedy for the situation, then, as a last resort, this oppressed people have a right to remedial secession. Under such circumstances, the larger state loses its right to its territorial integrity. Although remedial secession is discussed in the scholarly literature, the consensus of most is that it is not a legal right to achieve external self-determination (independence) outside the colonial context.[33] Interestingly, the Supreme Court of Canada, in its lengthy and useful discussion of the international legal status of secession, basically agreed with this reasoning when it ruled that Quebec did "not enjoy a right at international law to effect the secession of Quebec from Canada unilaterally."[34]

Nevertheless, the increasingly legally binding rules on maintaining and furthering human rights may ultimately challenge the territorial integrity of a state grossly violating human rights.[35] Humanitarian intervention, for example, is actions by states, international organizations, or other international groups to intervene, often with coercive force, to prevent human suffering without necessarily obtaining the consent of the state involved. The emerging Responsibility to Protect (R2P) doctrine holds that when domestic methods for protection against massive violations of human rights are ignored or fail, other states have a responsibility to intervene in the domestic affairs of the state where the abuses are occurring to provide security. Such actions might be seen as enforcing some sort of self-determination, while contradicting the Westphalian doctrines of state sovereignty and territorial integrity. As two UN officials have attested, this "marks the coming of age of the imperative of action in the face of human right abuses, over the citadels of state sovereignty."[36] Although such initiatives might eventually create a broader, more flexible application of the doctrines of sovereignty and territorial integrity, to date they have not. Territorial integrity still trumps self-determination.

Furthermore, how legitimate are such initiatives when employed only selectively? For example, why was intervention against Serbia in Kosovo (1998–1999) and Libya (2011) justified, while in Rwanda (1994) and Syria (2011–present) it was not? How massive do the violations against human rights have to be before intervention is justified? Who decides to implement intervention? In the past, some states have employed humanitarian intervention as a mere pretext for their own selfish interests of state. In the case of Karabakh, the Organization for Security and Cooperation's (OSCE) Minsk Group tasked to facilitate communication between Armenia and Azerbaijan to find a negotiated solution to the conflict has failed because neither Armenia or Azerbaijan wanted to compromise. As Svante Cornell noted when the conflict was beginning again in 1991, "there seems to have been no-one [sic] in a power position, in any of the republics, at any time, that was interested in a dialogue and a peaceful resolution of the conflict through compromise."[37]

Conclusion

The rugged mountainous geography of the Caucasus region partially explains the conflict over Karabakh.[38] Thus, the mountain ranges and watershed lines dictated small political units and their unique political boundaries. What roads that existed were often barely passable. When the Russians conquered the region early in the nineteenth century, they did create larger provinces or governorates, but at the lower levels kept the old, smaller frontiers dictated by geography. This perpetuated a bewildering ethnic and religious mix of people that ignited with the coming of nationalism by the end of the nineteenth century.

Karabakh with its Christian Armenian majority and Muslim Tatar (Turkic) minority was one of the regions where ethnic/nationalist conflicts arose. In 1905, there was a particularly violent Armenian-Tatar war. The regional geography made access to Karabakh considerably easier from the east than from the west where virtually impassable mountains lay. These geographic facts favored placement of Armenian-majority Karabakh within Muslim majority Azerbaijan. Thus, the Bolshevik approach to the Karabakh problem became an eclectic stew of several ingredients involving a genuine attempt to solve the problem, pursuing Bolshevik aims, and attempting to satisfy the conflicting interests of Armenia and Azerbaijan. The disputed area of Karabakh was left under Azerbaijani control with limited Armenian autonomy. Although the compromise satisfied neither adversary, as long as the Soviet Union stood strong these territorial conflicts remained obscured. However, once Soviet power began to weaken in the late 1980s, the submerged conflict reemerged and quickly degenerated into war. Indeed, nothing could more easily testify to the disintegration of the once mighty Soviet Union than internal civil war within its existing boundaries. Even bloodier wars resulted with the breakup of communist Yugoslavia. Despite all the damning Western rhetoric against communism, few had appreciated how it had dampened and even dropped into the memory hole these ancient conflicts that were now resurfacing.

In surveying the opposing internationally legal doctrines of self-determination and territorial integrity's implications for Karabakh, this chapter has concluded that the latter trumps the former. However, as was also noted, there is nothing in international law that prohibits secession from an existing state. Neither is there any rule of international law which prohibits the existing state from crushing the secession. International law simply will recognize the winner of such struggles as legitimate.[39] Thus, in Kosovo and Eritrea, cases with similarities to Karabakh, these former possessions of Serbia and Ethiopia won their independence by force of arms. South Sudan, East Timor, and Bangladesh are similar examples. Although resort to war violates UN Charter Article 2(4), "All Members [of the UN] shall refrain from the threat or use of force against the territorial integrity or political independence of any state," in such cases one might counter by citing UN Article 51, "Nothing in the present Charter shall impair the inherent right of individual or collective self-defense if an armed attack occurs." Thus, in the end attempting to further parse the distinction between self-determination and territorial integrity leads to the conclusion that force of arms becomes determinative, while recourse to legal doctrines secondary.

In an attempt to suggest a peaceful compromise based both on international law and political realities, one recent study has recommended the famous example of the Aland Islands located half way between Sweden and Finland at the entrance to the Gulf of Bothnia.[40] For many centuries, the Swedish-speaking Aland Islands were, together with mainland Finland, part of Sweden. In 1809, however, following its defeat during the Napoleonic Wars, Sweden was forced to cede Finland to Russia. The Aland Islands, along with the rest of Finland, became an autonomous Grand Duchy of the Russian Empire, with the Tsar as Grand Duke. (The Islands were also famously placed under an international servitude not to be fortified by an annex to the Treaty of Paris in 1856, but that narrative is beyond the scope of this article.) When the Tsar collapsed in 1917, Finland became independent. Sweden, the "kin-state," claimed the islands on the basis of self-determination, while Finland averred its sovereignty based on maintaining its territorial integrity. Under the auspices of the League of Nations, the Aland Islands successfully became an autonomous region of Finland, but were granted a very high level of self-government.

However, given the volatility of Caucasian politics compared to those in the Scandinavian states, whether such a solution would work for Karabakh remains problematic. Indeed, autonomy for Karabakh is exactly the solution that failed and led to the most recent war in 2020. Thus, we seem to need what another observer has termed "a bolder approach," along the lines post-World-War-II Europe had apparently finally achieved until Russia threw fire on it by invading Ukraine in February 2022. "The problem can only be solved if borders lose their significance."[41] Only in such a seemingly utopian world, would Karabakh find security. Unfortunately, that time does not appear imminent.

NOTES

1. For background on Karabakh, see Svante E. Cornell, *The Nagorno-Karabakh Conflict*, Report no. 46, Department of East European Studies, Uppsala University, Sweden, 1999; Thomas de Waal, *Black Garden: Armenia and Azerbaijan Through Peace and War* (New York: New York University Press, 2003); Gerard J. Libaridian, ed., *The Karabakh File: Documents and Facts on the Question of Mountainous Karabakh, 1918–1988* (Cambridge: Zoryan Institute, 1988); Thomas Goltz, *Azerbaijan Dairy: A Rogue Reporter's Adventures in an Oil-rich, War-torn, Post-Soviet Republic* (Armonk, NY: M.E. Sharpe Press, 1998); Michael Kambeck and Sargis Ghazaryan, eds., *Europe's Next Avoidable War: Nagorno-Karabakh* (New York: Palgrave Macmillan, 2013); Ohannes Geukjian, *Negotiating Armenian-Azerbaijani Peace: Opportunities, Obstacles, Prospects* (Farnham, England: Ashgate, 2014); and Arsene Saparov, *From Conflict to Autonomy in the Caucasus: The Soviet Union and the Making of Abkhazia, South Ossetia and Nagorno Karabakh* (London and New York: Routledge, 2015). More recently since the Second Karabakh War in 2020, see M. Hakan Yavuz and Michael M. Gunter, eds., *The Nagorno-Karabakh Conflict: Historical and Political Perspectives* (London and New York: Routledge, 2023, in which I published an earlier version of the present chapter on pp. 115–129; Fariz Ismailzade and Damjan Krnjevic Miskovic, eds., *Liberated Karabakh: Policy Perspectives by the ADA University Community* (Baku, Azerbaijan: ADA University Press, 2021); and M. Hakan Yavuz and Vasif Huseynov, "The Second Karabakh War: Russia vs. Turkey?" *Middle East Journal* 27 (Winter 2020), pp. 103–118.
2. Other recent examples that involve various elements of the inherent contradiction between these two conflicting doctrines, but in each case have their unique characteristics it should be noted, include Kosovo, Eritrea, Western Sahara, East Timor (Timor-Leste), Belize, Gibraltar, the Falkland Islands (Malvinas), the Basques, Biafra, Catalonia, Chechnya, Eastern Ukraine, the Kurds, Northern Cyprus, and Scotland, among numerous others. For background on over 40 self-determination conflicts including Karabakh outside the colonial context that have appeared virtually impossible to settle, see Marc Weller, "Settling Self-determination Conflicts: Recent Developments," *The European Journal of International Law* 20:1 (2009), pp. 111–164. For many further possible examples, see James Minahan, *Nations Without States: A Historical Dictionary of*

Contemporary National Movements (Westport, CT: Greenwood Press, 1996).
3. The legal doctrines of sovereignty meaning unlimited power or better just independence, and uti possidetis meaning that old administrative colonial boundaries would remain legal international boundaries upon independence are closely related to and tend to reinforce the concept of territorial integrity. In general, see Peter Malanczuk, *Akehurst's Modern Introduction to International Law*, 7th revised ed. (London and New York: Routledge, 1997), pp. 17–18 and 162, 163. For an encompassing historical approach to the concept of sovereignty, see Stephen D. Krasner, *Sovereignty: Organized Hypocrisy* (Princeton: Princeton University Press, 1999). For further analysis, see below. The most comprehensive analysis of statehood creation in international law is arguably James R. Crawford, *The Creation of States in International Law*, 2nd ed. (Oxford: Oxford University Press, 2006).
4. As Svante Cornell noted when the present conflict was still in its earlier stages: "The Armenians invoked the principle of peoples' right to self-determination, and the Azeris defended the principle of territorial integrity." *Nagorno-Karabakh Conflict*, p. 25. Thomas de Waal concurred: "A resolution of the issue had to reconcile the competing claims of Azerbaijan's territorial integrity and Karabakh's self-determination (or, in blunter language, de facto secession)." *Black Garden*, p. 255.
5. "Hundreds of Dead Armenian Soldiers Shown in Nagorno-Karabakh," Novinite.com (Sofia News Agency), November 13, 2020, https://www.novinite.com/articles/206519/Hundreds+of+Dead+Armenian+Soldiers+Shown+in+Nagorno-Karabakh, accessed November 14, 2020.
6. Congressional Research Service, "Azerbaijan and Armenia: The Nagorno-Karabakh Conflict," (written by Cory Welt and Andrew S. Bowen) R46651, January 7, 2021, https://sgp.fas.org/crs/row/R46651.pdf, accessed July 10, 2022.
7. UN General Assembly Resolution 1514 (XV), December 14, 1960.
8. UN General Assembly Resolution 2625 (XXV), October 24, 1970.
9. Boleslaw A. Boczek, *The A to Z of International Law* (Lanham: The Scarecrow Press, Inc., 2010), p. 114.
10. See "Conference on Security and Co-operation in Europe Final Act," Helsinki 1975, https://www.osce.org/files/f/documents/5/c/39501.pdf, accessed December 7, 2020. While Principle VIII of the Helsinki Final Act proclaims the right of self-determination, Principle IV calls for states to refrain from acting "against the territorial integrity, political independence or the unity of any participating State," and Principle III emphasizes "the inviolability of state frontiers."
11. UN World Conference on Human Rights, Vienna Declaration and Programme of Action, June 25, 1993, as cited in *International Legal*

Materials, 32 (1993), pp. 1661, 1665. However, it should be noted that this Declaration added that the sanctity of their territorial integrity assumed States "conducting themselves in compliance with the principle of equal rights and [internal] self-determination of peoples and thus possessed of a Government representing the whole people belonging to the territory without distinction of any kind." Ibid.

12. UN General Assembly Resolution 2200A (XXI), December 16, 1966.
13. Crawford, *Creation of States in International Law*, pp. 415, 417.
14. Joshua Castellino, "Territorial Integrity and the 'Right' to Self-Determination: An Examination of the Conceptual Tools," *Brooklyn Journal of International Law* 33:2 (2008), p. 566. "Internal self-determination, in the sense of the recognition of cultural identity and internal self-government for different groups or peoples within the State," that is some type of meaningful autonomy, is the recommended solution. Crawford, *Creation of States in International Law*, p. 418. See above and below.
15. *ICJ Reports*, 1986, p. 566.
16. Opinion No. 3 of 11 January 1992, cited in *International Legal Materials* 31 (1992), p. 1499.
17. UN General Assembly Resolution 47/134, December 18, 1992.
18. UN General Assembly Resolution 2131 (XX), December 21, 1965, https://legal.un.org/avl/pdf/ha/ga_2131-xx/ga_2131-xx_e.pdf, accessed April 16, 2021. The UN Declaration on Friendly Relations referred to above, repeats this principle in practically the same language.
19. Island of Palmas Case, 2 *United Nations Reports of International Arbitral Awards*, 4 April 1928, p. 829. This case is best known for its definition of prescription as a mode of territorial acquisition as well as its mention of the problem of intertemporal law.
20. Texts in *International Legal Materials* 17 (1978), p. 1488; and *International Legal Materials* 23 (1983), p. 306.
21. ICJ Rep., 1986, p. 566.
22. ICJ Rep., 1962.
23. The Indo-Pakistan Western Boundary (Rann of Kutch) between India and Pakistan (India, Pakistan), 17 *Reports of International Arbitral Awards*, 19 February 1968, pp. 1–576.
24. Opinion No. 3 of 11 January 1992, cited in *International Legal Materials* 31 (1992), pp. 1499–1500.
25. Eyassu Gayim, *The Eritrean Question: The Conflict Between the Right of Self-Determination and the Interest of States* (Uppsala: Iustus Folag, 1993). East Timor (Timor-Leste) went through a similar process of Portuguese colonization until 1975 followed by annexation by neighboring Indonesia claiming territorial integrity, and finally independence in

2002. Western Sahara, a similar case, remains disputed between an indigenous population claiming self-determination following the end of Spanish colonization in 1975 and neighboring Morocco claiming sovereignty through territorial integrity.
26. On this point, see Lassa F.L. Oppenheim (1858–1919), regarded by many as the father of modern international law, particularly its positivist school: Robert Jennings and Arthur Watts, eds., *Oppenheim's International Law*, vol. 1, 9th ed. (London: Oxford University Press, 2008), p. 677.
27. For background, see Independent International Commission on Kosovo, *The Kosovo Report: Conflict, International Response, Lessons Learned* (Oxford: Oxford University Press, 2000). The secession of Bangladesh (East Pakistan) from Pakistan in 1971 proved successful because of India's military support for the breakup of its existential enemy. Turkey's continuing solitary support for the potential separation of the Turkish Republic of Northern Cyprus from internationally recognized (Greek) Cyprus represents an additional exception to the generally recognized doctrine of territorial integrity. Indeed, in this case, Turkey's position would seem a double standard given its support for Azerbaijan's territorial integrity.
28. Incongruously with its long-established legal practice regarding an existing state's territorial integrity, many UN General Assembly resolutions declared the Black majority inhabitants of apartheid era South Africa were entitled to self-determination. See, for example, UN General Assembly Resolutions 2396 (XXIII), December 15, 1969; and 31/61, December 9, 1976.
29. Since 1970, the UN General Assembly has also frequently proclaimed that the Palestinians are entitled to self-determination. See, for example, UN General Assembly Resolutions 2672 C (XXV), December 8, 1970; 3236 (XXIX), November 22, 1974; and 33/23, November 29, 1978.
30. For a list of 21 "unsuccessful attempts at secession... by groups or territories within independent States" including Karabakh, see Crawford, *Creation of States in International Law*, p. 403. Subsequently, however, two of these then unsuccessful attempts, South Sudan and Kosovo, have now become independent. History does not stand still.
31. One day after it had virtually equated self-determination for colonial entities with complete independence in UN General Assembly Resolution 1514 (XV), December 14, 1960; UN General Assembly Resolution 1541 (XV), December 15, 1960 stated that self-determination might also result in "free association" or "integration" with another state. The Cook Islands' association with New Zealand is an example of the first option, while the former independent states of Texas and Hawaii becoming states in the United States might be cited as an example of the second. The UN Declaration on Friendly Relations referred to above added a fourth possible outcome for self-determination, "Any other political status freely

determined by the people of the territory in question." UN General Resolution 2625 (XXV), October 24, 1970. Suffice to say, independence has almost always been the preference.
32. Cited in "Self-determination and the Future of Democracy," tamilnation.org/selfdetermination/index.htm, accessed December 8, 2020. This site contains a great deal of information about "more than 2000 thousand ethnic groups but only 192 states," which theoretically might claim self-determination and independence.
33. On these points, see Jure Vidmar, "Remedial Secession in International Law: Theory and (Lack of) Practice," *St. Anthony's International Review* 6:1 (2010), pp. 37–56; and Turgut Kerem Tuncel, "The Karabakh Conflict and the Lawfare of Armenia: Armenia's Campaign for Remedial Secession (I)," Center for Eurasian Studies (AVIM), October 27, 2020, https://avim.org.tr/en/Analiz..., accessed December 22, 2020.
34. Supreme Court of Canada, "Reference re Secession of Quebec," [1998] 2 S.C.R. 217, Case number 25506 *Supreme Court Judgments*, https://scc-csc.lexum.com/scc-csc/scc-csc/en/item/1643/index.do, accessed April 10, 2021. The Court did elaborate that a "state whose government represents the whole of the people or peoples resident within its territory, on a basis of equality and without discrimination, and respects the principles of self-determination in its internal arrangements is entitled to maintain its territorial integrity under international law and have that territorial integrity recognized by other states." Ibid. This reasoning might imply that a territory denied such rights might have a right to secede.
35. Martha Finnemore, *The Purposes of Intervention: Changing Beliefs About the Use of Force* (Ithaca, NY: Cornell University Press, 2003).
36. Shashi Tharoor and Sam Daws, "Humanitarian Intervention: Getting Past the Reefs," *World Policy Journal* 18:2 (Summer 2001), p. 23.
37. Cornell, *Nagorno-Karabakh Conflict*, p. 27. See also de Waal, *Black Garden*, p. 83, interview on December 5, 2000, where he cites Vyacheslav Mikhailov, the Politburo of the Communist Party of the Soviet Union's adviser on nationalities in Mikhail Gorbachev's time and who had hundreds of conversations while travelling between the two republics of Armenia and Azerbaijan in 1988, "I didn't meet a single Armenian or a single Azerbaijani who held a compromise position on this question, from shepherds to academicians."
38. Much of the following discussion is based on Arsene Saparov, *From Conflict to Autonomy in the Caucasus: The Soviet Union and the Making of Abkhazia, South Ossetia and Nagorno Karabakh* (New York: Routledge, 2015), pp. 90–177. See also Arsene Saparov's earlier, "Why Autonomy? The Making of Nagorno-Karabakh Autonomous Region 1918–1925," *Europe-Asia Studies* 64 (March 2012), pp. 281–323.
39. Malanczuk, *Akehurst's Modern Introduction to International Law*, p. 78.

40. See Kamal Makili-Aliyev, *Contested Territory and International Law: A Comparative Study of the Nagorno-Karabakh Conflict and the Aland Islands Precedent* (London and New York: Routledge, 2020).
41. Frank Engel, "The Karabakh Dilemma: Right to Self-Determination, Imperative of Territorial Integrity, or a Caucasian New Deal?" in Michael Kambeck and Sargis Ghazaryan, eds., *Europe's Next Avoidable War: Nagorno-Karabakh* (New York: Palgrave Macmillan, 2013), pp. 207, 209. Lessening the significance of borders has similarities with what many years ago Karl Deutsch termed a security community, that is an area where relations are predictably peaceful and war for solving problems is inconceivable. *Political Community and the North American Area: International Organization in the Light of Historical Experience* (Princeton: Princeton University, 1957).

CHAPTER 7

The Second Nagorno-Karabakh War: Causes and Consequences

Neither the Azerbaijani opposition nor the scholars of the Karabakh conflict expected a second full-scale war to erupt. Even though some had speculated that the war would resume, none expected the total capitulation of Armenian forces. The dominant view maintained that Armenian forces were much better trained and more willing to fight than Azerbaijani troops and that Armenian forces formed major defense lines for controlling the high hills that were unbreachable. This view also indicated that the Azerbaijani leader would not dare start a war because he was risk averse, fearing that he might lose and thus be stripped of his political power. This perspective is summed up by Krista Goff, who, along with many scholars, anticipated a defeat for Azerbaijan. For instance, Goff, a scholar of Azerbaijani politics, argued:

> This [the war] can be a risky gamble for President Ilham Aliyev, though. He will face a lot of criticism at home if the fighting does not go well for Azerbaijan. This is not just a territorial dispute, but a foundational conflict central to Azerbaijan's national identity. War with Armenia has the potential to unite disaffected citizens and oppositionists behind the government, but the Azerbaijani public has not been primed for compromise or more losses. The death of an Azerbaijani general in the July clashes renewed public pressure on Baku to reclaim Azerbaijani territories under Armenian control and enable the return of internally displaced persons to their homes, but what will happen if Baku falls short again?[1]

The second war surprised many experts who studied the conflict.[2] For instance, Thomas de Waal wonders "we, the world, the Armenians and Azerbaijan, have had 26 years to forge a peace. There's been a fairly stable situation - not much violence in that time, although certainly outbreaks of violence." Moreover, he asserts that three major powers—the US, Russia, and France—were involved in sustaining the status quo, meaning Armenian control of the disputed territories. These experts generally were sympathetic to the Armenian claims, and ruled out a military solution because they argued Armenia was much stronger militarily. President Aliyev was less likely to initiate a war, and Russia, along with the Minsk Group, would not tolerate disruption to the status quo.

Not only the war's outbreak but, more importantly the outcome of the war upset the conventional wisdom. A US government official, who follows developments in the Caucasus, said:

> All our intelligence reports indicated that Azerbaijani leadership would not risk a war. In other words, we never expected Ilham Aliyev to go to the war by risking his presidency and the legacy of his father. He did, and this was a major shock. Not only he did, but he also totally transformed the conflict by defeating Armenia and pulling Turkey into the Caucasus. We underestimated President Aliyev and totally misread the dynamics of the forces in the region. The Armenian leadership's statements and change in policy in Yerevan played an important role in the eruption of the conflict.[3]

As scholars and policy experts of the South Caucasus, we must explain not only what happened, but why and how it ended with the total defeat of Armenia.[4] This chapter will explore the following questions:

What are the major political causes of the Second Karabakh War? How did Armenian rhetoric and its new position change Azerbaijani strategic? When and how did Ilham Aliyev, the president of Azerbaijan, conclude that there was no hope in negotiations but to retake its territories through, what in Azerbaijani eyes was, the legitimate use of force? How should we explain the shocking and rapid victory of Azerbaijan? What were the roles of Russia and Turkey in the process? Answering these questions, along with reviewing the consequences of the war, which started on September 27, 2020 and ended with the Russian-imposed truce on November 10, 2020, we briefly examine (1) the causes of the current war by tracing the major events; (2) the role of the two major regional powers (Russia and Turkey); and (3) the nine-item truce agreement and its potential consequences on Armenia, Azerbaijan, and the region.

Causes of the Second Karabakh War

Two perspectives compete to explain the war's outbreak. According to Armenian scholars and corresponding public opinion, there are two dominant reasons: Turkey pushed Azerbaijan to attack Armenian forces and therefore, this was a war unleashed by Turkey and Turkish forces, with Russia giving the green light to Turkey due to the evolving nature of their bilateral relations.[5] This perspective, however, ignores the roles of the past and present Armenian leadership and denies Azerbaijani agency while also underestimating the desires and the strengths of Azerbaijan. Moreover, many scholars rarely question the basic assumptions of the Armenian position on the Karabakh conflict, which have a dehumanizing effect regarding the Azerbaijani civilians and corresponding Azerbaijani claims. There has been surprisingly little criticism of Armenia's past and present political leadership; and practically no open nor honest debate over Nikol Pashinyan's provocative statements that dashed virtually any hope in diplomacy.

The Azerbaijanis, unlike the Armenians, had regarded the war as inevitable, at least since 2016. The debate in Baku was not about its outbreak but instead its outcome. They welcomed Aliyev's leadership during the war and are currently proud of the achievements of the Azerbaijani military forces. One scholar who has criticized the government in Baku stated,

> We should thank Pashinyan for giving us this opportunity. It was Pashinyan who destroyed any hope in diplomacy. Although it was a war of choice for Armenia, for us it was a war of necessity. We had no option but to grab this challenge to restore our dignity, safety and sovereignty. Our leadership and the army did it.[6]

For Goyusov, just like many Azerbaijanis, "Azerbaijan has been incomplete with the loss of Karabakh. The pain of Karabakh has become the womb of our second birth."[7] Another Azerbaijani scholar said:

Armenian politicians were very aggressive towards us. They were talking about 'new wars and new territories.' After killing our general and high-ranking officials in July 2020, the Azerbaijani public was very angry at the government's lack of response. The total failure of the Minsk initiative showed that there was no hope but to use all our means to end this humiliation. Our leadership responded at the right time with full preparation. Yet, we should also recognize Pashinyan who gave us the opportunity.[8]

A military officer in Baku amplified the point:

The Second Karabakh War was necessary for several reasons. It was necessary because of national identity, the legitimacy of the state and the regime, and especially the geographic unity of the homeland. Moreover, the war was short and it was successful in its aims at a relatively modest cost. This was a just war. We aimed to liberate our occupied and devastated territories.[9]

The overall opinion in Baku is that the Armenians destroyed any possibility of a diplomatic solution and forced the war on Azerbaijan. Unlike Armenians, Azerbaijanis believed that they had too much at stake: territorial integrity, national identity, dignity, and the sovereignty of the state. Aliyev's leadership to carry out the war, along with careful diplomacy orchestrated with neighbors, especially Russia and Turkey, was appreciated. Ordinary Azerbaijanis, along with the government officials, have stressed the diplomatic, military, and technological support of Turkey to liberate their territories.

From the collective scholarly perspective, there are several factors that led to the outbreak of the 2020 war[10]: (1) the calculating decision of the Azerbaijani leadership to pick the timing, while building proper alliances and executing the right war strategy; (2) the failure of the past 26 years of the Minsk Group of the Organization for Security and Co-operation in Europe (OSCE), the main international mission tasked with coordinating peace negotiations between Armenia and Azerbaijan to resolve the conflict; (3) the aggressive rhetoric of Pashinyan, who declared that Karabakh is part of Armenia[11]; (4) the July 2020 skirmishes that resulted in the killing of an Azerbaijani general, along with several military officials; (5) pressure from the Azerbaijani public on their government to restore their territorial integrity[12]: and (6) the shift in Russian and Turkish strategic thinking about the Karabakh conflict. The crux of the reason for Armenia's defeat revolved around the calculated risks that Azerbaijani political leaderships had determined to take for to prepare their army and to absorb the shock that such risk taking would entail.

ALIYEV VERSUS PASHINYAN

Aliyev sought to strengthen the nation and avoid the fate of other Caucasus republics, especially Georgia, at the hand of false Western expectations. He was a realistic leader with a canny sense of what was possible given the resources at his disposal. Despite the pressures on Azerbaijan, Aliyev avoided picking fights with Russia but also disregarded Russian goals in the region. He bided his time wisely in order to shape Azerbaijani identity while preparing the military to restore the dignity and territorial integrity of the nation. It was Aliyev who deserves credit for navigating the stormy Caucasus and ultimately retaking the territories for Azerbaijan. While periodically displaying a Western-friendly face, he managed to avoid irritating Russia's Vladimir Putin. Azerbaijan defined its national security concern as the "restoration of its territorial integrity/liberation of all territories." Three events had a major impact on Aliyev's strategic thinking: the 2008 Georgian war; the 2014 Crimean occupation; and the 2016 war. These events along with the indifferent stances of the Western powers drove changes in Aliyev's strategic assessment in how to deal with the Karabakh question.

Consequently, Aliyev concluded that there was no hope for a diplomatic solution. Azerbaijan lobbied to solve the Karabakh problem according to international legal principles of territorial integrity. It engaged in various diplomatic initiatives to put pressure on Armenia. Baku lobbied at the United Nations, parliaments in European countries, and numerous international organizations. However Washington and Brussels refused to guarantee the territorial integrity of Azerbaijan in rejecting Azerbaijani diplomatic initiatives. When the UN General Assembly voted on Resolution 10,693 (passed on March 14, 2008), which confirmed Azerbaijan's claim to territorial integrity and demanded the withdrawal of all Armenian forces from the occupied territories, the United States and France vetoed the resolution, with nearly every European Union member abstaining.

When the United States and European countries imposed sanctions against Russia over the annexation and occupation of Crimea, Aliyev asked the same countries to do the same against Armenia. Russia's war against Georgia in 2008, which resulted in the loss of Abkhazia and South Ossetia and crippled the Georgian state, incurred major regional consequences. It became clear that no country could expect any external help if they also faced a security problem with Russia. In addition, Russia made it clear that it would support separatism and secessionism as a political strategy to further its hegemonic position. No European country was willing to employ its resources to resist the practice of Russian occupation.

On the contrary, some EU countries, such as France, attempted to use the Abkhazian and South Ossetian conflicts to promote their own interest by appeasing Putin.[13] Western inaction over the fragmentation of Georgia was a wake-up call for Baku. Russia sought to legitimize its actions on the principle of self-determination in Georgia, and later in Crimea on the principle of territorial integrity. These developments disturbed Baku, especially when Armenia supported Russia's annexation of Crimea in 2014. These events, however, encouraged Azerbaijan not to seek an alliance with the West that might anger Russia. Rather, Aliyev pursued a policy of moderating Russia's perspective on Azerbaijan as a friendly country that also is sensitive toward Russia's historical fears and concerns.

The timing proved significant, given the policies of Pashinyan in Armenia, who came to power in 2018 via a popular uprising with the goal of developing closer ties with the West to counterbalance Russian influence.[14] When the war erupted, the entire international system was confronting the COVID-19 pandemic. Regional countries were distracted by their domestic or other foreign policy issues. No country had the desire nor resources to focus on the Karabakh War. The U.S. was occupied with the upcoming presidential election and Washington was overwhelmed in trying to bring the pandemic under control. The EU was busy with the pandemic and with negotiations regarding the U.K. and Brexit.

With sanctions in place against Russia due to its annexation of Crimea, the Russian economy gradually worsened. The sharp decline in oil and gas prices aggravated the economic crisis in Russia. Meanwhile, Russia was bogged down in the Donbas and Luhansk regions in its conflict against Ukraine. The worst crisis emerged from the political upheavals in Belarus where pro-Western forces were overwhelming the pro-Russian political regime. The Belarus presidential elections on 9 August 2020 and the surrounding crisis made Russia fear the impact of regime change in that country.[15] Russia was also dealing with the challenges of political opposition leader Alexei Navalny, who enjoyed a great deal of public support in some areas of the West.

Pashinyan represented a significant break from the hardline Karabakh Armenians who had dominated the state of Armenia since the war in the 1990s. At the outset, he signaled an intent to resolve the conflict, which the Azerbaijani government welcomed. According to recently declassified information, the governments of Armenia and Azerbaijan, at that time, had engaged in secret negotiations regarding the settlement process.[16] However, after consolidating his political power at home, Pashinyan abruptly abandoned this approach and called for the unification of Karabakh and Armenia, declaring, "Karabakh is Armenia, period."[17] Unlike the previous Armenian leadership, he worked hard to destroy the framework of the Minsk Group and rejected the recommended step-by-step process.[18]

Pashinyan's irredentist rhetoric not only angered the Azerbaijanis, it also provided the reason for Azerbaijani political opposition groups to challenge their own government on the principal grievance. That is, the stinging effect of 30 years of events in which historical cities of Azerbaijan identity were ceded to Armenia, and outcomes that implied the conflict had been resolved in favor of the Armenians. Pashinyan's raw nationalist rhetoric on behalf of his country, which included calling eastern Turkey a "historic land of Armenia," angered the Turkish government as well. Tensions reached unprecedented levels when the Armenian government officially feted the centennial anniversary of the defunct Treaty of Sevres, which would have dismantled the Ottoman Empire at the end of the wars in 1920 and divided Ottoman territories, including Turkey, into several chunks.[19] The treaty never entered into force and was replaced by the Treaty of Lausanne of 1923.[20] But, in August 2020, Pashinyan proclaimed:

> The Treaty of Sevres is a historical fact. It remains so to this day...in its Article 89, the Treaty of Sevres reaffirmed our nation's indisputable historical association with the Armenian Highland, wherein the Armenian people had originated, lived, developed their statehood and culture for millennia... The establishment of the independent Armenian statehood in its ancestral homeland was the fair solution of the Armenian Question. Historical justice was being restored. Favorable conditions were created for reinstating our people's economic and demographic potential and ensuring its natural development. ...We are bound by duty to remember it, realize its importance and follow its message.[21]

Amplifying this stance, Armenian Defense Minister Davit Tonoyan called for a "new war for new territories" during a meeting in New York City with representatives of the Armenian diaspora.[22] The Turkish security establishment read these statements as Pashinyan's intent to spread the conflict to Turkey and, provoked by Pashinyan's confrontational rhetoric, Ankara decided to openly support Azerbaijan.

Meanwhile, the Azerbaijani public and government apparently concluded that peace negotiations were never going to result in the return of their occupied territories. The point was confirmed in their view by attacks on civilians and the killing of a popular Azerbaijani general and his colleagues in a missile attack near the previously negotiated ceasefire lines of July 2020.[23] The Armenian attack was a test run to gage Azerbaijani resolve. It activated public opinion in Azerbaijan, propelled by the public display of grief at the funerals of the fallen soldiers and then by a massive demonstration in Baku and other towns demanding a corresponding response to Armenia's aggression. Protesters shouted, "Liberation of Karabakh" and "Martyrs do not die; the homeland will not be divided." Some protesters reached the parliament in Baku, caused some damage and called upon the government to act. The pro-war protests signaled a public concern that the government of Azerbaijan was not taking the conflict seriously enough to fight for the repatriation of the contested territories. The protests strengthened the hand of the Azerbaijani political opposition, which echoed the public sentiment favoring decisive action. Thus, Azerbaijanis bonded quickly around the premises and prospects of nationalism, igniting dormant passions behind the goal of integrating the occupied territories into the homeland. The Armenian government celebrated its military victory and Pashinyan orchestrated a ceremony where medals were presented to military personnel who participated in combat against Azerbaijan.

The Minsk Group, co-chaired by the US, Russia, and France, failed to resolve the conflict, according to the principles and norms of the OSCE, the UN Charter, and UNSC resolutions.[24] Armenia's desire to consolidate control over not only the region that previously belonged to the Nagorno-Karabakh Autonomous Oblast but also seven adjacent Azerbaijani districts, discouraged them from meaningfully participating in the negotiation process. The settlement formulas proposed by the Minsk Group, based on the UNSC resolutions, were not welcomed by the Armenian government, because they would have meant the withdrawal of Armenian military forces from the occupied Azerbaijani territories. On the other hand, Armenia interpreted the geopolitical situation in the region as a sign of continuous Russian support for the existence of Azerbaijani territories under the control of Armenia. The subsequent Armenian governments failed to read the changes in the geopolitical environment of the wider South Caucasus region, especially in trilateral relations among Russia, Azerbaijan, and Turkey.

Russia had taken a leading role by demonstrating that the Caucasus is legitimately inside its backyard as a national interest, therefore conveying the right to negotiate a solution to this conflict.[25] Russia's alliance with Armenia within the Collective Security Treaty Organization (CSTO), Armenia's economic dependence on Russia, and the existence of a Russian military base inside of Armenian territory further complicated the international dynamics to the detriment of efforts to resolve the Armenia-Azerbaijan conflict. The impasse had aggravated the animus on both sides and imparted a false sense of security to Armenians who saw Russian support as a signal that the occupied territories were part of their country and that the issue had already been resolved. The Armenian political leadership always used the term "never" for any compromise. On 1 August 2016, President Sargsyan said:

> I would like to speak about another issue, which we have spoken about on many occasions. It is about the Karabakh issue and so-called 'surrender of lands'. My personal statements with regard to our clear-cut position on that are probably numberless. I repeat once again: there will be no unilateral concessions in the resolution of the NK issue. Never. Nagorno-Karabakh will never be part of Azerbaijan. Never. I repeat once again: it is out of the question. I have given my entire adult life to this. To get to the solution acceptable for my nation, I have always been ready to sacrifice any position, and also my life. It is like that today; it will be like that tomorrow.[26]

> "Never" was the code word how the Armenian political leadership approached the negotiations. Their fundamental goal was to legalize the occupation with the support of the some of Western powers. In 2019, an Armenian scholar said, "There is no more Karabakh problem. It has been solved. Armenia took over what has always belonged to as Armenian. No Armenian would give up an inch of the territories we have liberated."[27]

Armenia considered Russia and its army as the most powerful military force in the Caucasus. And Russia continues to be the main supplier of arms to both Armenia and Azerbaijan. According to the Stockholm

International Peace Research Institute (SIPRI), a think tank that monitors military spending worldwide, oil-rich Azerbaijan spent more than $24 billion on arms between 2008 and 2018. Armenia, with limited resources, had received cheaper and older Russian weaponry, including some that were donated. It spent a mere $4 billion during the same period, but allocated one-fifth of its annual state budget to spending on arms. Nevertheless, the alliance with Russia allowed Armenia to acquire otherwise expensive arms without excessive cost burdens, significantly strengthening the country's defensive capabilities.

The 2016 border clashes between Azerbaijan and Armenia resulted in significant human losses and a loss of territory.[28] The war exposed the Azerbaijani weaknesses, and consequently Armenia became more lackadaisical about its military's capabilities. For instance, when Russia proposed a major peace plan in 2016, it was rejected by Armenia. After the clashes in 2016, Russian Foreign Minister Sergey Lavrov, a Russian-Armenian with deep sympathies toward Armenian causes, proposed a compromise plan that comprised two parts ensuring the Karabakh region would have special status. Armenia would return the five adjacent regions to Azerbaijan and keep the Lachin and Karavajar districts until a final status on Karabakh would be decided in a referendum. Armenia rejected this plan, which would have avoided the disastrous defeat of the Armenian forces in 2020.

Pashinyan's visit to Karabakh on August 5, 2019, and his open declaration that it is part of Armenia erased realistic hopes for a peaceful solution. Turkey concluded that there was no room for a peaceful resolution and thus supported the Azerbaijani right to defend its territories. Turkey was worried about the potential for public anger to deepen the leadership crisis in Azerbaijan and lead the most powerful Caucasian country into a downward spiral of uncontrollable political turmoil.[29] Pashinyan's statements about Karabakh, his visit to the city of Shusha—considered by Azerbaijanis to be the cradle of their culture—and his declaration that Shusha would remain part of Armenia portended the forthcoming war.

After the First Karabakh War, Armenian nationalism was transformed into a more self-confident and assertive stance. Yet, the same Armenia, due to its aspirations to unify with the Karabakh region, also became a Russian outpost in the Caucasus. Given Armenia's relatively small demography (as compared to that of Azerbaijan) and its fighting spirit which was informed by the *fedayi* model (sacrificing oneself for a bigger goal), Armenia succeeded in a military victory and occupation of the

20% of Azerbaijani territories in the 1990s. Armenian individual and communal identity coalesced with a militarized and self-assured national body. After the First Karabakh War, Armenian intellectuals and politicians agreed nearly unanimously that "not even an inch" of territory would be returned to Azerbaijani Turks.

This uncompromising position was built on a narrative of an invincible army that could go all the way to Baku. This narrative shaped Armenian political positions for the next quarter of a century, as Armenians constructed an image of the Azerbaijani Turk as lazy, cowardly, and uncivilized. Self-criticism and foresight about potential problems were all negated, or at least ignored, and the majority of Armenians rallied around this new form of victorious and conquering Armenian nationalism. The First Karabakh War signified the rebirth of Armenia as an aspiring hegemon in the Caucasus, with hopes of surpassing its neighbors. As a result, every Armenian either in the global diaspora or inside Armenia has been dedicated to adding their own voice and resources to achieve Armenia's vision of victorious nationalism.

The military victory in the 1990s provided an opportunity for Armenians to reimagine themselves as instrumental pieces of the mythologized Armenian body as a potent entity. Jirair [Gerad]Libaridian, an American-Armenian historian and diplomat, argues that Armenians "became obsessed with [their] dreams instead of focusing on the possible."[30] One of the results of this cognitive transformation was the "otherization" of the Azerbaijanis as lazy, backward Turks. The enmity toward Azerbaijanis carried dehumanizing consequences and effectively blocked any political compromise or even sincere acknowledgment of the sufferings of Azerbaijani refugees. The Armenian elite never imagined the possibility that Azerbaijan could fight and regain these territories; the Armenians became hostage to a blind nationalistic worldview. As events in 2020 portrayed, the Armenian stubbornness would prove costly.

Before the Velvet Revolution in Armenia, Pashinyan was a leading critic of Armenia's pro-Russian foreign policy.[31] As a member of the parliament he voted against Armenia's accession to the Russian-dominated Eurasian Economic Union (EEU). He campaigned for Armenia to leave the EEU and develop closer relations with the European Union. Pashinyan's worldview was shaped by his admiration of European economic and cultural development and he treated Europe as the future of what Armenia could become. And, just like the new Armenian political elite, he saw in everything Soviet or Russian, backwardness, imperialism, and antidemocracy.

As prime minister, Pashinyan reversed his thinking about Russia by insisting that Armenia's security situation constrained its foreign policy options. Furthermore, not only Pashinyan but many Armenian foreign policy scholars also insisted that Armenia does not have any alternative but to rely on Russia and remain as a Russian "outpost" in the Caucasus. This group insists that Armenia's geography determines its foreign policy because it is sandwiched between two hostile neighbors, Turkey and Azerbaijan. Thus, these geographic circumstances forced Armenia to rely on Russia.[32] Moreover, the majority of Armenians believed that Moscow would defend Armenia militarily if it were attacked by either of these two states. For instance, Col. Andrey Ruzinsky, commander of the 102nd Military Base at Gyumri in Armenia, indicated Russian readiness for "armed conflict against Azerbaijan if it decides to restore jurisdiction over Nagorno-Karabakh by force."[33]

Russia never hesitated to limit Armenia's foreign policy options by using the Turkish or Azerbaijani threat card. The vast majority of Armenians view Turkey as the existential enemy of the Armenian people and in order to remove this danger they accept the role of acting as a vassal for Russia. But, this essentialist view ignores the fact that Armenian irredentist nationalism and its occupation of Karabakh and its surrounding regions made it reliant on Russia. This manufactured an irrational threat perception confused by its nationalism rather than informed realistically by its geographic position. As a result, Armenian foreign policy options were tainted and hopelessly out of touch with geopolitical realism. Armenia would have had many foreign policy options had it ceded its dream of nullifying the terms of the Treaty of Sevres or if it had accepted the territorial integrity claims of Azerbaijan.

Turkey's Role and Erdoğan's Determination

Although international media and Armenian representatives, along with France, have blamed Turkey for instigating the Second Karabakh War, there is no concrete evidence that would suggest this to be true. President Recep Tayyip Erdoğan's combative personality and his international posture have subjected him to criticism in Europe and the Middle East.[34] True, Erdoğan never hesitates to use gunboat diplomacy whenever he deems it necessary. However, he did not instigate this conflict and was not involved in the ceasefire negotiations. Yet, he also exposed the Minsk

Group's failures and Armenian intentions to annex the occupied territories. Indeed, he has fully supported Azerbaijan, offering to provide whatever assistance the country needs—a position that aligns with both Azerbaijani and Turkish public opinion. Erdoğan has always been critical of the failure of former Turkish leaders to act resolutely on the side of Azerbaijan. His position reflects a sense of guilt on the part of the Turkish state for failing to help Azerbaijan during its most fateful period in the early 1990s, a point to which Erdoğan has referred previously.[35] For instance, Turgut Özal, then Turkish president during the height of the war in the 1990s, refused to offer aid to Azerbaijan and declared, "Azerbaijanis are closer to Iranian culture and they are Shia; we are Sunni."[36]

There are several factors that help decipher Erdoğan's daring alliance with Azerbaijan.[37] Erdoğan has always regarded the Karabakh issue as an illegitimate occupation and humiliation of the Azerbaijani nation, carried out with the support of major (Christian) powers. Karabakh, for Erdoğan, was a just cause and it must be supported at all costs. Erdoğan was sure that Putin could not intervene in the conflict because Russia had numerous problems to deal with and would not risk alienating both Turkey and Azerbaijan for Armenia. The Turkish president was sure about the military preparedness of the Azerbaijani army to win the war. Likewise, Erdoğan told members of his inner circle that neither France nor the United States would intervene in this conflict because they have other issues to deal with in their countries. Erdoğan's personality, as a risk taker who is suspicious of the West, decided to support Azerbaijan with as many available means as possible. Some have also referred to Erdoğan's image that Turkey could not have any critical role in Central Asia if Azerbaijan were to be crippled and too ineffective to play any role in the Caucasus. Finally, the 2009 Turkish-Armenian rapprochement and the reactions to a normalizing bilateral process was a moment of epiphany for Erdoğan.

Several factors clarify Turkey's shift from indifference toward Azerbaijan to full support as a strategic partner: (1) the Turks' view of the Azerbaijanis as ethnic kin whom they are obligated to support; (2) the fact that Azerbaijan is not attacking another country but seeking to restore its own territorial integrity—a cause that for many Turks is morally and legally just; (3) the ingrained and politically motivated feeling among the majority of Turks that Armenia has always been subservient to Europe and Russia in its quest to restore its status as a major power; and, most critical, (4) the role of economic relations between Turkey and Azerbaijan.

The recent wave of nationalism is behind Turkey's current assertive foreign policy. As its public opinion stances have become more nationalistic, so have the policies of its government. Erdoğan, for example, has allied himself with the nationalist party of Devlet Bahçeli to secure a majority bloc in parliament and in presidential elections. This alliance has had a major impact on foreign policy. The Karabakh conflict has provided an opportunity for Erdoğan to polish his nationalist credentials and enhance his legitimacy before those Turkish voters who identify as nationalists.[38] Moreover, from the perspective of international law, Turkey has had firm ground for its rationale in siding with Azerbaijan.

At the same time that Armenians have worked tirelessly to see their suffering during World War I recognized as genocide, the Turkish public has increasingly distanced itself from the Armenians, whom they regard as a convenient pawn of Turkey's enemies to weaken the country and destroy its hard-earned positive image.[39] Unfortunately, the use of Armenian suffering by the U.S. Congress or the European Parliament against Turkey in well publicized formal resolutions has not helped to elucidate an unbiased historical account of what occurred, nor to raise Turkish consciousness and bolster diplomacy in the region.[40] Whenever these countries have thought they were aggrieved because of Turkey's actions, both historical or current, the response has often been to frame it as Turkey's unwillingness to recognize the events of 1915 as genocide.

Perceived as abusing the historical record by seeking an acknowledgment that atrocities affected all groups in the relevant territories during the wars, contemporary generations of Turks have chafed at the insistence of Armenians to return repeatedly to the events of 1915 as the source of their grievances. Moreover, Armenian attempts to justify the occupation and ethnic cleansing of Azerbaijanis as revenge for the events of 1915 have forced the Turkish public to identify with the cause of Azerbaijan. Erdoğan, in this instance, is not shaping public opinion but responding to it. Rather than seeking to pause and understand the societal image and public standing of Armenia and Armenians in Turkey, more than a few experts and scholars are quick to blame Erdoğan for antagonizing this particular conflict.

Finally, the economic and geopolitical situations compel Turkey to support Azerbaijan. Although Turkey and Azerbaijan describe their relationship in terms of "one nation, two states," their economic interdependence has played a critical role in changing its dynamics.[41] As a growing economy with a growing population, Turkey is an energy-dependent country that buys a significant part of its oil and gas from Azerbaijan. Moreover, major Azerbaijani oil and gas pipelines pass through Turkey, which has been collecting fees from them. The two countries built the Baku-Tbilisi-Kars railway and two pipelines to integrate their economies, and Azerbaijan is the biggest investor in the Turkish energy sector. Its state-owned oil company (SOCAR) owns the biggest refineries in Izmir. The trade volume between the two countries is close to $5 billion and likely to increase to $15 billion by 2024. As Turkey becomes more dependent on Azerbaijani oil and gas, its foreign policy will reflect these facts. Economics also clarifies the general understanding behind Turkey's unquestioned support for Azerbaijan but it also does not explain why the 2020 war erupted.

When the United States pressured Turkey to open its border with Armenia and establish diplomatic relations, Ankara moved forward by signing a set of documents, known as the Zurich Protocols, with Armenia in 2009.[42] The goal was to open the borders with Armenia that were closed because of the Armenian invasion of Azerbaijani territories, and to establish diplomatic relations between the two countries.[43] The Foreign Ministry of Azerbaijan reacted to the protocols by claiming that Turkey's decision "directly contradicts the national interests of Azerbaijan and overshadows the spirit of brotherly relations between Azerbaijan and Turkey built on deep historical roots."[44] The Azerbaijani government worried that with the opening of borders between Turkey and Armenia, the result would end the isolation of Armenia. Thus, Azerbaijan would lose crucial leverage to influence any talks on the future status of Nagorno-Karabakh.[45] Baku used persuasive means, including its oil pipeline over Turkey, along with the volumes of Azerbaijani oil companies' investments, to mobilize Turkish public opinion against the diplomatic overtures to open relations between Turkey and Armenia. Eventually, the Turkish government retreated from the protocols and submitted to Baku's inclinations. This crisis showed Baku that it could deploy Turkish public opinion to strengthen Azerbaijan's relationship with Turkey.

Russia's Enduring Yet Declining Influence

The Caucasus is a region of global economic significance, as gas and oil pipelines run through Azerbaijan, Georgia, and Turkey. Georgia has had poor relations with Russia since the 2008 war, which resulted in the fragmentation of Georgian territory when Russia occupied and recognized the breakaway regions of Abkhazia and South Ossetia. Azerbaijan has pursued a sophisticated foreign policy by recognizing Russia's hegemonic role in the Caucasus, and Baku has taken care not to provoke Russia. Yet, while Aliyev has developed cordial relations with Putin, he has also cultivated ties with Turkey, Israel, and major European countries. In return, Russia has tried to keep Azerbaijan close, emphasizing to Aliyev that Moscow holds "the key to the Karabakh conflict."

According to some in the Azerbaijani opposition, it was Putin who allowed Aliyev to move in and, in turn, Aliyev promised something to Putin, but we do not know what it was. This reading, which exaggerates the extent of Russian power and the role of Putin and denies any agency of the Azerbaijani leadership, is inaccurate. Russia had very little ability to stop Azerbaijan. Putin, aware of Aliyev's determination, used his secret channels to upgrade the Armenian military including providing Iskender missiles. Russia did not want to intervene on the side of Armenia because this might have compromised its standing with Azerbaijan, a major Caucasian power. Azerbaijan has more to offer to Russia than the economically poor Armenians. Moreover, Russia did not want to ruin relations with Turkey. It was fully aware of Turkish engagement and did not want to spark another conflict. Thus, as one assessment noted, "Putin, as far as we know, was on the side of Armenia emotionally and even militarily helped during the war, but he was fully aware what Russia can and cannot do under those conditions. He put Russian national interests above his pro-Armenian sympathies. Our reports indicate that he was also surprised by the quick Azerbaijani military victory and especially Azerbaijan's strong determination to fight."[46]

Russia has a shared identity with Armenia and historically has defended Armenian interests in the Caucasus.[47] However, although the entire Russian establishment and media were on the side of Armenia, Putin pursued a balanced policy. Aliyev was a first-order strategist as well as an excellent tactician. He did not give the impression to Putin that he was part of the encirclement plan of the West or NATO. He avoided poking the Russian bear and fully understood Russian fears and anxieties. Meanwhile, Georgia's dalliances with the West had provoked Russia and instigated Russian support for separatists within Georgia. Putin does not want Azerbaijan to engender pro-NATO sentiments, and he assumed that Armenia under Pashinyan was more likely to go along with Western interests than Aliyev. This is the most important conclusion he accepted in his thinking.

7 THE SECOND NAGORNO-KARABAKH WAR: CAUSES AND CONSEQUENCES   169

Another major cause of instability in the Caucasus seems to be nostalgia for Russian imperialism. Russia still sees itself as a great power and treats the Caucasus as its backyard. Moscow's heavy-handed imperialist policies, however, have resulted in the loss of any possible alliance with Ukraine or Georgia and the possible estrangement of Azerbaijan. According to Armenians including Pashinyan, Russia's main goal has been to keep the Karabakh conflict in limbo so that it can reduce Armenia to a vassal state while ensuring Baku does not follow a foreign policy independent of Russian interests.[48] Russia has a military base in Gymri, Armenia, and Armenia's borders with Turkey and Azerbaijan were closed in 1993 as a result of the first Karabakh conflict. This, in turn, has stifled Armenia's economy in the long term. Its able-bodied young people are emigrating to Russia, Europe, and the U.S. The more vulnerable Armenia becomes, the more it risks lapsing into the vassal status that Russia desires. Armenia is the poorest state in the Caucasus, with a failing infrastructure and a shrinking population, evidence of how irredentist Armenian nationalism has destroyed the country's social fabric and well-being and compromised its independence from Russia.

Upon Russia's arrival in the Caucasus in the nineteenth century, its main challenger was Iran, followed by Ottoman Turkey.[49] Today, Turkey enjoys excellent economic relations with Georgia and has close ties with many North Caucasian Muslim communities. Turkey is home to more than five million Muslims from the North Caucasus who were ethnically cleansed or deported by Tsarist Russia.[50] As Russia seeks to restrain Turkey's efforts in Syria, Turkey is also seeking to expand its influence in Russia's southern and most vulnerable border regions. Presently, the Russia-Turkey relationship has been damaged by disputes over Syria and Libya, though the two regularly find common ground for addressing their differences. Erdoğan and Putin, it appears, respect each other. Yet, there are numerous disagreements between them.[51]

Turkey has never recognized the Russian annexation of Crimea and has defended the rights of Crimean Tatars. As Russia becomes increasingly dependent on oil and gas—a commodity whose market prices have been volatile during and since the pandemic as well as with the outbreak of the war in Ukraine and because of green-energy commitments around the world—it in turn is becoming increasingly vulnerable economically. Today, Russia sells raw materials and buys most of its manufactured goods from China. This is not the global image it prefers to portray, and Turkey is not what it was in the early twentieth century—the sick man of Europe.

As Russia continues to anger the people of the Caucasus with excessive campaigns of meddling and aggression, it will ironically open more opportunity spaces for Turkey and other countries in the region to exploit. Moreover, there is a shared feeling in Europe and the U.S., though perhaps not in Baku or Ankara, that Russia is a declining power in the Caucasus. Turkey has been careful not to challenge Russia directly, but Ankara is also acutely aware of Russia's limitations in the region and is biding its time for future opportunities. If Russia allies itself completely with Armenia or fails to respect the territorial integrity of Azerbaijan, it is more likely to lose influence in Azerbaijan and turn Armenia into a garrison state in the service of Russia. Today, Azerbaijan is much richer and more developed than in the 1990s, when it was defeated and lost 20% of its territories. Azerbaijan's military is also better trained and equipped, and its morale projects a fresh national confidence.

Armenia's "Clash of Civilizations"?

The Armenians portray Azerbaijanis as Turks and treat them as the children of the Ottoman Empire. David Laitin and Ronald Suny explain that "much of Armenian identity is wrapped up in what they have suffered at the hands of the Turks, and since the Azerbaijanis are 'Turks' (Azerbaijani is a Turkic language), hostility felt toward one people is transferred to another."[52] Azerbaijani Turks were not part of the Ottoman Empire and were never involved in the events of 1915, which the Armenians consider as genocide. This hostility has been regularly activated to justify Armenian irredentist nationalism. During the Karabakh conflict of the early 1990s, Laitin and Suny noted, "Armenian militias along with civilian compatriots systematically cleansed [of its indigenous Azerbaijani population] the corridors separating Armenia from Karabakh in a cold-blooded campaign."[53] The hatred of Turks was realized against the Azerbaijanis who became the victims of systematic killings and ethnic cleansing.

Pashinyan prefers to portray the conflict as a war between Muslims and Christians, claiming that the Turks had to be stopped in Karabakh or they would have seized Vienna again.[54] Although Armenia worked to frame the war as a clash of Islam versus Christianity and presented itself as the outpost of Christianity against Islamic terrorism, only a few radical groups adopted this line of propaganda. For instance, European fascists and some extremist faction groups rushed to defend the Armenian cause not because they see them as a right but rather because they are Christian.

For instance, in October 2020, Marc de Cacqueray-Valmenier, the leader of the French extreme-right group Zouaves Paris, declared on his social media accounts that he had left to fight alongside the Christian Armenians in the Nagorno-Karabakh against Muslims. This irresponsible response to the war was expressed at the highest level in France, when Emmanuel Macron openly supported Armenian occupation of the Azerbaijani territories and deliberately tried to portray the conflict as a religious conflict by insisting that Syrian jihadists are fighting on the side of Azerbaijani troops.

Pashinyan's rhetoric echoes that of two convicted genocidal Serbian leaders: Slobodan Milosevic and Radovan Karadcic. Pashinyan wants to defend his occupation of another country and ethnic cleansing of 700,000 people on the basis of orientalist images of Muslims and Turks. Yet, in this conflict, the Islamic Republic of Iran is fully supporting (Christian) Armenia.[55] Meanwhile, Turkey, Israel, Great Britain, and Hungary have supported Azerbaijan. This is neither a religious nor a civilizational war.[56] The rhetoric ignores that this is a war over territory and a conflict involving rival nationalist movements. Pashinyan has claimed that Armenia is defending the West against Turkey because Turkey wants once again to be at the gates of Vienna. The expressions of orientalism and otherization of the Azerbaijani Turks recycle repugnant motifs that the historical record has refuted. In order to gain the sympathy of other countries, Pashinyan presents the conflict between Christian Armenia and Muslim Azerbaijan as a "civilizational front line," even though Shia Iran stands with Armenia in the dispute. In many surveys and studies, Azerbaijan is consistently recognized as a predominantly secular country, similar to Finland or Vietnam.

There have been several threads of persistent disinformation throughout the war. The first is attributed to France's Macron. Apparently catering to Armenian-origin voters in the 2022 French presidential elections, he falsely claimed that Syrian-Islamist mercenaries were fighting on the Azerbaijani side. Rather than being sensitive to global justice, international law and norms, France has supported the occupation of Karabakh for 26 years. Erdoğan angered Macron by exposing French intentions in Karabakh as well as in Libya. Meanwhile, Armenians from France, the US, Canada, and Lebanon joined the fight, and those who died in the conflict were acclaimed as heroes in social media posts. But, there is yet to be any evidence of a Syrian fighter fatality in Karabakh. This calculated stream of disinformation, similar in respects to the claim of chemical weapons raised before the 2003 US invasion of Iraq, has been advanced not only by France, but also by Russian interests. When the ceasefire was signed on November 10, 2020, neither France nor Russia raised the issue of mercenaries.

Moreover, in order to mobilize the Armenian diaspora around the world, Pashinyan portrayed Armenia once again as a victim of Turkey, vulnerable to being wiped off the global map. The Armenian president and prime minister presented the Karabakh war as "the continuation of the genocide against the Armenian people."[57] This instrumentalization of past human suffering is an unmistakable example of how a victim can become the victimizer under specific circumstances when it seeks to use the scars of healed wounds to justify a new round of retribution. Regrettably, the Armenian officials have selective memories, failing to accept the worst atrocities of the 1991–94 Karabakh war, such as a series of massacres carried out in Khojaly and elsewhere, in which hundreds of innocent civilians were murdered.

THE CEASEFIRE: THE TRANSFORMATION OF THE CONFLICT

Russia has always maneuvered to exploit the fears and insecurities of both sides in the conflict to promote its own interests and status as the hegemon of the Caucasus.[58] More than the Azerbaijanis, it has been the Armenians who relied on and demanded a Russian presence in the Caucasus, which Russia has sought to legitimize on its own accord. Facing decisive defeat and the loss of the entire Karabakh area to the Azerbaijani army, Armenia had no option but to ask for Russia's assistance. Russia used its leverage over Azerbaijan to prevent complete control of Karabakh by Azerbaijan, as reflected in the truce that was signed by Putin, Aliyev, and Pashinyan. Armenia had no option but to capitulate to Russian demands, while Azerbaijan reluctantly agreed, even as they reacquired their territories. Reiterating an earlier point, Armenia had long ago accepted vassal status under Russian protection, but a historical analysis of conflicts in the region also leads to the following conclusion: Russia consistently exploits the fears of these ethnic groups by pitting one against another. Whenever Russian troops enter a region under the pretext of peacekeeping (as in the case in Georgia), it becomes much more difficult to get rid of them. In the Caucasus, the idea of Russian troops as peacekeepers is an oxymoron. Russia is always tempted to behave unilaterally with the hope of reclaiming some level of imperialist intentions. Moscow never seeks a true resolution to the conflict but rather a framework for managing it to advance its interests. The current truce agreement is just that: a vague, open-ended, unclarified instrument to deepen Russian presence in the region.

The nine-point truce agreement portends historical significance, as it will become the foundation for the final peace treaty.[59] As news of the truce spread, celebrations broke out in Azerbaijani cities, while protests, unrest, and chaos reigned in the Armenian capital of Yerevan, with people pouring into the streets, chanting, "Where is Nicol? Where is that traitor?" Armenian opposition parties, including nationalist diaspora communities, have called for the Pashinyan government to resign. Azerbaijan won the war, but Russia did not allow it to be translated into a full diplomatic victory, which would encompass recognizing the claim of territorial integrity and sovereignty of Azerbaijan. Still, Azerbaijan recovered the territories around Karabakh, including 30% of the former Nagorno-Karabakh autonomous region. Of course, this carries the caveat that Russian troops will guarantee the truce. Azerbaijan liberated its most important cultural center, Shusha, allowing displaced Azerbaijanis from the first Karabakh war to return to their homes—constituting a symbolic strategic victory for Azerbaijan. Russia is also a winner, as it crafted the truce while saving Armenia from total defeat. Moreover, it will deploy close to 2,000 troops in the conflict zone as a peacekeeping force—meaning a Russian presence not only in Armenia but also in formerly occupied Azerbaijani territories.

Meanwhile, Armenia bears the greatest losses. It paid a heavy price by losing over 4,000 soldiers, resources and territory, along with the failure of its state institutions to be honest to their population about the war conditions. The poorly trained, inadequately armed Armenian forces had no feasible option but to withdraw. They paid the greatest price because of the failure of their politicians, who refused to compromise and differentiate the circumstances of the possible from the desirable. They cared little for the well-being of their people, with the exception of those cliques who were the most loyal to the ruling government and most financially capable. Armenia could have salvaged much better terms had they pursued diplomacy after their military victory in 1994. With this truce, there is no mention of an autonomous Karabakh nor any recognition of its political status. In his address, Aliyev announced to the nation, "What happened to the [political] status? The status has gone to hell. No status. And there won't be any status. It won't happen as long as I am president." However, the widespread belief among Armenians is that there will be some form of autonomy regarding Azerbaijan's territorial integrity.

SocioPolitical Implications of the Second War

There are several consequences of the 44-day war and the truce agreement signed by Russia, Armenia, and Azerbaijan.[60]

The war and the truce have exposed the weakness of international institutions, particularly the fact that Western governments focus more on arms sales and the support of powerful lobbies with specific geopolitical interests than on broader human rights guarantees. This realization may encourage players in other frozen (dormant) conflicts to take matters into their own hands without relying on the support or guidance of international institutions. The Karabakh war suggests that frozen conflicts are likely to be reactivated with little advance notice or preparation. International institutions should address genuine concerns rather than focus on the status quo. As a result of the failure of the negotiations mediated by the OSCE's Minsk Group beginning in the mid-1990s, the Azerbaijani public had become disillusioned and gradually consolidated their resolve to make amends on the defeat they suffered during the first war.

The Karabakh war has already transformed the balance of power in the region. As Russia crafted and imposed a truce agreement resulting in the surrender of Armenia, this, in turn, has angered many in Armenia and its diaspora. As a result, there are calls to shift dramatically the orientation of Armenia away from Russia.[61] These calls will have little impact because Armenia cannot turn against Russia for reasons of economy, energy, and security. Russia is aware of Armenia's dependence and does not want to make an enemy of Azerbaijan. If Armenia fails to improve its economy, this would compel its able and young population to move away; its cities could become virtual ghost towns without an able labor force to sustain basic services. The truce agreement has prompted intense soul searching in Armenia and critical thinking about the balance of risks and benefits associated with irredentist nationalism.

Although Turkey is not mentioned in the truce agreement, the country stepped forward from the back channels to be a partner to the center of monitoring the ceasefire between the parties.[62] Azerbaijan has insisted on including Turkey, and Aliyev made it clear that Turkey's military role in Karabakh is inevitable and indispensable. Yet, due to Armenian opposition and Russian reluctance, Turkey's role has not been fully articulated in the agreement. Nevertheless, Turkey stands as the second-most prominent regional power in shaping the outcome. On November 11, 2020, Turkish Defense Minister Hulusi Akar and his Russian counterpart, Sergei Shoigu, signed an agreement to establish a joint ceasefire-monitoring center in Azerbaijani-controlled territories.

The Impact on Azerbaijani State and Society

The dynamics of victimhood and nationalism intersected with each other, as Azerbaijanis witnessed the level of destruction in the cities and villages of the Karabakh region. These dynamics are accompanied by intensified anger against Armenians. When the author visited the region in May 2022, it was shocking to observe the extent of looting, along with the damage affecting entire Azerbaijani villages and cities, including graveyards. One could sense the feelings of shock and anger among the Azerbaijanis who accompanied the author on this tour. The author watched several Azerbaijanis break into tears, when they saw the widespread scale of destruction of once vibrant urban centers.

Following the Azerbaijani victory of the Second Karabakh war, the collective identity is now composed of a pair of opposite, but ultimately complementary images of Azerbaijan: Azerbaijan as a victim state, its suffering and occupation was ignored by the international community, and Azerbaijan as a victorious power, ready to take its proper place on the world stage. These two nationalist narratives co-exist to show where Azerbaijan was before the latest war and where it is today. The dualism between Azerbaijan as a victim and Azerbaijan as a victor is reflected in recent public opinion reflecting the mood of Azerbaijani society. The sense of victimhood generated a necessary momentum in moving Azerbaijani foreign and domestic politics. As far as Azerbaijan is concerned, it won the war on the battlefield but has yet to advance its claim at the negotiating table to assume full control over the former Nagorno-Karabakh region. The truce agreement is open-ended, and many people have genuine concerns about the presence of Russian troops in Azerbaijan.

Aliyev cemented this new version of Azerbaijani nationalism with the military victory over Armenia in 2020. He has transformed victim nationalism into a proud and self-confident brand of Azerbaijani Turkish nationalism. Yet, Aliyev's expression of nationalism has remained statecentric, as he used all available means to enhance the legitimacy of the state. A key argument to develop in this book is that the First Karabakh War led to a victim identity and a unified grief-based national identity for Azerbaijan while the Second Karabakh War enhanced the process of state-building and enhanced the legitimacy of the state institutions, especially the military. Although the state tradition has remained weak in the Caucasus, the new independent states sought to overcome this problem with hyperbolized renditions of national identities and thorny mythologies. These states have lacked a critical historical and cultural depth so they have had to enhance their sovereignty and consolidate the state-building processes through conflict.

The Impact on Armenian State and Society

> Our country is still in denial about what happened at the end of the 44-day war. We have not fully grasped the consequences yet.[63]

Why did Armenia lose the war? There are several factors to explain the catastrophic defeat: (a) the lack of societal support for the war, as the Armenian public was tired of being manipulated by the Karabakh clan; (b) the military did not prepare for and never acknowledged the magnitude of Azerbaijani will and determination; (c) Armenian political leaders misread the regional changes and new conditions in the Caucasus, especially the role of Russia and the will of Turkey to support Azerbaijan; and (d) it was not tenable to maintain Armenian control over huge territories and international law was united against Armenian claims, which lacked any legal support for the Armenian side.[64] Although the reasons for the failure are not the same as the consequences, they are closely related.

The post-war electoral victory of Pashinyan indicates that Armenian society wants normalization and the country to focus on the issues affecting the Armenian state and society, not Karabakh. According to Ruslan Pukhov, a Russian military strategist, who edited several books and defends the Armenian perspective, Armenia lost the war because there was no societal support. He asserts that "the war was lost before it was started," because there was no widespread support or proper preparation.[65] The Karabakh clan's manipulation of state power and its penchant for enriching themselves have angered the majority of Armenians, who are more concerned about the economic and social welfare of their families and the state's capacity to deliver essential services. Pukhov argues that

> Armenians--locals and especially diaspora should stop thinking about it [Armenia] as a theme park. Many Armenians, even if they come here to Armenia, they still think about their future elsewhere: Russia, France and the US. People should treat their homeland seriously; not as a certain transitional period. At the end, it is about the state. I do not think that the Armenian nation is at stake. Armenians, as Jews did for 2,000 years, lived without a state. You should make a decision where you value your state on this territory or you are fine without it.[66]

Echoing this sentiment, an Armenian, whom the author interviewed, said "the Second Karabakh War has destroyed our faith in the state and the military. We are ignoring its impact. It is very hard to swallow the loss of our dreams."[67]

The November Agreement in 2020 among the three leaders—Putin, Aliyev, and Pashinyan—did not solve the problem but rather "Russified" the conflict. By Russification, this means the realization of the Russian long-term goal of having troops in Azerbaijan and using the conflict to control the foreign policies of both states and also make them dependent on Russia. The Russification of the Karabakh conflict will have a long-term impact on Azerbaijan's perception of Russia. As far as Armenia is concerned, the war eroded the stable sovereignty of Armenia, and Russia fully controls the Armenian borders and serves as the only power able to deliver something to Armenians in Karabakh.

The most ominous act during the war occurred when Armenia emptied Karabakh of its civilian population, weakening Karabakh's claim to autonomy more than its defeat on the battlefield had accomplished. According to the International Crisis Group, one-half of the population and 90% of children, women and the elderly have fled to Armenia proper.[68] There was no resistance to their leaving. Despite all this, the government of Azerbaijan has indicated that it would welcome the Armenian inhabitants of Karabakh back to their homes. But, the future of the Karabakh region will be decided between Azerbaijan, Armenia, Turkey, and Russia. Any solution will depend on the size of the Armenian population who live in Karabakh. In Karabakh, the population has declined to 45,000, as of July 2022, its smallest number yet. So the issue is Armenians are leaving the region and there will not be a viable population to discuss autonomy or the justification for the presence of the Russian troops in the long run. Although de Waal claims that the Azerbaijani goal is the "gradual emptying of Karabakh" of Armenians, this actually is happening without any Azerbaijani pressure.[69] Rather than the threat of assimilation, it is the search for better economic opportunities, which is driving the current emigration out of Karabakh.

Armenians have articulated two positions, in their own words: "first, we lost the war and therefore we lost Karabakh and there is no way to get it back, and let's improve the economic situation in Armenia." The second view contends that Armenia lost the war, not the argument and they should rearm and prepare for a third war. This group does not question the fact it failed, not because of the war but instead because of what it saw as a faulty framework about preparing for military action. It believes that Karabakh should either unify with Armenia or become an independent state. There is a third option being developed: Karabakh should become a Russian protectorate.

The war provided more critical perspectives for the Armenian intellectuals to debate. For instance, if one reads Gerard Libaridian's first report on the Karabakh conflict in 1988, and then his response to the Second Karabakh War, one sees a major shift in thinking. Libaridian is the most prominent Armenian historian and diplomat who in recent years has offered the most insightful analyses about what went wrong. In 1988, Libaridian, like other nationalist Armenians, pursued his dreams without comprehending the issues holistically. He advanced the Armenian nationalist cause without checking the facts. In that report, he accepted the claim that Armenians had legitimate "grievances" and he even agreed with the statement that "the knife had reached the bone" but then barely cites any social, political, or economic factor as to how the "knife reached the bone, representing the limit of tolerance for the painful condition."[70] In the same report, Libaridian indicated that the issue is not grievances, but for Armenians in Yerevan, the "Karabagh [cause] is a natural answer to the scarcity of arable land and mineral resources. Armenia itself is too precarious not to be easily damaged by too much antagonism." This sentence suggests that the issue for the people of Yerevan is more about resources and less about the self-determination of Karabakh Armenians.

According to Libaridian, Karabakh "has become the code word for change, rejuvenation, daring, the ability to be true to oneself, to speak one's mind." Again, the post-Soviet project of democratization and the building of civil society institutions was hijacked by the Karabakh cause and no Armenian intellectual at that time dared use the debate to criticize how the Karabakh issue would envelop and overwhelm the entire state and nation. Karabakh has "produced a new leadership that is not drawn from the official circles of Soviet Armenia," but rather an emerging class of people who wanted political power and access to resources. One should treat them as ethnic entrepreneurs who use nationalism to promote their ambitions. Libaridian avoided discussing what happened to the Azerbaijanis, whom he calls Turks, in Armenia and only mentioned them when he reported the meeting between Azerbaijani and Armenian communist leaders in the village of Ghazakh. They agreed on the "population exchanges: Sumgait Armenians would take over houses in Armenia now belonging to Turks living there who wish to move to Azerbaijan and Turkish citizens of Armenia would occupy Armenian houses in Sumgait." However, in the report, there was no mention of the deportation of the Azerbaijanis (Turks) from Armenia. In conclusion, Libaridian called upon the global Armenian diaspora to coordinate their actions to facilitate the liberation of Karabakh Armenians.

However, in 2020, there was a shift with the Second Karabakh War, as Libaridian offered a more sobering analysis of Armenian political thinking and the mistakes Armenians have made. He explains what went wrong:

> Our fundamental problem is in the way we think. (By "we" in this case I mean most of our political parties and leaders.) Our problem is the way we looked at the Karabakh conflict and the way we framed the questions related to its resolution: we started by the conclusion that corresponded to our dreams, and then asked only those questions that confirmed our conclusions and did not challenge our assumptions and logic. Our problem is our political culture that relies on dreams rather than hard facts; the way we strategize, the way we easily set aside what the outside world and our antagonists say and do if these disturb any of our prejudices and predetermined beliefs. We adjust political strategy to our wishes, to what will make us feel good about ourselves rather than take into consideration the simple facts that collectively make up the reality around us. Our problem is the way we allow our judgment to be obscured by the highest, noblest and ideal solutions of our problems, our illusions. Our problem is the way we insist on overestimating our capabilities so that we would not question our strategy and compromise our dreams. We thought that our strategy "not give an inch back" was the right one because our cause was just. And we believed we could bend the will of the enemy and of the international community and have them think and feel the way we do.
>
> We thought our dreams were so noble that just having them constituted a political program and telling the world about them could replace strategic thinking. We did not want to disturb our comfortable way of feeling patriotic.[71]

With the humiliating defeat, Armenian society and state lost the self-confidence born from the victory in the First Karabakh War. The war has led to the out-migration of the best and brightest Armenians to US, Russia, and EU countries. This defeat could encourage the Armenian elite to rethink their assumptions about nationalism and the state-society relations. Armenian nationalism is a stateless nationalism and it evolved in opposition to the Ottoman state (i.e., they called it a Turkish state) with a guerrilla movement. It is a romantic form of nationalism and its idols have always been the rebels, alternatively known as *fedayin*. This form of nationalism focused on dreams poised to fight against real or imagined injustices. Although Armenia became independent in 1991, the society could not construct a functioning state-centric culture. They hardly internalized the existence, needs, and political power of the state. The elite and the general public are still exploring and debating what should be the proper interest of the state. Armenia "remains stuck in this binary choice between populist nihilism, and a nationalistic romanticism."[72] Armenian idols are not statesmen or diplomats but remain stuck in their roles as rebels and freedom fighters (*fedayin*). Each ideological group seeks to capture the state to impose its own will on Armenian society. Except for Levon Ter-Petrosyan, the last three Armenian presidents have acted and modeled themselves as *fedayin*. The latest defeat is expected to force the Armenian elite to give up the *fedayin* model and its networks, as the nation hopefully comes to terms with the "reasons of state" and enacts policies for realizing the needs of the state.

Debate Over the Final Status of Karabakh: Independence, Autonomy or Minority Rights

In recent discussions, some Armenian and Azerbaijani scholars have advanced three options for addressing the post-war situation in Karabakh. These are: independence or union with Armenia, territorial autonomy, and minority cultural rights without any territorial dimension.

Although Armenians of Karabakh declared the Republic of Arshak, no country, even Armenia, recognized this illegal entity since it violated international norms. The first option (independence or union with Armenia) was defeated on the battlefield. However, after the Second Karabakh War, some Armenian nationalists seek to promote secessionism as a remedial right principle. This is a weak argument.[73] The remedial right argument treats secession as a last resort in response to grave injustices and the policies of the central government to deny the survivability of an ethnic group. In the case of Azerbaijan, the Armenian minority had a high degree of autonomy and Baku did not attempt to strip away autonomy until the NKAO declared its independence.

Armenians never experienced the sort of "grave injustices" they claimed. On the contrary, they occupied, ethnically cleansed, and massacred the Azerbaijanis, which violated the basic principles of international law. As a consequence, they have no moral or legal basis to claim remedial rights to advance their argument for secession. The exercise of the principle of self-determination does not encompass a right to secession, outside the colonial context. The ideals of remedial right and "remedial' secession are new and they only allow secession if and only if grave injustices are exacted against a minority, as they occurred in Kosova.

Some scholars have insisted on autonomy for the Armenian minority in the Karabakh region.[74] But, their argument is flawed in its interpretation of international law, as well as the legacy of the violent conflict, and, most importantly, the number of affected Armenians who presently constitute less than 0.5% of the Azerbaijani population. In a recent op-ed, Vahagn Avedian aptly argued that autonomy "is not a solution for the future of Karabakh."[75]

I agree with his conclusion but for different reasons. Avedian contends that the Armenian minority cannot live together with Azerbaijanis and thus, they either need to be independent or be unified with Armenia. I would argue that for the security and well-being of Armenia and Azerbaijan as well as the welfare of the Armenian minority, there should not be any form of territorial autonomy. The Karabakh conflict is the key reason why the population of the Republic of Armenian declined from 3.6 million in 1994 to 2.8 million in 2020, which coincides with a drop in the number of Armenians in Karabakh from 132,000 to 52,000, as of July 2022.

As far as international law is concerned, ethnic minorities in a sovereign state do not have the right to secede.[76] It is up to the sovereign state to offer autonomy. International law offers good reasons for why such decisions remain with the sovereign state: stability of the international system, peace and security of states, and economic prosperity of communities, all of which emphasize territorial integrity over the principle of self-determination.

In examining a conflict which has lasted more than 30 years, the massive ethnic cleansing of Azerbaijanis from their ancient lands and the Armenian refusal to live together with Azerbaijanis make the case that

Armenians have forfeited their right to claim territorial autonomy. They have violated every rule of international law by occupying close to 20% of Azerbaijani territories and presiding over the ethnically cleansing of more than one million Azerbaijanis.

Those who have proposed the Aland Island model for the Karabakh, such as Kamal Makili Aliyev, fail to understand the differences between the two cases. Swedes, who enjoyed a high degree of autonomy within Finland, barely used arms to dismantle their state or carry out mass campaigns of ethnic cleansing. On the contrary, they supported Finland's war to be liberated from Russia. Moreover, regarding the Aland Island, when the Swedes claimed that they have a right to self-determination and return from Finland to the Kingdom of Sweden, the Council decided that, "positive international law does not recognize the right of national groups, as such, to separate themselves from the State of which they form a part by the simple expression of a wish."[77] International law prohibits secessionism and especially those acts which violate the norms of the international legal system. By seeking to secede, using force, ethnically cleansing Azerbaijanis, and carrying out massacres in Khojaly, Armenians have no justifiable legal or moral argument to call for the principle of self-determination.

Thus, the Aland Island solution is neither feasible nor sensible, given the characteristics of the Karabakh conflict and, notably, the secessionist brand of nationalism among Armenians in seven occupied areas of the Azerbaijani regional territories. Armenians in the NKAO had a high degree of autonomy within the former Azerbaijani socialist republic of the Soviet empire. But, Karabakh Armenians instead engaged in a devastating campaign. The recent literature on territorial autonomy indicates that this was more perilous than any other arrangement.

The scholarship on ethnic and nationalist management is divided over the success and failures of ethnic-territorial autonomy.[78] Those who have worked on post-Soviet ethnic tensions usually argue that territorial autonomy promotes nationalism and undermines stability in newly independent countries. In many cases, ethnic autonomy triggers separatism. After a bloody violent conflict, ethnic autonomy, when proposed as a solution, is more likely to deepen the cleavages and institutionalize the conflict.

A group of prominent scholars who work on ethnic management, such as Rogers Brubaker,[79] Valerie Bunce,[80] and Philip G. Roeder[81] offer compelling arguments and evidence against territorial autonomy, which is seen as perpetuating the conflict and wasting the resources of both the affected minority and the central state.[82] On the basis of events in former Yugoslavia and the Soviet Union, as well as more recently in Iraq, I would argue that ethnic-territorial autonomy risks becoming the most destructive arrangement for all parties in the conflict.

There are four reasons against territorial autonomy. One, it usually deepens insecurities and expands polarization. Two, it prevents national integration between diverse ethnic groups. Three, it usurps the formulation of a shared identity and memory among diverse groups. Fourth, it helps to create autonomous and conflict-ridden enclaves with nationalistic political entrepreneurs who care more about their individual interests than the well-being of the group. In short, territorial autonomy promotes primordial ethnic or religious loyalties and sharpens divisions between groups. This leads to the phenomenon of an ethnic prison for these groups, as it has become for the Armenians in Karabakh. The studies of Svante Cornell independently exemplifies how territorial autonomy has become destructive and has led to wars.[83] Scholars who work on conflict resolution in culturally pluralist societies argue that, in areas with a history of violent conflict, territorial autonomy could fuel secessionist movements. To reiterate: Armenians enjoyed a high degree of administrative and territorial autonomy in the former Soviet state of Azerbaijan but they also leveraged it to establish a secessionist movement and weaken, if not dismantle, the central state. It is this historical evidence which I believe argues the point that the presence of such autonomy germinated the Armenian movement of separatist nationalism and led to a full-blown war in the Karabakh region.

To stop a ceaseless cycle of violence, which has already wasted scarce economic resources, and instead move toward cultivating conditions of coexistence and integration, the Armenian minority should give up its unrealistic dream of independence. Azerbaijan should not grant territorial autonomy, if Baku desires to establish good neighbor relations with Armenia and free themselves from Russian interference. In Georgia, the Armenian and Azerbaijani minorities together comprise approximately 12% of the republic's population and while there are no threats to territorial integrity on the scale as in autonomous areas of Ossetia and Abkhazia, which eventually seceded, there are suggestions that the Georgian government could do more to accommodate the minority rights of both groups.

Philip G. Roeder's analytically guided and empirically rooted studies indicate that autonomy incentivizes ethnic separatism by providing *resources* and *motives* to nationalist entrepreneurs to advocate for secession. In the Caucasus, especially in the case of the NKAO, autonomy absorbed the already limited resources of newly independent Azerbaijan as much as with the resources of the Republic of Armenia, which hampered both countries from realizing the benefits of full independence.[84]

The Karabakh conflict ended up with both states compromising their sovereignty in their relations with Russia. If Armenia wants to become fully independent and integrate into the Caucasus region, it must not depend on Russia to the extent that it has. This could only be possible if Yerevan policymakers focus on Armenian well-being and work with Azerbaijan to secure minority cultural rights for 50,000 Armenians in the Karabakh region.

Because of the violent conflict's history and the evidence of past actions suggesting how ethnic groups are most likely to act in the future, autonomy is likely to foster vengeance and hatred against Azerbaijanis. The scale of destruction of once lively and productive Azerbaijani cities in newly liberated territories also has underscored the trauma and deep scarring imposed upon by the Azerbaijani population during the Armenian occupation. Thus, one can see why there is little to no will among the Azerbaijanis to grant any form of autonomy to Armenians. Araz Aslanli, a political scientist in Baku, confirmed the above in a May 2022 interview with the author: "No autonomy because of two reasons. First, Armenians will use autonomy to prepare for a new war. Second, Armenians of Karabakh are less than 0.5% of the population, and who would pay the costs of these separate political institutions? The Republic of Armenia used to divert over $20 million every year to keep these institutions of the Nagorno-Karabakh running. Baku will not and should not do that."

The Second Karabakh War had a major impact on Armenian society. There are signs of radicalization in Armenia and the Karabakh. There are calls for violence against the Pashinyan government. Under the current conditions, the quest for territorial autonomy would be untenable. (The paragraph I cut was repeated earlier in the paper).

To conclude, no form of territorial or ethnic autonomy will improve relations between Armenia and Azerbaijan. While some nationalist Armenians may find it more convenient to welcome the aid of Russia and its military for its objectives, there are also other groups, which heretofore have been silent, that would prefer both parties to the conflict pursue a diplomatic compromise and build bridges of economic opportunity to fortify the integrity of their respective independent republics. The disproportionately loud voices of Karabakh Armenians have hijacked the normal project of development and sustainability for Armenia to become a thriving state with economic promise, political stability, and regional integration.

The whole of Armenia should not have to sacrifice its economic and stable political potential for a minority group of 52,000 Armenians in Azerbaijan, a group that continues to shrink in size. The time is overdue for Armenia to try a different path, mainly by negotiating with Azerbaijan to ensure that the cultural rights of those minority group Armenians are fully guaranteed.

Conclusion

The war did not fully resolve the conflict but the dimensions of it have been transformed. Azerbaijan retook the formerly occupied seven districts and 30% of the Karabakh region. The Republic of Armenia, a Russian ally, was defeated resoundingly. Moreover, the war exposed (as the present Ukraine war is now doing) just how outdated Russian military technology is. As a new military actor, Turkey entered the equation in the South Caucasus as an Azerbaijan ally and key supporter of the Georgian republic. Although the war will not heal or ameliorate the deep geopolitical wounds in this region, it did restore a modicum of justice for the Azerbaijani public, which was persecuted, ethnically cleansed, and humiliated by previous events surrounding this conflict.

A majority of the Armenian population left the war zone despite calls from local Armenian authorities in Khankendi (Stepanakert) to remain. Those Armenians who departed from the region, because they could not tolerate living under Azerbaijani sovereignty, left behind serious damage and environmental destruction. International and Armenian news outlets reported variously that Armenians burned their homes, gardens, and nearby forest areas surrounding Kalbajar and other regions before the territories were to be handed over to Azerbaijan. These scorched earth measures defying the option to live side by side with the "Turks" (a pejorative term chosen deliberately by Armenians) elude rational analysis and undermine any hope of coexistence.

The main obstacle in achieving coexistence persists, as past events always have been portrayed to exclude consideration of the other side.[85]

Despite these actions, however, there is hope for regional cooperation among the three South Caucasian states (Georgia, Armenia and Azerbaijan) if they set aside nationalist rhetoric to recognize that regional integration mutually would improve the economic and social conditions, respectively, for their citizens. The ultimate peace treaty for Karabakh should address the genuine concerns of all parties and recognize the territorial integrity of Azerbaijan. It should also provide full minority rights for Armenians to preserve and perpetuate their language, religion, and culture. If no party is satisfied with the terms in a final deal, the risk of resentment sparking a new round of conflict will increase. Armenians and Azerbaijanis should commit to developing a shared language to acknowledge each other's fears constructively and provide the essential space for their respective desires to be realized within the scope of international law. They should furthermore commit to building an integrated economic future for the region to promote prosperity for all its inhabitants.

Notes

1. Krista Goff, "The Nagorno-Karabakh Conflict: An Expert Analysis," https://www.wilsoncenter.org/article/nagorno-karabakh-conflict-expert-analysis, accessed March 9, 2022.
2. Thomas de Waal, a leading expert on the conflict, whose work has been funded by Armenian business interests through the Carnegie Endowment, has always advanced the Armenian claims and often underemphasizes the necessity of understanding in greater depth the sufferings of the Azerbaijanis. See his interview in 'Salvage: A Conversation on Nagorno-Karabakh," https://www.opendemocracy.net/en/odr/salvage-conversation-nagorno-karabakh/, accessed March 19, 2022.
3. Interview with the US Government Official, Washington, May 12, 2022.
4. Students and scholars should consider reading other sources to gain a comprehensive understanding of the conflict and the Karabakh region. In addition to the widely cited book by de Waal, several lesser known studies of the Karabakh conflict have been published. These include works by former Armenia parliament member and educator Suren Zolian, journalist Tatul Hakobyan, former Azerbaijani official Yevgeniy Aliyev and historian Mamed Velimamedov. Memoirs or biographies of former Armenian military commanders Arkady Ter-Tadevosyan, Samvel Babayan and Monte Melkonian, and retired Russian diplomats Vladimir Kazimirov and Vladimir Stupishin have also been published, as have been a number of interviews and articles by early nationalist activists Igor Muradyan, Vache Sarukhanyan, Arkady Karapetyan and Zardusht Alizade.

Likewise, previously unpublished official information has also emerged in the public statements of the former Azerbaijani president Heydar Aliyev (1993–2003), as well as in recently published documents from the Ayaz Mutalibov presidency (1990–1992). The list of published research about these countries and this conflict in particularly should be expanded, as it will focus visibility on converging upon a broad common base for a constructive diplomatic solution.

5. Yeghia Tashjian, "Russia and the Future Status of Shusha," *Armenian Weekly*, November 17, 2020; https://armenianweekly.com/2020/11/17/russia-and-the-future-status-of-shushi/, accessed November 23, 2021.
6. My interview with Altay Goyusov, Baku, 28 April 2022.
7. My Interview with Altay Goyusov, Baku, 28 April 2022.
8. My interview with Araz Aslanli, Baku, 29 April 2022.
9. My Interview with an Azerbaijani General, Baku, 30 April 2022.
10. Rovshan Ibrahimov and Mehmet Fatih Oztarsu, "Causes of the Second Karabakh War: Analysis of the Positions and the Strength and Weakness of Armenia and Azerbaijan," *Journal of Balkan and Near Eastern Studies* 24:4 (2022), pp. 595–613.
11. Joshua Kucera, "Pashinyan Calls for Unification Between Armenia and Karabakh," *Eurasianet*, August 6, 2020, https://eurasianet.org/pashinyan-calls-for-unifi-cation-between-armenia-and-karabakh, accessed September 12, 2021.
12. Robert M. Cutler, "The Second Karabakh War and Western strategic thinking," *The Wilson Center*, January 5, 2021, https://www.wilsoncenter.org/blog-post/second-karabakh-war-and-western-strategic-thinking, accessed February 20, 2021.
13. Richard G. Whitman and Stefan Wolff, "The EU as a Conflict Manager? The Case of Georgia and Its Implications." *International Affairs* 86:1 (2010), pp. 87–107.
14. For a thorough analysis of Pashinyan's worldview, see David Batashvili, "Nikol Pashinyan's Russian Problem," *Security Review*, January 12, 2019, https://www.gfsis.org/publications/view/2684, accessed March 12, 2022.
15. Cain Burdeau, "Tension Builds in Belarus as EU, Russia Get Involved," August 19, 2020, *Courthhousenewsservice*, https://www.courthousenews.com/tension-builds-in-belarus-as-eu-russia-get-involved/, accessed May 22, 2022.
16. Haqqin.az, "Secret Talks Between the Envoys of Nikol Pashinyan and Ilham Aliyev," September 24, 2020, https://haqqin.az/news/190193, accessed April 8, 2021.
17. Eurasianet, "Pashinyan Calls for Unification Between Armenia and Karabakh," August 6, 2020, https://eurasianet.org/pashinyan-calls-for-unification-between-armenia-and-karabakh, accessed June 10, 2021.

18. "Farid Shafiyev Comments on Armenia's Refusal from Madrid Principles," September 4, 2020, Azərbaycan24, https://www.azerbaycan24.com/en/farid-shafiyev-comments-on-armenia-s-refusal-from-madridprinciples/, accessed March 18, 2021.
19. Gerard Libaridian, a leading scholar on Armenian foreign policy and former adviser to President Ter Petrosiyan, criticized Pashinyan's remarks. He called these statements equivalent to a declaration of a diplomatic war, See Gerard Labaridian, "Step, This Time a Big Step Back," *Aravot*, September 2, 2020 https://www.aravot-ru.am/2020/09/02/335325/, accessed May 21, 2022.
20. The Treaty of Alexandrapol (December 1920) between Turkey and Armenia annulled the Treaty of Sevres. Moreover, the Treaty of Kars (October 1921) between Turkey and the Armenian Soviet Government also annulled the terms of the Sevres Treaty.
21. Panorama, "Pashinyan: Treaty of Sevres Continues to be a Historical Fact," August 8, 2020, https://www.panorama.am/en/news/2020/08/10/Pashinyan-Treaty-of-Sevres/2341518, accessed May 3, 2022.
22. Asbarez.com, "'New Territories in the Event of New War,' Says Defense Minister," April 1, 2019, http://asbarez.com/178701/new-territories-in-the-event-of-new-war-says-defense-minister/, accessed January 8, 2022.
23. Jamestown Foundation, "Armenia-Azerbaijan Conflict Escalates with Intense Border Confrontation", July 14, 2020, https://jamestown.org/program/armenia-azerbaijan-conflict-escalates-with-intense-border-confrontation/, accessed June 12, 2022.
24. For more on the Minsk Group negotiations, see Esmira Jafarova, "Evaluating the OSCE Minsk Group's Mediation of the Armenia-Azerbaijan Conflict," 2020, Center for Analysis of International Relations (Vienna), https://www.institutfuersicherheit.at/wp-content/uploads/2020/10/ISP-Working-Paper-Esmira-JAFAROVA-Evaluating-the-OSCE-Minsk-Group%E2%80%99s-mediation-of-the-Armenia%E2%80%93Azerbaijan-conflict.pdf, accessed March 10, 2022.
25. Kavus Abushov, "Russian Foreign Policy Towards the Nagorno-Karabakh Conflict: Prudent geopolitics, Incapacity or Identity?" *East European Politics* 35:1 (2019), pp. 72–92.
26. http://www.president.am/en/press-release/item/2016/08/01/President-Serzh-Sargsyan-meeting-with-government-civiland-spiritual-representatives
27. Interview with an Armenian scholar, March 12, 2021.
28. Zaur Shiriyev, 'The "Four-Day War": New Momentum for Nagorno-Karabakh resolution?' *The Central Asia-Caucasus Analysis*, May 2, 2016 https://www.cacianalyst.org/publications/analytical-articles/item/13356-the-four-day-war-new-momentum-for-nagorno-karabakh-resolution?.html, aaccessed April 17, 2021.

29. Interview with a high-ranking Turkish government official, November 19, 2020.
30. For the quote, see Carlotta Gall, "Roots of War: When Armenia Talk Tough, Azerbaijan Took Action," *The New York Times*, October 27, 2020.
31. Alexander Iskandaryan. "The Velvet Revolution in Armenia: How to Lose Power in Two Weeks," *Demokratizatsiya: The Journal of Post-Soviet Democratization*. 26:4 (2018), pp. 465–482.
32. Alexander Iskandaryan, "Armenia-Russia Relations: The Revolution and the Map," *Russian Analytical Digest*, No. 232 (February 2019), pp. 2–4.
33. Alexandros Petersen, "Russia Shows Its Hand on Karabakh," *EU Observer*, November 18, 2013, http://euobserver.com/opinion/122032, accessed February 12, 2021.
34. For more on Erdoğan and his foreign policy see, M. Hakan Yavuz, *Nostalgia for the Empire: The Politics of Neo-Ottomanism* (New York: Oxford University Press, 2020); Yavuz, *Erdoğan: Making of an Autocrat* (Edinburg: Edinburg University Press, 2021).
35. Svante E. Cornell, "Turkey and the Conflict in Nagorno-Karabakh: A Delicate Balance," *Middle Eastern Studies* 34:1 (1998), pp. 51–72.
36. See Özal's statement, *Milliyet*, February 16, 1990.
37. H. Yalçınkaya, "Turkey's Overlooked Role in the Second NagornoKarabakh War." January 21, 2021, The German Marshall Fund of the United States. https://www.gmfus.org/publications/tur keys-overlooked-role-second-nagorno-karabakh-war, accessed March 20, 2022.
38. Some scholars suggest that especially in the last decade, Erdoğan turned back to the nationalist discourse of his former political party (National Salvation Party [MSP]) which is representative of the ideology of *Milli Görüş* (National Outlook) where Islamism is articulated with nationalism to a great extent. Mehmet Arısan, "From 'Clients' to 'Magnates': The (Not So) Curious Case of Islamic Authoritarianism in Turkey," *South East European and Black Sea Studies* 19:1 (2020), pp. 11–30.
39. M. Hakan Yavuz, "The Turkish-Armenian Historical Controversy: How to name the events of 1915," *Middle East Critique* 29:3 (2020), pp. 345-365.
40. Brendon J. Cannon, *Legislating Reality and Politicizing History: Contextualizing Armenian Claims of Genocide* (Hamburg: Manzara Verlag, 2016).
41. It was President Haydar Aliyev who coined the motto, 'one nation, two state' to describe the deep emotional connection between Turkey and Azerbaijan. More on the relations between the two states, see Murad Ismayilov and Norman A. Graham, eds, *Turkish-Azerbaijani Relations. One Nation—Two States?*, (Abingdon: Routledge, 2016).

42. Nona Mikhelidze (2010, March 5). "The Turkish-Armenian Rapprochement at the Deadlock," *Istituto Affari Internazionali*. March 5, 2010.
43. Vahram Ter-Matevosyan,"Deadlocked in History and Geopolitics: Revisiting Armenia-Turkey Relations," *Digest of Middle Eastern Studies* 30:3 (2021), pp. 155–169.
44. Azerbaijan Ministry of Foreign Affairs, Statement of the Ministry of Foreign Affairs of the Republic of Azerbaijan, October 12, 2009, http://mfa.gov.az/eng/index.php?option=com_content&task=view&id=580, accessed July1, 2022.
45. "Azerbaijan Threatens Turkey Over Armenia Agreement", Radio Free Europe/Radio Liberty, October 21, 2009, http://www.rferl.org/content/Azerbaijan_Threatens_Turkey_Over_Armenia_Agreement/1857198.html, accessed July 7, 2022.
46. Interview with Eldar Abbasov, April 10, 2022.
47. Dumitru Minzarari, 'Russia's Stake in the Nagorno-Karabakh War: Accident or Design?' *German Institute for International and Security Affairs*, November 12, 2020, https://www.swp-berlin.org/en/publication/russias-stake-in-the-nagorno-karabakh-war-accident-or-design/, accessed June 12, 2022.
48. For more on Pashinyan's love and hate relations with Russia, see David Batashvili, "Nikol Pashinyan's Russian Problem," *Security Review*, 2019, Georgian Foundation for International Studies, https://www.gfsis.org/publications/view/2684, accessed May 5, 2022.
49. Akdes Nimet Kurat, *Rusya Tarihi: Başlangıçtan 1917'ye Kadar* (Ankara: Türk Tarih Kurumu, Yayınları, 1999); Kamuran Gürün, *Türk-Sovyet İlişkileri (1920–1953)* (Ankara: Türk Tarih Kurumu Yayınları, 1991).
50. Mithat Celikpala, "Türkiye'de Kafkas Diyasporası ve Türk Dış Politikası'na Etkileri," *Uluslarası Ilişkiler* 2:5 (2005), pp. 71–108.
51. Pavel Baev, "Russia and Turkey. Strategic Partners and Rivals." French Institute of International Affairs. May, 2021. https://www.ifri.org/en/publications/etudes-delifri/russieneireports/russia-and-turkey-strategic-partners-and-rivals, accessed June 26, 2022.
52. Laitin and Suny, "Armenia and Azerbaijan," p. 147.
53. Laitin and Suny, "Armenia and Azerbaijan," p. 153.
54. France24, "'Turkey Has a Clear Objective of Reinstating the Turkish Empire', Armenian PM Says," October 2, 2020, https://www.france24.com/en/20201002-turkey-has-a-clear-objective-of-reinstating-the-turkish-empire-armenian-pm-says, accessed June11, 2022.
55. For more on the relations between Iran and Armenia, see Maziar Motemedi, "Iran's Delicate Balancing Act in the Nagorno-Karabakh Conflict," Aljazeera, October 5, 2020. https://www.aljazeera.com/news/2020/10/5/iran-nk, accessed March 3, 2022.

56. Jamestown Foundation, "Armenian-Azerbaijani Conflict: Clash of Civilizations?" October 13, 2020, https://jamestown.org/program/armenian-azerbaijani-conflict-clash-of-civilizations/, accessed April 20, 2022.
57. Ben Judah, "Armenian President Wants NATO to Explain Turkey's Involvement in Nagorno-Karabakh," October 17, 2020, https://www.politico.eu/article/armenia-president-armen-sarkissian-nato-turkey-involvement-nagorno-karabakh/, accessed March 10, 2022.
58. J. Herbst, "Putin Gains and Losses from Armenia-Azerbaijan Ceasefire Deal," Atlantic Council, November 12, 2020, https://www.atlanticcouncil.org/blogs/new-atlanticist/putingains-and-loses-from-armenia-azerbaijan-ceasefire-deal/, accessed May 8, 2022.
59. The Truce Agreement of November 9, 2020 represents more than an end to the conflict, as it provides a framework for negotiating future treaties.
60. Michael Rubin, "The Problem with the Nagorno-Karabakh Ceasefire Agreement," *The National Interest*, November 10, 2020, https://www.aei.org/op-eds/the-problem-with-thenagorno-karabakh-ceasefire-agreement/, accessed June 1, 2022; M. Russell, "Russia–Turkey Relations," European Parliamentary Research Service, February, 2021, https://www.europarl.europa.eu/RegData/etudes/BRIE/2021/679090/EPRS_BRI(2021)679090_EN.pdf, accessed March 12, 2022; Narek Sukiasyan, "Appeasement and Autonomy: Armenian-Russian Relations from Revolution to War," February 1, 2021, European Union Institute for Security Studies (EUISS), http://www.jstor.org/stable/resrep28789, accessed April 15, 2022.
61. Herbst, "Putting Gains and Losses".
62. Kemal Kirişci, and Behlul Özkan, "After Russia's Nagorno-Karabakh Ceasefire, Could Turkey Step Up Next for a Lasting Peace?" November 17, 2020, https://www.brookings.edu/blog/order-from-chaos/2020/11/18/after-russias-nagornokarabakh-ceasefire-could-turkey-step-up-next-for-a-lasting-peace/, accessed April 5, 2022.
63. An e-mail exchange with an Armenian journalist in Yerevan, May 12, 2021.
64. "Armenia Economy Minister Says Weak Army and Unpopulated Territories Reasons for Defeat in Karabakh War', *News.am*, February 11, 2011, https://news.am/eng/news/628226.html, accessed February 17, 2021.
65. Ruslan Pukhov's interview, See "Armenia's Mistakes in the Second Karabakh War," October 20, 2021, https://www.youtube.com/watch?v=LXUm7SDP6CM.
66. Pukhov's interview, https://www.youtube.com/watch?v=LXUm7SDP6CM.
67. An e-mail exchange with an Armenian analysts, June 10, 2022.

68. For more information, see https://www.crisisgroup.org/europe-central-asia/caucasus/nagorno-karabakh-conflict/reducing-human-cost-new-nagorno-karabakh-war, accessed March 12, 2021.
69. Gerard Libaridian and Thomas De Waal, "Salvage: A Conversation on Nagorno-Karabakh," December 8, 2020, https://www.opendemocracy.net/en/odr/salvage-conversation-nagorno-karabakh/, accessed June 9, 2022.
70. Gerard J. Libaridian, "The Question of Karabakh: An Overview," Zoryan Institute, June, 1988, http://libaridian.com/wp-content/uploads/2018/09/Report-on-the-Karabakh.pdf, Accessed April 2, 2022.
71. Jirair Libaridian, "What Happened and Why: Six Theses," *Armenian Mirror-Spectator*, November 24, 2020. https://mirrorspectator.com/2020/11/24/what-happened-and-why-six-theses/, accessed April 25, 2021.
72. Kevork Oskanian, "Why Armenia Needs Realpolitik, Now." EVN, June 1, 2022, https://evnreport.com/opinion/why-armenia-needs-realpolitik-now/, accessed July 18, 2022.
73. Vahagn Avedian, "The Question of Remedial Secession in the case of Nagorno-Karabakh," June 22, 2022, https://www.e-ir.info/2022/06/22/opinion-the-question-of-remedial-secession-in-the-case-of-nagorno-karabakh/, accessed July 13, 2022; David Manukyan, "What is "Remedial Secession" and Why is it Applicable to Nagorno-Karabakh?', *The Armenian Weekly*, November 4, 2020, https://armenianweekly.com/2020/11/04/what-is-remedial-secession-and-why-it-is-applicable-to-nagorno-karabakh/, accessed May 19, 2022.
74. Kamal Makili Aliyev, "Opinion: Autonomy is One Way in Which Some of the Problems in Armenia-Azerbaijan Relations can be Resolved," June 21, 2022,
    https://karabakhspace.commonspace.eu/opinion/opinion-autonomy-one-way-which-some-problems-armenia-azerbaijan-relations-can-be-resolved-0, July1, 2022.
75. Vahagn Avedian, "Autonomy Within Azerbaijan is Not a Solution for the Future of Karabakh." June 21, 2022, https://karabakhspace.commonspace.eu/opinion/opinion-autonomy-within-azerbaijan-not-solution-future-karabakh, accessed July 4, 2022.
76. Advisory Opinion on the Accordance with International Law of Unilateral Declaration of Independence in Respect of Kosovo, 2010 I.C.J. 141 (July 22); Artashes Khalatyan, "Nagorno-Karabakh Conflict in light of the ICJ's Advisory Opinion on Kosovo: Whether the Nagorno-Karabakh Case Meets the Criteria Elaborated by the UN Court," American University of Armenia, Unpublished Master's Thesis, 2011, https://law.aua.am/files/2012/02/Artashes_Khalatyan.pdf, accessed July 14, 2022.

77. The Question of the Aaland Islands: Report of the Commission of Jurists, (1920) League of Nations Official Journal Spec Supp 3, 5, https://www.ilsa.org/Jessup/Jessup10/basicmats/aaland1.pdf, accessed July 16, 2022.
78. Liam Anderson," Ethnofederalism and the Management of Ethnic Conflict: Assessing the Alternatives," *Publius: The Journal of Federalism*, 46:1 (2016), pp. 1–24.
79. R. Brubaker, *Nationalism Reframed: Nationhood and the National Question in the New Europe* (Cambridge: Cambridge University Press, 1996).
80. Valerie Bunce, "Federalism, Nationalism, and Secession: The Communist and Postcommunist Experience," in U. Amoretti and N.G. Bermeo, eds. *Federalism and Territorial Cleavages*. Johns Hopkins University Press, 2004),
81. Philip G. Roeder, "Ethnofederalism and the Mismanagement of Conflicting Nationalisms," *Regional & Federal Studies*, 19:2 (2009), pp. 203–219.
82. Alan Buchanan, "Theories of Secession', *Philosophy and Public Affairs* 26:10 (1997), pp. 1–12; Buchanan, *Justice, Legitimacy and Self-Determination: Moral Foundations for International Law* (Oxford: Oxford University Press, 2003). Buchanan criticizes Wellman's theory of ethnic or territorial autonomy and argues that autonomy fosters secessionism and deepens the conflict. Christopher Wellman, "A Defense of Secession and Self-Determination," *Philosophy and Public Affairs* 24:2 (1995), pp. 142–171.
83. Svante E. Cornell, "Autonomy as a Source of Conflict: Caucasian Conflicts in Theoretical Perspective." *World Politics*, 54:2 (2002), pp. 245–276.
84. Erik Melander; "The Nagorno-Karabakh Conflict Revisited: Was the War Inevitable?" *Journal of Cold War Studies* 3:2 (2001), pp. 48–75.
85. Getting from Ceasefire to Peace in Nagorno-Karabakh. Crisis Group. (2020, November 10). https://www.crisisgroup.org/europe-central-asia/caucasus/nagorno-karabakhconflict/getting-ceasefire-peace-nagorno-karabakh; The Nagorno-Karabakh Conflict: A Visual Explainer. Crisis Group. (2021, May 7). https://www.crisisgroup.org/content/nagorno-karabakh-conflict-visual-explainer#1.

CHAPTER 8

Conclusion

Our book has analyzed the long-running conflict between Armenia and Azerbaijan over Nagorno-Karabakh. We began by briefly examining the controversial historical origins of the conflict in the ancient past and saw that both sides have staked plausible historical claims. Although the Armenian presence in the Caucasus dates back to before the common era—that is more than 2,000 years ago—the Turkic peoples only began to arrive about 1,000 years ago. However, we also saw that today's Azerbaijani people—although speaking a Turkic language—are nevertheless likely an assimilated, amalgamated nation that includes ancient peoples such as the Caucasian Albanians. Ironically, both Armenians and Azerbaijanis are probably correct when they claim Caucasian Albanian origins. Possibly, realizing these partial common origins might help ameliorate their deep differences.

Our historical analysis quickly arrived in the early nineteenth century when the Russians began their conquest of the Caucasus, largely replacing the Iranians and to a lesser extent the Ottomans. Despite these much more recent times, however, the Armenians and Azerbaijanis (called Tatars into the twentieth century) debate about who was in Karabakh the majority and when. In addition, as recently as 1905–1906 and again in the early 1920s, they fought deadly wars against each other in which ownership of Nagorno-Karabakh was part of the dispute. Only the final

Bolshevik (Communist) victory ended this overt violence. Most important for our book is that the eventual Bolshevik triumph in the 1920s decided that Nagorno-Karabakh's large Armenian majority would possess formal governmental autonomy within the overall territorial integrity of Azerbaijan.

Although there was an even larger Azerbaijani minority living in Armenia, the Armenian minority living as the majority in Nagorno-Karabakh constituted the only minority in the Soviet Union that had its own separate governmental institutions within another Soviet Socialist Republic (SSR) even though it also had its own SSR elsewhere. Still this was not satisfactory for the Armenians because as the Soviet Union began to disintegrate in the late 1980s, the Karabakh Committee in Yerevan began increasingly to agitate for Moscow to hand over Nagorno-Karabakh to Armenia even though it was formally part of Azerbaijan. Under the Soviet legal regime of that day, this was illegal unless Azerbaijan agreed and of course Baku did not. Instead, the two sides began their deadly struggle which finally resulted in the Armenians seizing approximately 20% of Azerbaijan by the time a cease-fire went into effect in 1994. Thus, began a frozen post-Soviet ethnic conflict that the OSCE's Minsk Group/Process co-chaired by Russia, the United States, and France miserably failed to solve even thought the UN Security Council on four separate occasions passed resolutions that called for the immediate and unconditional withdrawal of Armenian troops and recognition of Azerbaijan's territorial integrity over Armenia's claim to some type of self-determination.

International law clearly held that Nagorno-Karabakh belonged to Azerbaijan despite misleading arguments to the contrary about supposed Armenian rights of self-determination often parsed into claims of some type of internal and/or remedial self-determination. However, none of these later theories took precedence over the hard fact of Azerbaijan's sovereignty and territorial integrity as such arguments would threaten the sovereignty and territorial integrity of every single member of the United Nations. This existential fact is arguably the most important point that this book makes! Despite the Armenian narrative that the Azerbaijanis were simply continuing a century's old genocide against them, international law and international organization speaking through the United Nations, unambiguously sided with the Azerbaijani position. If this book does nothing else, it will make a major contribution by explicating this existential point. Yet the Armenians were partially successful at Orientalizing[1] and Otherizing[2] the Azerbaijanis as the instigator of war and injustice.

For more than 25 years, the Azerbaijanis attempted to regain their honor and territory by legal, diplomatic means, but the Armenians refused to respond to the dictates of international law and international organization. Instead they engendered ceaseless arguments on behalf of their supposed rights to Nagorno-Karabakh through some type of self-determination and historical right. When international law and its determinative principle of territorial integrity refuted the Armenian position, they fell back on their military victory in the First Karabakh War from 1988–1994 and refused to return the occupied Azerbaijani territories.

In 2019, as detailed in previous chapters, the new Armenian president Nikol Pashinyan progressively began to magnify his state's position by calling for the unification of Karabakh and Armenia. Disdaining sincere negotiations, Pashinyan now declared, "Artsakh [Karabakh] is Armenia, and that's it"[3] A few months earlier, while dressed in a military uniform, Davit Tonoyan, the Armenian defense minister, had already told the Armenian diaspora in the United States that if Azerbaijan dared attempt to regain its lost territories by force his state's policy was no longer "land for peace," but "war for new territories."[4] Other Armenians even began to speak about Armenian soldiers "drinking tea in Baku."[5] Adding further fuel to these incendiary boasts, the Armenian prime minister also rehashed the long dead Treaty of Sevres, by declaring that defunct treaty still was a "historical fact."[6] This gratuitous remark was a not-so-subtle threat against the territorial integrity of Turkey. It amounted to a declaration of diplomatic war against Turkey as well as Azerbaijan, bringing into question the most rudimentary judgment of the Armenian leader. Whom the gods would destroy, they first make mad.

Thus, when it became clear that even though international law and organization were on their side, the Azerbaijanis were not going to regain their occupied territories through peaceful negotiations, they finally turned to the only possible solution, war. UN Charter 2(4) not only prohibited what Armenia had done in conquering Nagorno-Karabakh and seven surrounding Azerbaijani provinces, but also permitted under Article 51, Azerbaijani counter force in self-defense.

Despite attempts to Orientalize and Otherize him, Azerbaijani president Ilham Aliyev proved a very effective leader in regaining his country's occupied territories. In a wide-ranging question-and-answer session held during an international forum on the "South Caucasus: Development and Cooperation" on April 29, 2022 and attended by the two authors of this book, Aliyev made the following realistic points concerning his country's victory in the Second Karabakh War. (1). Do not accept the occupation of your territory. Continue to maintain your territorial integrity. (2). Do not depend on international organizations. The unanimous UN resolutions supporting the Azerbaijani position alluded to above, did nothing to return occupied Azerbaijani territory. There was no effective help from the international community. (3). Build and maintain a strong military to regain your lost territory.[7] Unfortunately for an ideal world, Aliyev's realistic prescriptions proved correct.

Thus, this book unambiguously and unabashedly defends the Azerbaijani position on the status of Nagorno-Karabakh and their inherent right to use force in self-defense in the autumn of 2020 to regain their occupied territory. In so doing, this book stands firmly against Armenian counter claims of Azerbaijani aggression even though Armenia still has so many supporters, especially in those states such as the United States, Russia, and France, among others, which have politically strong Armenian diasporas instrumentalizing their cause despite the clear verdict of international law and organization. In taking this firm pro-Azerbaijani position, this book covers in detail the historical origins of the conflict, the First Karabakh War from 1988–1994, the debate between advocates of the political and international principles of territorial integrity and self-determination, the long-simmering failed negotiations from 1994–2020, and finally the Second Karabakh War in the autumn of 2020 that returned Azerbaijan's occupied territories and its current aftermath.

However, despite the resounding Azerbaijani victory, ultimate peace remains elusive until the Armenians finally sign on to it. Unfortunately, there is little to indicate that they will. Here this book takes a second, most important position. The Armenian people are victims of their own selfish, misguided leaders who continue to see themselves as perpetual victims entitled to territory legally belonging to Azerbaijan and Turkey. Given the geostrategic situation and despite supposed Russian support, this is an impossible Armenian position that continues to curse the Armenian nation from successfully developing politically and economically. Thus, this book strongly argues that Armenia accepts its current borders so that the resulting peace can enable it to enter into a mutually profitable relationship with its neighbors including most importantly Azerbaijan and

Turkey. If this occurs, Azerbaijan and Turkey should sincerely offer its new found partner a magnanimous peace. Given the historical memory, this will not be easy to implement, but it is the only way for Armenia to finally begin to prosper and develop in peace as a modern, successful state.

Notes

1. On this famous, critical concept to describe the West's contemptuous depiction of the Orient, see Edward W. Said, *Orientalism* (New York: Pantheon Books, 1978).
2. On this critical concept describing the treatment of people from a different group as essentially inferior to your group, see Gayatri Chakravorty Spivak, "The Rani of Sirmur: An Essay in Reading the Archives," *History and Theory* 24:3 (October 1985), pp. 247–272.
3. Cited in Joshua Kucera, "Pashinyan Calls for Unification between Armenia and Karabakh," Eurasianet, August 6, 2019, https://eurasianet.org/pashinyan-call-for-unificaton-bewteen-armenia-and-karabakh, accessed February 27, 2021.
4. Cited in "'New Territories in the Event of New War,' Says Defense Minister," *Asbarez*, April 1, 2019, http://asbarez.com/178701/new-territories-in-the-event-of-new-war-says-defense-minister/, accessed February 28, 2021.
5. Cited in Michael A. Reynolds, "Confidence and Catastrophe: Armenia and the Second-Karabagh War," War on the Rocks, January 11, 2021, https://warontherocks.com/2021/01/confidence-and-catastrophe-armenia-and-the-second-nagorno-karabakh-war/, accessed February 28, 2021.
6. Cited in Ibid.
7. "Keynote Speech by H. E. Ilham, President of the Republic of Azerbaijan, Shusha International Forum, 'South Caucasus: Development and Cooperation,'" Baku and Shusha, Azerbaijan, April 29, 2022.

Selected Bibliography

Abbasov, Eldar. "Armenian Irredentist Nationalism and Its Transformation into the Mass Karabakh Movement, "MIATSUM" (1965–1988)." In M. Hakan Yavuz and Michael Gunter, eds., *The Nagorno-Karabakh Conflict: Historical and Political Perspectives*. New York: Routledge, 2022, pp. 59–88.

Abilov, Shamkhal and Ismayil Isayev. "The Consequences of the Nagorno-Karabakh War for Azerbaijan and the Undeniable Reality of Khojaly Massacre: A View from Azerbaijan." *Polish Political Science Year Book* 45 (2016), pp. 291–303.

Abushov, Kavus. "Russian Foreign Policy Towards the Nagorno-Karabakh Conflict: Prudent Geopolitics, Incapacity or Identity?" *East European Politics* 35:1 (2019), pp. 72–92.

Akcam, Taner. *A Shameful Act: The Armenian Genocide and the Question of Turkish Responsibility*. New York: Henry Holt and Company, 2006.

Aklar, Yasemin. Kilit. "Nation and History in Azerbaijani School Textbooks." *AB Imperio* 2 (2005), pp. 469–497.

Aliyev, Ilham. "Keynote Speech by H. E. Ilham Aliyev, President of the Republic of Azerbaijan, Shusha International Forum, 'South Caucasus: Development and Cooperation.'" Baku and Shusha, Azerbaijan, April 29, 2022.

Altstadt, Audrey L. *Frustrated Democracy in Post-Soviet Azerbaijan*. Columbia University Press, 2017.

Altstadt, Audrey L. "Nagorno-Karabagh—'Apple of Discord' in the Azerbaijan SSR." *Central Asian Survey* 7:4 (1988), pp. 63–78.

Altstadt, Audrey L. "O Patria Mia: National Conflict in Mountainous Karabagh." In W. R. Duncan, and G. P. Holman, eds., *Ethnic Nationalism and Regional*

Conflict: The Former Soviet Union and Yugoslavia. Boulder, CO: Westview Press, 1994.

Altstadt, Audrey L. *The Azerbaijani Turks: Power and Identity Under Russian Rule*. Stanford, CA: Hoover Institution Press, 1992.

Altstadt, Audrey et al. "The Nagorno-Karabakh Conflict: An Expert Analysis." The Wilson Center, October 2, 2020, https://www.wilsoncenter.org/article/nagorno-karabakh-conflict-expert-analysis.

Anderson, Liam. "Ethnofederalism and the Management of Ethnic Conflict: Assessing the Alternatives." *Publius: The Journal of Federalism* 46:1 (2016), pp. 1–24.

Arısan, Mehmet. "From 'Clients' to 'Magnates': The (Not So) Curious Case of Islamic Authoritarianism in Turkey." *South East European and Black Sea Studies* 19:1 (2020), pp. 11–30.

"Armenia Economy Minister Says Weak Army and Unpopulated Territories Reasons for Defeat in Karabakh War." News.am, February 11, 2011, https://news.am/eng/news/628226.html, accessed February 17, 2021.

Askerov, Ali. "The Nagorno Karabakh Conflict: The Beginning of the Soviet End." In Ali Askerov et al., *Post-Soviet Conflicts: The Thirty Years' Crisis*. Rowman and Littlefield, 2020.

Askerov, Ali and Thomas Matyok. "The Upper Karabakh Predicament from the UN Resolutions to the Mediated Negotiations: Resolutions or Hibernation?" *European Journal of Interdisciplinary Studies* 2:1 (2015), pp. 154–164.

Astourian, Stephan H. "In Search of Their Forefathers: National Identity and the Historiography and Politics of the Armenian and Azerbaijani Ethnogenesis." In Donald V. Schwartz and Razmik Panossian, eds., *Nationalism and History: The Politics of Nation-Building in Post-Soviet Armenia, Azerbaijan and Georgia*. Toronto: University of Toronto Press, 1994, pp. 43–45.

Astourian, Stephan H. "Killings in the Armenian Parliament: Coup d'Etat, Political Conspiracy, or Destructive Rage?" *Contemporary Caucasus Newsletter in Soviet and Post-Soviet Studies* 9 (Spring 2000).

Atkin, Muriel. "The Strange Death of Ibrahim Khalil Khan of Qarabagh." *Iranian Studies* 12:1/2 (Winter/Spring 1979), pp. 79–107.

Avdaliani, Emil. "With the EU's Help, Armenia Is Inching Closer to Peace with Azerbaijan." *World Politics Review*, July 15, 2022, https://www.worldpoliticsreview.com/articles/30680/two-years-after-azerbaijan-armenia-war-a-new-hope-for-peace, accessed July 15, 2022.

Avedian, Vahagn. "Autonomy Within Azerbaijan Is Not a Solution for the Future of Karabakh." June 21, 2022, https://karabakhspace.commonspace.eu/opinion/opinion-autonomy-within-azerbaijan-not-solution-future-karabakh, accessed July 4, 2022.

Avedian, Vahagn. "The Question of Remedial Secession in the Case of Nagorno-Karabakh." June 22, 2022, https://www.e-ir.info/2022/06/22/opinion-the-question-of-remedial-secession-in-the-case-of-nagorno-karabakh/, accessed July 13, 2022.

Aves, Jonathan. *Post-Soviet Transcaucasia*. London: Royal Institute of International Affairs, 1993.

Azadian, Edmond Y. "Paul Goble Is for Real." *The Armenian Mirror-Spectator*, May 18, 2020, https://mirrorspectator.com/2020/05/18/paul-goble-is-for-real/, accessed February 3, 2021.

Baev, Pavel. "Russia and Turkey. Strategic Partners and Rivals." French Institute of International Affairs, May 2021. https://www.ifri.org/en/publications/etudes-delifri/russieneireports/russia-and-turkey-strategic-partners-and-rivals, accessed June 26, 2022.

Baser, Baher. "Third Party Mediation in Nagorno-Karabakh: Part of the Cure or Part of the Disease?" *OAKA* 3:1 (2008), pp. 86–114.

Batashvili, David. "Nikol Pashinyan's Russian Problem." *Security Review*, January 12, 2019, https://www.gfsis.org/publications/view/2684, accessed March 12, 2022.

Betts, Wendy. "Third Party Mediation: An Obstacle to Peace in Nagorno Karabakh." *SAIS Review* 19:2 (1999), pp. 161–183.

Bloxham, Donald. *The Great Game of Genocide: Imperialism, Nationalism, and the Destruction of the Ottoman Armenians*. New York: Oxford University Press, 2005.

Boczek, Boleslaw A. *The A to Z of International Law*. Lanham: The Scarecrow Press, Inc., 2010.

Bolukbasi, Suha. *Azerbaijan: A Political History*. London and New York: I.B. Tauris, 2001.

Bournoutian, George A. *A History of Qarabagh: An Annotated Translation of Mirza Jamal Javanshir Qarabaghi's Tarikh-e Qarabagh*. Costa Mesa, CA, Mazda Publishers, 1994.

Bournoutian, George A. *Armenians and Russia, 1626–1796: A Documentary Record*. Costa Mesa, CA: Mazda Publishers, 2001.

Bournoutian, George A. "The Politics of Demography: Misuse of Sources on the Armenian Population of Mountainous Karabakh." *Journal of the Society for Armenian Studies* 9 (1996–1997), pp. 99–103.

Bournoutian, George A. *Two Chronicles on the History of Karabagh*. Costa Mesa, CA: Mazda Publishers, Inc., 2004.

Boyajian, David. "Why Russia Needs Armenia and Vice Versa." *The Armenian Weekly*, February 5, 2019, https://armenianweekly.com/2019/02/05/why-russia-needs-armenia-and-vice-versa/.

Broers, Laurence. *Armenia and Azerbaijan: Anatomy of a Rivalry*. Edinburgh: Edinburgh University Press, 2021.

Brown, Michael. "The Causes of Internal Conflict: An Overview." In Michael Brown et al., eds., *Nationalism and Ethnic Conflict*. Cambridge, MA: The MIT Press, 1997, pp. 3–25.

Brubaker, Rogers. *Nationalism Reframed: Nationhood and the National Question in the New Europe*. Cambridge: Cambridge University Press, 1996.

Brzezinski, Zbigniew. *The Grand Chessboard: American Primacy and Its Geostrategic Imperatives*. New York: Basic Books, 1997.

Buchanan, Alan. *Justice, Legitimacy and Self-Determination: Moral Foundations for International Law*. Oxford: Oxford University Press, 2003.

Buchanan, Alan. "Theories of Secession." *Philosophy and Public Affairs* 26:10 (1997), pp. 1–12.

Bunce, Valerie. "Federalism, Nationalism, and Secession: The Communist and Postcommunist Experience." In Ugo M. Amoretti and Nancy Gina Bermeo, eds., *Federalism and Territorial Cleavages*. Johns Hopkins University Press, 2004, pp. 417–440.

Candar, Cengiz. "South Caucasus Deal Echoes Plan from 30 Years Ago." Al-Monitor, November 13, 2020, https://www.al-monitor.com/pulse/ori ginals/2020/11/turkey-russia-nagorno-karabakh-deal-armenia-azerbaijan. html, accessed November 24, 2020.

Cannon, Brendon J. *Legislating Reality and Politicizing History: Contextualizing Armenian Claims of Genocide*. Hamburg: Manzara Verlag, 2016.

Castellino, Joshua. "Territorial Integrity and the 'Right' to Self-Determination: An Examination of the Conceptual Tools." *Brooklyn Journal of International Law* 33:2 (2008), pp. 503–568.

Cederman, Lars-Eric et al. "Territorial Autonomy in the Shadow of Conflict: Too Little, Too Late?" *The American Political Science Review* 109:2 (May 2015), pp. 354–370.

Celikpala, Mithat. "Türkiye'de Kafkas Diyasporası ve Türk Dış Politikası'na Etkileri." *Uluslarası Ilişkiler* 2:5 (2005), pp. 71–108.

Cheterian, Vichen. "Dialectics of Ethnic Conflicts and Oil Projects in the Caucasus." In Bulent Gokay, ed., *The Politics of Caspian Oil*. New York: Palgrave, 2001, pp. 11–37.

Cheterian, Vichen. "Is the Political Status of the Nagorno-Karabakh That Important?" https://bakuresearchinstitute.org/en/is-the-political-status-of-nagorno-karabakh-that-important/#_edn2, accessed April 12, 2022.

Chorbajian, Levon. *The Making of Nagorno-Karabakh: From Secession to Republic*. New York: Palgrave, 2001.

Chorbajian, Levon, Patrick Donabedian, and Claude Mutafian. *The Caucasian Knot: The History and Geopolitics of Nagorno-Karabagh*. London and New Jersey: Zed Books, 1994.

"Conference on Security and Co-operation in Europe Final Act." Helsinki 1975, https://www.osce.org/files/f/documents/5/c/39501.pdf, accessed December 7, 2020.

Congressional Research Service. "Azerbaijan and Armenia: The Nagorno-Karabakh Conflict." (Written by Cory Welt and Andrew S. Bowen.) January 7, 2021, https://sgp.fas.org/crs/row/R46651.pdf, accessed February 22, 2021.

Cornell, Svante E. "Autonomy as a Source of Conflict: Caucasian Conflicts in Theoretical Perspective." *World Politics* 54:1 (January 2001), pp. 245–276.

Cornell, Svante E. *Azerbaijan Since Independence.* New York: M. E Sharpe, 2011.

Cornell, Svante E. *The Nagorno-Karabakh Conflict.* Report no. 46, Department of East European Studies, Uppsala University, Sweden, 1999.

Cornell, Svante E. *Small Nations and Great Powers: A Study of Ethnopolitical Conflict in the Caucasus.* Richmond, Surrey, England: Curzon, 2001.

Cornell, Svante E. "Undeclared War: The Nagorno-Karabakh Conflict Reconsidered." *Journal of South Asian and Middle Eastern Studies* 20 (Summer 1997), pp. 51–72.

Cox, Caroline and John Eibner. *Ethnic Cleansing in Progress: War in Nagorno-Karabakh.* London: Institute for Religious Minorities in the Islamic World, 1993.

Coyle, James J. *Russia's Border Wars and Frozen Conflicts.* New York: Palgrave, 2018.

Coyle, James J. *Russia's Interventions in Ethnic Conflict: The Case of Armenia and Azerbaijan.* Palgrave, 2021.

Crawford, James R. *The Creation of States in International Law*, 2nd ed. Oxford: Oxford University Press, 2006.

Croissant, Michael P. *The Armenian-Azerbaijani Conflict: Causes and Implications.* Westport, CT: Praeger, 1998.

Cutler, Robert M. "The Second Karabakh War and Western Strategic Thinking." The Wilson Center, January 5, 2021, https://www.wilsoncenter.org/blog-post/second-karabakh-war-and-western-strategic-thinking, accessed 20 February 2021.

Danielyan, Emil. "Armenia: 1996 Presidential Election Was Rigged, Aide Suggests." Radio Free Europe/Radio Liberty, January 9, 1999, https://www.rferl.org/a/1090270.html.

Deutsch, Karl W. *Political Community and the North Atlantic Area.* Princeton: Princeton University Press, 1957.

de Waal, Thomas. *Black Garden: Armenia and Azerbaijan Through Peace and War.* New York: New York University Press, 2003.

Dragadze, Tamara. *Azerbaijan.* London: Melisende, 2000.

Emmers, Ralf. "Securitization." In Alan Collins, ed., *Contemporary Security Studies*. Oxford: Oxford University Press, 2007, pp. 109–125.

Engel, Frank. "The Karabakh Dilemma: Right to Self-Determination, Imperative of Territorial Integrity, or a Caucasian New Deal?" In Michael Kambeck and Sargis Ghazaryan, eds. *Europe's Next Avoidable War: Nagorno-Karabakh*. New York: Palgrave Macmillan, 2013.

Ergun, Ayca. "Citizenship, National Identity, and Nation-Building in Azerbaijan: Between the Legacy of the Past and the Spirit of Independence." *Nationalities Papers* (2021), pp. 1–18.

Finnemore, Martha. *The Purposes of Intervention: Changing Beliefs About the Use of Force*. Ithaca, NY: Cornell University Press, 2003.

Frye, R. N. "Iran v. Peoples of Iran (1) A General Survey." *Encyclopaedia Iranica* XIII:3 (2004), pp. 321–326.

Fuller, Elizabeth. *Azerbaijan at the Crossroads*. London: Royal Institute of International Affairs, 1994.

Fuller, Elizabeth. "Ethnic Strife Threatens Democratization." *RFL/RL Research Report* 2:1 (January 1993).

Fuller, Elizabeth. "Nagorno-Karabakh: Internal Conflict Becomes International." *RFL/RL Research Report* 1:11 (March 13, 1992), pp. 1–2.

Fuller, Elizabeth. "What Lies Behind the Current Armenian-Azerbaijani Tensions?" *Report on the USSR* 3:21 (May 24, 1991), pp. 12–15.

Gahramanova, Aytan. "Paradigms of Political Mythologies & Perspectives of Reconciliation in the Case of the Nagorno-Karabakh Conflict." *International Negotiation* 15:1 (2010), pp. 133–152.

Gall, Carlotta. "Roots of War: When Armenia Talked Tough, Azerbaijan Took Action." *New York Times*, October 27, 2020, https://www.nytimes.com/2020/10/27/world/europe/armenia-azerbaijan-nagorno-karabakh.html, accessed November 3, 2020.

Gall, Carlotta and Anton Troianovski. "After Nagorno-Karabakh War, Trauma, Tragedy and Devastation." *New York Times*, December 31, 2020, https://www.nytimes.com/2020/12/11/world/europe/nagorno-karabakh-armenia-azerbaijan.html, accessed March 19, 2021.

Garagozov, Rauf. "Collective Memory and Narrative Toolkit in Turkish-Armenian Mnemonic Standoff over the Past." *Review of Armenian Studies* 30 (2014), pp. 79–99.

Garagozov, Rauf. "Memory, Emotions, and Behavior of the Masses in an Ethnopolitical Conflict: Nagorno-Karabakh." *The Caucasus & Globalization* 5:3–4 (2011), pp. 77–88.

Garagozov, Rauf. "The Khojaly Tragedy as a Collective Trauma and Factor of Collective Memory." *Azerbaijan in the World* 2:20. Baku: Azerbaijan

Diplomatic Academy, 2010, http://biweekly.ada.edu.az/vol_3_no_5/The_Khojaly_tragedy_as_a_collective_trauma_and_factor_of_collective_memory.htm, accessed July 10, 2022.

Gayim, Eyassu. *The Eritrean Question: The Conflict Between the Right of Self-Determination and the Interest of States.* Uppsala: Iustus Folag, 1993.

Gazıyev, Yusif. "Karabakh in 1920–1980." Virtual Karabakh, 2009; as cited in "When Was the Nagorno-Karabakh Autonomous Oblast (NKAO) Created?" https://karabakh99.com/2020/10/31/when-was-the-nagorno-karabakh-autonomous-oblast-nkao-created/, accessed January 29, 2021.

Gellner, Ernest. *Nations and Nationalism*, 2nd ed. Hoboken, NJ: Blackwell, 2008.

Gerhard, Simon. *Nationalism and Policy Toward the Nationalities in the Soviet Union from Totalitarian Dictatorship to Post-Stalinist Society.* Boulder: Westview Press, 1991.

Geukjian, Ohannes. *Ethnicity, Nationalism and Conflict in the South Caucasus: Nagorno-Karabakh and the Legacy of Soviet Nationalities Policy.* Farnham, England and Burlington, VT: Ashgate, 2012.

Geukjian, Ohannes. *Negotiating Armenian-Azerbaijani Peace: Opportunities, Obstacles, Prospects.* Farnham, England and Burlington, VT: Ashgate, 2014.

Ghaplanyan, Irina. *Post-Soviet Armenia: The New National Elite and the New National Narrative.* New York: Routledge, 2018.

Goble, Paul. "Coping with the Nagorno-Karabakh Crisis." *The Fletcher Forum* 16:2 (Summer 1992), pp. 18–26.

Goldberg, Jeffrey. "Getting Crude in Baku: The Crude Face of Global Capitalism." *The New York Times*, October 4, 1998.

Golden, Peter B. "The Turkic Peoples and Caucasia." In Ronald Grigor Suny, ed., *Transcaucasia: Nationalism and Social Change*, rev. ed. Ann Arbor: University of Michigan, 1996.

Goldenberg, Suzanne. *Pride of Small Nations: The Caucasus and Post-Soviet Disorder.* London: Zed Books, 1994.

Goltz, Thomas T. *Azerbaijan Dairy: A Rogue Reporter's Adventures in an Oil-Rich, War-Torn, Post-Soviet Republic.* Armonk, NY: M.E. Sharpe Press, 1998.

Goltz, Thomas T. "The Successes of the Spin Doctors: Western Media Reporting on the Nagorno-Karabakh Conflict." *Journal of Muslim Minority Affairs* 32: 2 (2012), pp. 186–195.

Gozalova, Nigar. "Massacre of the Azerbaijani Turkic Population (1918–1920) According to the Documents of the British Diplomats." *International Crimes and History*, Issue 18 (2017), pp. 37–53.

Gozalova, Nigar. "The Karabakh Issue in Relation with Armenia and Azerbaijan (1918–1920)." *AVIM Conference Book*, No. 24 (2019), pp. 37–53.

Gozalova, Nigar and Eldar Amirov, eds. *Armenian-Azerbaijani Conflict of 1905–1906 According to "The New York Times" Coverage*. Baku, Azerbaijan: Elm, 2021.

Gozalova, Nigar and Eldar Amirov. "The South Caucasus in 1905-1906 According to "The New York Times" Coverage." *Review of Armenian Studies*, Issue 43 (2021), pp. 83–108.

Grigoryan, Arman. "The Karabagh Conflict and Armenia's Failed Transition to Democracy," *Nationalities Papers* 46:5 (April 2018), pp. 844–860.

Gunter, Michael M. *Armenian History and the Question of Genocide*. New York: Palgrave Macmillan, 2011.

Gurr, Ted. "People Against States: Ethnopolitical Conflict and the Changing World System." *International Studies Quarterly* 38:3 (1994), pp. 344–377.

Gurr, Ted. *Why Men Rebel*. Princeton, NJ: Princeton University Press, 1971.

Gürün, Kamuran. *Türk-Sovyet İlişkileri (1920–1953)*. Ankara: Türk Tarih Kurumu Yayınları, 1991.

Haqqin.az. "Secret Talks Between the Envoys of Nikol Pashinyan and Ilham Aliyev." September 24, 2020, https://haqqin.az/news/190193, accessed April 8, 2021.

Hasanli, Jamil. *The Sovietization of Azerbaijan: The South Caucasus in the Triangle of Russia, Turkey, and Iran, 1920–1922*. Salt Lake City: University of Utah Press, 2018.

Helsinki Commission Report. "The Nagorno-Karabakh Conflict." June 15, 2017.

Herbst, John E. "Putin Gains and Losses from Armenia-Azerbaijan Ceasefire Deal." Atlantic Council, November 12, 2020, https://www.atlanticcouncil.org/blogs/new-atlanticist/putingains-and-loses-from-armenia-azerbaijan-ceasefire-deal/, accessed May 8, 2022.

Hewsen, Robert H. *Armenia: A Historical Atlas*. Chicago: The University of Chicago Press, 2001.

Hewsen, Robert H. "Ethno-History and the Armenian Influence upon the Caucasian Albanians." In Thomas J. Samuelian, ed., *Classical Armenian Culture: Influences and Creativity*. Chicago: Scholars Press, 1982.

Hewsen, Robert H. "The Meliks of Arc'ax." In Thomas J. Samuelian and Michael E. Stone, eds., *Armenian Texts and Studies*. Chico, CA: Scholars Press, 1984, pp. 52–53.

Hewsen, Robert H. "The Meliks of Eastern Armenia: A Preliminary Study." *Revue des etudes Armeniennes* NS: IX (1970).

Ho, Ben. "The Second Nagorno-Karabakh War: Takeaways for Singapore's Ground-Based Air Defense." *The Air Force Journal of Indo-Pacific Affairs* 4:5 (Fall 2021), pp. 24–39.

Horowitz, Donald L. *Ethnic Groups in Conflict*. Berkeley: University of California Press, 1985.

Hovannisian, Richard G. *Armenia on the Road to Independence, 1918*. Berkeley: University of California, 1967.
Hovannisian, Richard G. *The Republic of Armenia: From London to Sevres, February–August 1920*, Vol. III. Berkeley: University of California, 1996.
Hovannisian, Richard G. *The Republic of Armenia: From Versailles to London, 1919–1920*, Vol. II. Berkeley: University of California Press, 1982.
Hovannisian, Richard G. *The Republic of Armenia: The First Year, 1918–1919*, Vol. I. Berkeley: University of California Press, 1971.
"How the 'Goble Plan' Was Born and How It Remains a Political Factor." Reliefweb, June 9, 2000, https://reliefweb.int/report/armenia/how-goble-plan-was-born-and-how-it-remains-political-factor, accessed February 3, 2021.
Human Rights Watch. "Azerbaijan: Seven Years of Conflict in Nagorno-Karabakh." December 1, 1994.
Huseynov, Vasif. "Armenia-Azerbaijan Conflict Escalates with Intense Border Confrontation." Eurasia Daily Monitor (The Jamestown Foundation), July 14, 2020, https://jamestown.org/program/armenia-azerbaijan-conflict-escalates-with-intense-border-confrontation/, accessed June 12, 2022.
Huysmans, Jef. "Revisiting Copenhagen: Or, On the Creative Development of a Security Studies Agenda in Europe." *European Journal of International Relations* 4:4 (1998), pp. 479–505.
Ibrahimov, Royshan and Mehmet Fatih Oztarsu. "Causes of the Second Karabakh War: Analysis of the Positions and the Strength and Weakness of Armenia and Azerbaijan." *Journal of Balkan and Near Eastern Studies* 24:4 (2022), pp. 595–613.
Independent International Commission on Kosovo. *The Kosovo Report: Conflict, International Response, Lessons Learned*. Oxford: Oxford University Press, 2000.
"The Indo-Pakistan Western Boundary (Rann of Kutch) Between India and Pakistan (India, Pakistan)." *Reports of International Arbitral Awards* 17, February 19, 1968, pp. 1–576.
Internal Displacement Monitoring Centre. "Azerbaijan: After Some 20 years, IDPs Still Face Barriers to Self-Reliance." December 2010.
International Crisis Group. "Armenia: Internal Instability Ahead." Report No. 158, October 18, 2004, https://d2071andvip0wj.cloudfront.net/158-armenia-internal-instability-ahead.pdf.
International Crisis Group. "Getting from Ceasefire to Peace in Nagorno-Karabakh." November 10, 2020, https://www.crisisgroup.org/europe-central-asia/caucasus/nagorno-karabakhconflict/getting-ceasefire-peace-nagorno-karabakh.

International Crisis Group. "Nagorno-Karabakh's Gathering War Clouds." June 1, 2017, No. 244, https://www.crisisgroup.org/europe-central-asia/caucasus/nagorno-karabakh-azerbaijan/244-nagorno-karabakhs-gathering-war-clouds, accessed December 3, 2020.

International Crisis Group. "Tackling Azerbaijan's IDP Burden." Briefing No. 67, February 27, 2012.

International Crisis Group. "The Nagorno-Karabakh Conflict: A Visual Explainer." May 7, 2021, https://www.crisisgroup.org/content/nagorno-karabakh-conflict-visual-explainer.

Iskandaryan, Alexander. "Armenia-Russia Relations: The Revolution and the Map." *Russian Analytical Digest*, No. 232 (February 2019), pp. 2–4.

Iskandaryan. Alexander. "The Velvet Revolution in Armenia: How to Lose Power in Two Weeks." *Demokratizatsiya: The Journal of Post-Soviet Democratization* 26:4 (2018), pp. 465–482.

Island of Palmas Case. 2 *United Nations Reports of International Arbitral Awards*. April 4, 1928, p. 829.

Ismailzade, Fariz and Damjan Krnjevic Miskovic, eds. *Liberated Karabakh: Policy Perspectives by the ADA University Community*. Baku, Azerbaijan: ADA University Press, 2021.

Ismayilov, Aslan. *Sumgayit-Beginning of the Collapse of the USSR*. Baku: Casioglu, 2011.

Ismayilov, Murad and Norman A. Graham, eds. *Turkish-Azerbaijani Relations. One Nation—Two States?* Abingdon: Routledge, 2016.

Isqandarova, Nazila. "Rape as a Tool Against Women in War: The Role of Spiritual Caregivers to Support the Survivors of an Ethnic Violence." *Cross Currents* 63:2 (2013), pp. 174–184.

Jafarova, Esmira. "Evaluating the OSCE Minsk Group's Mediation of the Armenia-Azerbaijan Conflict." Center for Analysis of International Relations (Vienna), 2020, https://www.institutfuersicherheit.at/wp-content/uploads/2020/10/ISP-Working-Paper-Esmira-JAFAROVA-Evaluating-the-OSCE-Minsk-Group%E2%80%99s-mediation-of-the-Armenia%E2%80%93Azerbaijan-conflict.pdf, accessed March 10, 2022.

Jennings, Robert and Arthur Watts, eds. *Oppenheim's International Law*, Vol. 1, 9th ed. London: Oxford University Press, 2008.

Judah, Ben. "Armenian President Wants NATO to Explain Turkey's Involvement in Nagorno-Karabakh." Politico, October 17, 2020, https://www.politico.eu/article/armenia-president-armen-sarkissian-nato-turkey-involvement-nagorno-karabakh/, accessed March 10, 2022.

Kambeck, Michael and Sargis Ghazaryan, eds. *Europe's Next Avoidable War: Nagorno-Karabakh*. New York: Palgrave Macmillan, 2013.

Kasim, Kamer. "The Nagorno-Karabakh Conflict, Caspian Oil and Regional Powers." In Bulent Gokay, ed., *The Politics of Caspian Oil*. New York: Palgrave, 2001, pp. 185–198.

Katchaznouni, Hovhannes. *The Armenian Revolutionary Federation (Dashnagtzoutium) Has Nothing to Do Anymore*. (Reprint), trans. from the original by Matthew A. Callender and ed. by John Roy Carlson (Arthur A. Derounian). New York: Armenian Information Service, 1955.

Kaufman, Stuart J. "Ethnicity as a Generator of Conflict." In Karl Cordell and Stefan Wolff, eds., *Routledge Handbook of Ethnic Conflict*. London: Routledge, 2011, pp. 91–102.

Kaufman, Stuart J. "Spiraling to Ethnic War: Elites, Masses, and Moscow in Moldova's Civil War." *International Security* 21:2 (1996), pp. 108–138.

Kazemzadeh, Firuz. *The Struggle for Transcaucasia (1917–1921)*. Birmingham: Templar Press, 1951.

Keppel, George. *Personal Narrative of a Journey from India to England*. London: Henry Colburn, 1827, as reprinted by Elibron Classics replica edition, 2005.

Khalatyan, Artashes. "Nagorno-Karabakh Conflict in Light of the ICJ's Advisory Opinion on Kosovo: Whether the Nagorno-Karabakh Case Meets the Criteria Elaborated by the UN Court." American University of Armenia, Unpublished Master's thesis, 2011, https://law.aua.am/files/2012/02/Artashes_Khalatyan.pdf, accessed July 14, 2022.

Khoshnood, Arvin and Ardavan Khoshnood. "Iran's Quandary on Nagorno-Karabakh." *Middle East Policy* 28 (Spring 2021).

Kirişci, Kemal and Behlul Özkan. "After Russia's Nagorno-Karabakh Ceasefire, Could Turkey Step up Next for a Lasting Peace?" Just Security, November 17, 2020, https://www.brookings.edu/blog/order-from-chaos/2020/11/18/after-russias-nagornokarabakh-ceasefire-could-turkey-step-up-next-for-a-lasting-peace/, accessed April 5, 2022.

Krasner, Stephen D. *Sovereignty: Organized Hypocrisy*. Princeton: Princeton University Press, 1999.

Kruger, Heiko. *The Nagorno-Karabakh: A Legal Analysis*. New York: Springer Press, 2010.

Kucera, Joshua. ""Between Europe and Asia": Geography and Identity in Post-Soviet Nation-Building Narratives." *Central Asian Affairs* 4:4 (2017), pp. 331–357.

Kucera, Joshua. "Pashinyan Calls for Unification Between Armenia and Karabakh." Eurasianet, August 6, 2019, https://eurasianet.org/pashinyan-call-for-unificaton-bewteen-armenia-and-karabakh, accessed February 27, 2021.

Kurat, Akdes Nimet. *Rusya Tarihi: Başlangıçtan 1917'ye Kadar*. Ankara: Türk Tarih Kurumu, Yayınları, 1999.

Kurkhiyan, Maria. "The Karabagh Conflict: From Soviet Past to Post-Soviet Uncertainty." In Edmund Herzig and Marina Kurkchiyan, eds. *The Armenians: Past and Present in the Making of National Identity*. New York: Routledge, 2004.

Kuznetsov, Oleg. "The Coup That Never Happened and 'the Karabakh Clan' in the Armenian Army." Politics Today, March 2, 2021, https://politicstoday.org/the-coup-that-never-happened-and-the-karabakh-clan-in-the-armenian-army/.

Laitin, David D. and Ronald Grigor Suny. "Armenia and Azerbaijan: Thinking a Way Out of Karabakh." *Middle East Policy* 7 (October 1999), pp. 145–176.

Lang, David M. *Armenia: Cradle of Civilization*. London: George Allen and Unwin, 1970.

Libaridian, Gerard. "Step, This Time a Big Step Back." *Aravot*, September 2, 2020, https://www.aravot-ru.am/2020/09/02/335325/, accessed May 21, 2022.

Libaridian, Gerard J. *The Challenge of Statehood: Armenian Political Thinking Since Independence*. Watertown, MA: Blue Crane Books, 1999.

Libaridian, Gerard J., ed. *The Karabakh File: Documents and Facts on the Question of Mountainous Karabakh, 1918–1988*. Cambridge: Zoryan Institute, 1988.

Libaridian, Jirair. "What Happened and Why: Six Theses." *Armenian Mirror Spectator*, November 4, 2020, https://mirrorspectator.com/2020/11/24/what-happened-and-why-six-theses/, accessed July 16, 2022.

Magnusson, Marta-Lisa. "Why No Settlement in the Nagorno-Karabakh Conflict?—Which Are the Obstacles to a Negotiated Solution?" In Karina Vamling, ed., *Language, History and Cultural Identities in the Caucasus: Papers from the Conference, June 17–19, 2005*, Malmo University, 2010, pp. 114–143, https://www.academia.edu/1265456/M%C3%A4rta_Lisa_Magnusson_Why_No_Settlement_in_the_Nagorno_Karabakh_Conflict_Which_are_the_obstacles_to_a_negotiated_solution, accessed July 12, 2022.

Mahmudlu, Ceyhan. "Theorizing Nation Building in Azerbaijan." In Aliaga Mammadli, Adeline Braux, and Ceyhun Mahmudlu, eds., *"Azerbaijan" and Beyond: Perspectives on the Construction of National Identity*. Berlin: Verlag Dr. Köster, 2017, pp. 124–150.

Mahmudlu, Ceyhan and Shamkhal Abilov. "The Peace-Making Process in the Nagorno-Karabakh Conflict: Why Did Iran Fail in Its Mediation Effort?" *Journal of Contemporary Central and Eastern Europe* 26:1 (2018).

Makili-Aliyev, Kamal. *Contested Territory and International Law: A Comparative Study of the Nagorno-Karabakh Conflict and the Aland Islands Precedent*. London and New York: Routledge, 2020.

Makiki-Aliyev, Kamal. "International Law and the Changes in the Status Quo of the Nagorno-Karabakh Conflict in 2020." In M. Hakan Yavuz and Michael

Gunter, eds., *Nagorno-Karabakh Conflict: Historical and Political Perspectives*. New York: Routledge, 2023, pp. 203–220.

Makili-Aliyev, Kamal. "Opinion: Autonomy Is One Way in Which Some of the Problems in Armenia-Azerbaijan Relations Can Be Resolved." June 21, 2022.

Malanczuk, Peter. *Akehurst's Modern Introduction to International Law*, 7th revised ed. London and New York: Routledge, 1997.

Malkasian, Mark. *"Gha-Ra-Bagh!" The Emergence of the National Democratic Movement in Armenia*. Detroit: Wayne State University Press, 1996.

Manukyan, David. "What Is "Remedial Secession" and Why Is It Applicable to Nagorno-Karabakh?" *The Armenian Weekly*, November 4, 2020, https://armenianweekly.com/2020/11/04/what-is-remedial-secession-and-why-it-is-applicable-to-nagorno-karabakh/, accessed May 19, 2022.

Maresca, John. "Lost Opportunities in Negotiating the Conflict over Nagorno-Karabakh." *International Negotiation* 1 (December 1996), pp. 471–499.

Melander, Erik. "The Nagorno-Karabakh Conflict Revisited: Was the War Inevitable?" *Journal of Cold War Studies* 3:2 (2001), pp. 48–75.

Melkonian, Markar. *My Brother's Road: An American's Fateful Journey to Armenia*. London and New York: I.B. Tauris, 2005.

Minahan, James. *Nations Without States: A Historical Dictionary of Contemporary National Movements*. Westport, CT: Greenwood Press, 1996.

Minassian, Gaidz. *Armenia, a Russian Outpost in the Caucasus?* February 2008, Paris: Ifri Russie. Nei.Visions 27, IFRI Russia/NIS Center, https://www.ifri.org/sites/default/files/atoms/files/ifri_RNV_minassian_Armenie_Russie_ANG_fevr2008.pdf, accessed March 23, 2022.

Minasyan, Sergey. "The Nagorno-Karabakh Conflict in the Context of South Caucasus Regional Security Issues: An Armenian Perspective." *Nationalities Papers* 45:1 (2017), pp. 131–139.

Minzarari, Dumitru. "Russia's Stake in the Nagorno-Karabakh War: Accident or Design." German Institute for International and Security Affairs, November 12, 2020, https://www.swp-berlin.org/en/publication/russias-stake-in-the-nagorno-karabakh-war-accident-or design/, accessed June 12, 2022.

Mirzayev, Farhad. "The Nagorno-Karabakh Conflict: International Law Appraisal." In M. Hakan Yavuz and Michael Gunter, eds., *Nagorno-Karabakh Conflict: Historical and Political Perspectives*. New York: Routledge, 2023, pp. 168–202.

Mirzeler, Mustafa. "Narrating the Memories of *Ermeni Mezalimi*." *Middle East Critique* 23:2 (2014), pp. 225–240.

Mirzoyan, Alla. *Armenia, the Regional Powers, and the West: Between History and Geopolitics*. New York: Palgrave, 2010.

Mkrtchyan, Tigran. "Democratization and the Conflict of Nagorno-Karabakh." *Turkish Policy Quarterly* 6:3 (2007), pp. 79–92.

Motemedi, Maziar. "Iran's Delicate Balancing Act in the Nagorno-Karabakh Conflict." Aljazeera, October 5, 2020, https://www.aljazeera.com/news/2020/10/5/iran-nk, accessed March 3, 2022.

Nahaylo, Bohdan and Victor Swoboda. *Soviet Disunion: A History of the Nationalities Problem in the USSR*. New York: Hamish Hamilton, 1990.

Najafizadeh, Mehrangiz. "Ethnic Conflict and Forced Displacement: Narratives of Azeri IDP and Refugee Women from the Nagorno-Karabakh War." *Journal of International Women's Studies* 14:1 (2013), pp. 161–183.

Najafizadeh, Mehrangiz. "Poetry, Azeri IDP/Refugee Women, and the Nagorno-Karabakh War." *Journal of Third World Studies* 32:1 (2015), pp. 13–43.

"'New Territories in the Event of New War,' Says Defense Minister." *Asbarez*, April 1, 2019, http://asbarez.com/178701/new-territories-in-the-event-of-new-war-says-defense-minister/, accessed February 28, 2021.

Oskanian, Kevork. "Why Armenia Needs Realpolitik, Now." EVN Report, June 1, 2022, https://evnreport.com/opinion/why-armenia-needs-realpolitik-now/, accessed July 18, 2022.

Panossian, Razmik. "The Diaspora and the Karabagh Movement: Oppositional Politics Between the Armenian Revolutionary Federation and the Armenian National Movement." In Levon Chorbajian, ed. *The Making of Nagorno-Karabagh: From Secession to Republic*. New York: Palgrave, 2001.

Panossian, Razmik. "The Irony of Nagorno-Karabakh: Formal Institutions Versus Informal Politics." *Regional & Federal Studies*, 11:3 (2001), pp. 143–164.

Papazian, Taline. "From Ter-Petrossian to Kocharian: Explaining Continuity in Armenian Foreign Policy, 1991–2003." *Demokratizatsiya* 14: 2 (2006), pp. 235–251.

Papazian, Taline. "State at War, State in War: The Nagorno-Karabakh Conflict and State-Making in Armenia, 1991–1995." *The Journal of Power Institutions in Post-Soviet Republics* 8 (2008), https://journals.openedition.org/, accessed 31March 2022.

"Pashinyan: Treaty of Sevres Continues to Be a Historical Fact." Panorama, August 8, 2020, https://www.panorama.am/en/news/2020/08/10/Pashinyan-Treaty-of-Sevres/2341518, accessed May 3, 2022.

Petersen, Alexandros. "Russia Shows Its Hand on Karabakh." *EU Observer*, November 18, 2013, http://euobserver.com/opinion/122032, accessed February 12, 2021.

Pipes, Richard. *The Formation of the Soviet Union: Communism and Nationalism, 1917–1923*, revised ed. Cambridge, MA: Harvard University Press, 1997.

Rahimov, Rahim. "Armenian-Azerbaijani Conflict: Clash of Civilizations?" Eurasia Daily Monitor (The Jamestown Foundation), October 13, 2020, https://jamestown.org/program/armenian-azerbaijani-conflict-clash-of-civilizations/, accessed April 20, 2022.

Remnick, David. "Ethnic Conflict Overwhelms Caucasus Enclave." *The Washington Post*, September 15, 1991, https://www.washingtonpost.com/arc hive/politics/1991/09/15/ethnic-conflict-overwhelms-caucasus-enclave/ c30e5465-3f2e-4004-9a85-d29759612768/.

Reynolds, Michael A. "Confidence and Catastrophe: Armenia and the Second-Karabagh War." War on the Rocks, January 11, 2021, https://waronther ocks.com/2021/01/confidence-and-catastrophe-armenia-and-the-second-nagorno-karabakh-war/, accessed February 28, 2021.

RFL/RL. "Amnesty Calls for Probe into Civilian Casualties in Nagorno-Karabakh Conflict." RadioFreeEurope/RadioLiberty, January 14, 2012, https://www.rferl.org/a/amnesty-probe-civilian-casualties-nagorno-kar abakh/31045850.html, accessed February 12, 2012.

Roeder, Philip. "Ethnofederalism and the Mismanagement of Conflicting Nationalisms." *Regional & Federal Studies* 19:2 (2009), pp. 203–219.

Rubin, Michael. "The Problem with the Nagorno-Karabakh Ceasefire Agreement." *The National Interest*, November 10, 2020, https://www.aei.org/op-eds/the-problem-with-thenagorno-karabakh-ceasefire-agreement/, accessed June 1, 2022.

Rubin, Uzi. "The Second Nagorno-Karabakh War: A Milestone in Military Affairs." Tel Aviv: Begin-Sadat Center for Strategic Studies, 2020.

Russell, Martin. "Russia–Turkey Relations." European Parliamentary Research Service, February 2021, https://www.europarl.europa.eu/RegData/etudes/ BRIE/2021/679090/EPRS_BRI(2021)679090_EN.pdf, accessed March 12, 2022.

Rutland, Peter. "Democracy and Nationalism in Armenia." *Europe-Asia Studies* 46: 5 (1994), pp. 839–861.

Said, Edward W. *Orientalism*. New York: Pantheon Books, 1978.

"Salvage: A Conversation on Nagorno-Karabakh." Open Democracy, December 8, 2020, https://www.opendemocracy.net/en/odr/salvage-conversation-nag orno-karabakh/, accessed March 19, 2022.

Saparov, Arsene. *From Conflict to Autonomy in the Caucasus: The Soviet Union and the Making of Abkhazia, South Ossetia and Nagorno Karabakh*. London and New York: Routledge, 2015.

Saparov, Arsene. "Why Autonomy? The Making of Nagorno-Karabakh Autonomous Region 1918–1925." *Europe-Asia Studies* 64 (March 2012), pp. 281–323.

Shafiyev, Farid. *Resettling the Borderlands: State Relocations and Ethnic Conflict in the South Caucasus*. McGill-Quinn University Press, 2018.

Shahmuratian, Samvel, compiler and editor. *The Sumgait Tragedy: Pogroms against Armenians in Soviet Azerbaijan. Eyewitnesses Accounts*, Vol. I. New Rochelle, NY and Cambridge, MA: Aristide D. Caratzas and Zoryan Institute, 1991.

Shnirelmann, Victor. *The Value of the Past: Myths, Identity and Politics in Transcaucasia*. Senri Ethnological Studies, No. 57. Osaka, National Museum of Ethnology, 2001.
Smith, Graham, Vivien Law, Andrew Wilson, Annette Bohr, and Edward Allworth. *Nation-Building in the Post-Soviet Borderlands: The Politics of National Identities*. Cambridge: Cambridge University, 1998.
Spivak, Gayatri Chakravorty. "The Rani of Sirmur: An Essay in Reading the Archives." *History and Theory* 24:3 (October 1985), pp. 247–272.
"Statement: Azerbaijan President Heydar Aliyev in Key West, Florida." *Azerbaijan International*, April 3, 2001, https://www.azer.com/aiweb/categories/karabakh/karabakh_current/keywest_aliyev.html.
Sukiasyan, Narek. "Appeasement and Autonomy: Armenian-Russian Relations from Revolution to War." European Union Institute for Security Studies (EUISS), February 1, 2021, http://www.jstor.org/stable/resrep 28789, accessed April 15, 2022.
Suny, Ronald G. *Looking Toward Ararat: Armenia in Modern History*. Bloomington: Indiana University Press, 1993.
Suny, Ronald G. *The Revenge of the Past: Nationalism, Revolution and the Collapse of the Soviet Union*. Stanford: Stanford University Press, 1993.
Supreme Court of Canada. "Reference re Secession of Quebec." [1998] 2 S.C.R. 217, Case number 25506 *Supreme Court Judgments*, https://scc-csc.lexum.com/scc-csc/scc-csc/en/item/1643/index.do, accessed April 10, 2021.
Swietochowski, Tadeusz. "Azerbaijan: A Borderland at the Crossroads of History." In Frederick S. Starr, ed., *The Legacy of History in Russia and the New States of Eurasia*. New York: S. Starr, 1994.
Swietochowski, Tadeusz. "Russia's Transcaucasian Policies and Azerbaijan: Ethnic Conflict and Regional Unity." In Marco Buttino, ed., *In a Collapsing Empire*. Milan: Feltrinelli, 1993, pp. 191–192.
Swietochowski, Tadeusz. "The Problem of Nagorno-Karabakh: Geography Versus Demography Under Colonialism and in Decolonization." In Hafeez Malik, ed., *Central Asia*. Basingstoke: MacMillan, 1994.
Synovitz, Ron and Susan Badalian. "Fear and Loathing vs. Trade Across the Armenian-Azerbaijani Border." RadioFreeEurope/Radio Liberty, February 7, 2012, https://www.rferl.org/a/fear-and-loathing-vs-trade-across-the-armenian-azerbiajani-border/31090569.html, accessed February 12, 2021.
Tang, Shipping. "The Security Dilemma and Ethnic Conflict: Towards a Dynamic and Integrative Theory of Ethnic Conflict." *Review of International Studies* 37:2 (2011), pp. 511–536.
Tashjian, Yeghia. "Russia and the Future Status of Shusha." *Armenian Weekly*, November 17, 2020, https://armenianweekly.com/2020/11/17/russia-and-the-future-status-of-shushi/, accessed November 23, 2021.

Tchilingurian, Hratch. "Nagorno Karabagh: Transition and the Elite." *Central Asian Survey* 18:4 (1999), pp. 435–461.

Ter-Matevosyan, Vahram. "Deadlocked in History and Geopolitics: Revisiting Armenia-Turkey Relations." *Digest of Middle Eastern Studies* 30:3 (2021), pp. 155–169.

Ter Minassian, Anahide. "The Revolution of 1905 in Transcaucasia." *Armenian Review* 42 (Summer 1989), pp. 1–23.

Ter-Petrossian, Levon and Arman Grigoryan. *Armenia's Future, Relations with Turkey, and the Karabakh Conflict*. New York: Palgrave, 2017.

Terzyan, Aram. "The Evolution of Armenia's Foreign Policy Identity: The Conception of Identity Driven Paths. Friends and Foes in Armenian Foreign Policy Discourse." In K. Kakachia and A. Markarov, eds., *Values and Identity as Sources of Foreign Policy in Armenia and Georgia*. Tibilisi: Publishing House Universal, 2006, pp. 145–183.

Tharoor, Shashi and Sam Daws. "Humanitarian Intervention: Getting Past the Reefs." *World Policy Journal* 18:2 (Summer 2001), pp. 21–30.

Tokluoglu, Ceylan. "The Political Discourse of the Azerbaijani Elite on the Nagorno-Karabakh Conflict (1991–2009)." *Europe-Asia Studies* 63:7 (2011), pp. 1223–1252.

Toloylan, Khachig. "National Self-Determination and the Limits of Sovereignty: Armenia, Azerbaijan, and the Secession of Nagorno-Karabakh." *Nationalism and Ethnic Politics* 1 (Spring 1995), pp. 86–110.

Tuncel, Turgut Kerem. "The Karabakh Conflict and the Lawfare of Armenia: Armenia's Campaign for Remedial Secession (I)." Center for Eurasian Studies (AVIM), October 27, 2020, https://avim.org.tr/en/Analiz, accessed December 22, 2020.

UN General Assembly Resolution 1514 (XV), December 14, 1960.
UN General Assembly Resolution 1541 (XV), December 15, 1960.
UN General Assembly Resolution 2131 (XX), December 21, 1965.
UN General Assembly Resolution 2200A (XXI), December 16, 1966.
UN General Assembly Resolution 2396 (XXIII), December 15, 1969.
UN General Assembly Resolution 2625 (XXV), October 24, 1970.
UN General Assembly Resolution 2672 C (XXV), December 8, 1970.
UN General Assembly Resolution 31/61, December 9, 1976.
UN General Assembly Resolution 3236 (XXIX), November 22, 1974.
UN General Assembly Resolution 33/23, November 29, 1978.
UN General Assembly Resolution 47/134, December 18, 1992.
UN General Assembly Resolution 62/243, March 14, 2008.
UN Security Resolution 822, April 30, 1993.
UN Security Resolution 853, July 29, 1993.
UN Security Resolution 874, October 14, 1993.
UN Security Resolution 884, November 12, 1993.

UN World Conference on Human Rights. Vienna Declaration and Programme of Action. June 25, 1993.
van der Leeuw, Charles. *Azerbaijan: A Quest for Identity: A Short History.* London: Curzon Press, 2000.
Van Evera, Stephen. "Hypotheses on Nationalism and War." *International Security* 18:4 (1994), pp. 5–39.
Vaserman, Arie and Rami Ginat. "National, Territorial or Religious Conflict? The Case of Nagorno-Karabakh." *Studies in Conflict & Terrorism* 17:4 (1994), pp. 345–362.
Vidmar, Jure. "Remedial Secession in International Law: Theory and (Lack of) Practice." *St. Anthony's International Review* 6:1 (2010), pp. 37–56.
Voronkova, Anastasia. "Understanding the Dynamics of Ethnonationalist Contention: Political Mobilization, Resistance and Violence in Nagorno-Karabakh and Northern Ireland." Unpublished PhD thesis, Quinn Mary University, 2011.
Walker, Christopher. *Armenia and Karabagh: The Struggle for Unity.* London: Minority Rights, 1991.
Waever, Ole. "Securitization and Desecuritization." In Ronnie D. Lipschutz, ed., *On Security.* New York: Columbia University Press, 1995, pp. 46–86.
Weller, Marc. "Settling Self-Determination Conflicts: Recent Developments." *The European Journal of International Law* 20:1 (2009), pp. 111–164.
Wellman, Christopher. "A Defense of Secession and Self-Determination." *Philosophy and Public Affairs* 24:2 (1995), pp.142–171.
Wertsch, James V. "Deep Memory and Narrative Templates: Conservative Forces in Collective Memory." In Aleida Assmann and Linda Shortt, eds., *Memory and Political Change.* New York: Palgrave Macmillan, 2012.
Whitman, Richard G. and Stefan Wolff. "The EU as a Conflict Manager? The Case of Georgia and Its Implications." *International Affairs* 86:1 (2010), pp. 87–107.
Whitmore, Brian. "Armenia Spotlights 'Karabakh Clan.'" Radio Free Europe, March 5, 2008, https://www.rferl.org/a/1079586.html.
Witt, Stephen. "The Turkish Drone That Changed the Nature of Warfare." *The New Yorker*, May 9, 2022, https://www.newyorker.com/magazine/2022/05/16/the-turkish-drone-that-changed-the-nature-of-warfare?utm_source=nl&utm_brand=tny&utm_mailin, accessed May 9, 2022;
Yalçınkaya, Haldun. "Turkey's Overlooked Role in the Second Nagorno-Karabakh War." January 21, 2021, The German Marshall Fund of the United States, January 21, 2021, https://www.gmfus.org/publications/turkeys-overlooked-role-second-nagorno-karabakh-war, accessed March 20, 2022.
Yamskov, Anatoly N. "Ethnic Conflict in the Transcaucasus: The Case of Nagorno-Karabakh." *Theory and Society* 20:5 (1991), pp. 631–660.

Yavuz, M. Hakan. *Erdoğan: Making of an Autocrat*. Edinburg: Edinburg University Press, 2021.
Yavuz, M. Hakan. *Nostalgia for the Empire: The Politics of Neo-Ottomanism*. New York: Oxford University Press, 2020.
Yavuz, M. Hakan. "The Turkish-Armenian Historical Controversy: How to Name the Events of 1915?" *Middle East Critique* 29 (May 2020), pp. 345–365.
Yavuz, M. Hakan and Michael M. Gunter, eds. *The Nagorno-Karabakh Conflict: Historical and Political Perspectives*. London and New York; Routledge, 2023.
Yavuz, M. Hakan and Vasif Huseynov. "The Second Karabakh War: Russia vs. Turkey?" *Middle East Journal* 27 (Winter 2020), pp. 103–118.
Yilmaz, Harun. "The Soviet Union and the Construction of Azerbaijani National Identity in the 1930s." *Iranian Studies* 46:4 (2013), pp. 511–533.
Zaman, Amberin. "Turkey's Talk of Peace with Armenia Rings Hollow." Al-Monitor, February 4, 2021, https://www.al-monitor.com/pulse/originals/2021/02/erdogan-turkey-normalize-united-states-azerbakjan.html, accessed February 12, 2021.
Zurcher, Christopher. *The Post-Soviet Wars: Rebellion, Ethnic Conflict, and Nationhood in the Caucasus*. New York: New York University Press, 2007.

Index

A
Abbas I (Shah), 17
Abbasid, 16
Abhazia, 24
Abilov, Shamkhal, 115
Abkhazia, 138
Ak Koyunlu, 16
Aland Islands, 125, 145
Albania (Caucasus), 1, 16, 28, 104
Aliyev, Heydar, 99, 111, 187, 189
Aliyev, Ilham, 8, 119, 124, 132, 133, 153–158, 168, 172–175, 177, 182, 187, 197, 198
Armenia, 4–8, 10, 13, 15, 16, 20–26, 107–127, 135, 137–139, 143, 144, 186, 188, 190
Armenian diaspora/lobby (US), 109, 117–119
Armenian nationalism, 35, 36, 38, 40–43, 53
Armenian National Movement (ANM), 70–72, 74, 77
Artsakh, 4, 16, 28, 135, 197
Aturpatkan (Atropatene), 16
Autonomy, 142, 144, 145, 148, 192, 193
Avars, 26
Azerbaijan, 2–8, 10, 12–26, 31, 101, 104, 105, 107–124, 126, 127, 131, 135, 137–139, 141, 143, 144, 189
Azerbaijani identity, 68, 85, 92–94
Azerbaijani nationalism, 37, 46, 52
Azerbaijani Special Function Militia Troops (OMON), 108

B
Bagratid, 16
Bangladesh, 145, 149
Basques, 11, 146
Belarus, 118, 130
Belize, 11, 146
Belt and Road Initiative (BRI), 1, 15
Biafra, 11, 146
Black Sea, 110
Black Sea Economic Cooperation Organization (BSEC), 109, 111
Blumenbach, Johann, 9

Bodin, Jean, 138
Bryza, Matthew, 113, 121
Brzezinski, Zbigniew, 7, 10
Burkina Faso, 137–139
Bush, George H.W., 111

C
Canada, 143
Candar, Cengiz, 110, 111, 128
Caspian Sea, 1, 3, 7, 15
Catalonia, 11, 146
Caucasian, 1
Caucasus, 1, 2, 5, 7–9, 13–17, 31, 33
Causes of ethnic conflict, 1
Ceasefire agreement, 160, 172
Chechnya, 11, 146
China, 1
Churchill, Winston, 15
Collective Security Treaty Organization (CSTO), 120
Conference on Security and Cooperation in Europe (CSCE), 115–118, 120, 130
Cornell, Svante, 10, 11, 25, 26, 29, 32, 62, 64, 130, 146, 147, 150
Crimea, 138
Cyprus, Northern, 11, 130, 146, 149

D
Dashnak Party, 76, 77
Demirel, Suleyman, 105, 109, 111
Deutsch, Karl, 125, 133, 151
Dizak, 17
Drones, 2, 8, 14

E
East Timor (Timor-Leste), 11, 145, 146, 148
Elisabethpol governorate, 19

Erdoğan, Recep Tayyip, 164–166, 169, 171, 189
Eritrea, 11, 140, 142, 145, 146
European Union (EU), 2, 14

F
Falkland Islands (Malvinas), 11, 146
Fedayin, 180
Finland, 118, 125
First Karabakh War, 3, 5, 8, 109, 122
France, 118, 128, 130
Freedom Support Act 907a (US), 117

G
Gellner, Ernest, 3, 9, 15, 27
Genocide, 4–6, 9, 10, 30, 63, 100, 101, 166, 170, 172
Georgia, 21, 23, 24, 26
Germany, 118, 121, 130, 139, 141
Ghazanchetosts Cathedral, 19, 20
Gibraltar, 11, 146
Goble Plan, 111–113, 128, 129
Gulistan, 17

H
Hai Dat, 41, 101
Hans-Adam II (Liechtenstein), 142
Helsinki Final Act of 1975, 14, 116, 136, 138
Huber, Max, 138
Human Rights Covenants, 136

I
Iberians (Caucasian), 1, 16, 28
Ibrahim-Khalil Khan, 17
Ilkhanate, Mongol, 16
International Court of Justice (ICJ), 14, 137, 139, 140
International law, 196–198

International organization, 196–198
Iran, 2, 6, 14, 18, 107, 110, 112–116, 126, 190
Islam, 170
Isle of Palmas case, 138
Israel, 6, 7
Italy, 118, 130

J
Jraberd, 17

K
Karabakh clan, 69–72, 74–78, 100
Karabakh Committee, 69, 71, 72, 74
Katchaznouni, Hovannes, 123, 132
Kavburo, 21, 23, 24, 31
Kazimirov, Vladimir, 121, 186
Kelbajar, 117
Keppel, George, 19, 30
Key West (Florida) meeting, 112, 118
Khachen, 17
Khamsa, 17
Khankendi (Stepanakert), 24
Khojaly, 3, 10, 110
Khojaly massacre, 54, 56
Kin-state, 137, 145
Kocharyan, Robert, 112
Korenizatsiaa (indigenization), 25
Kosovo, 11, 140, 142, 143, 145, 146, 149
Kurds, 11, 68, 141, 146
Kurekchai, Treaty of, 17

L
Lachin Corridor, 6, 56
Lezgins, 26
Libaridian, Jirair, 62, 122–124, 132, 146, 192
Libya, 143

M
Madrid Principles, 6, 108, 119, 188
Mahmudlu, Ceyhan, 104, 115, 129
Mali, 137–139
Mammadov, Yagub, 99, 114, 115
Mammadov, Zaur, 17, 18
Medes, 16
Melikdoms (Armenians principalities), 17
Minsk Group, 130, 154, 159, 160, 165, 174, 188
Minsk Process, 6, 8, 108, 112, 113, 119, 123, 125, 128
Moscow Treaty of 1921, 22
Mutalibov, Ayaz, 109–111, 187
Mythomoteur, 14

N
Nader Shah, 17
Nagorno-Karabakh, 1–3, 6–8, 10, 13, 15–18, 21, 22, 24, 29, 66, 109, 110, 112, 114–116, 124, 126, 186, 195–198
Nakhichevan, 22, 26, 63, 104, 110–113, 126, 131
Natevan, 19
Nazarbaev, Nursultan, 108
Norway, 142

O
Oghuz, 16
Oil, 2, 8, 14, 20
Operation Ring, 108, 109, 120
Organization for Security and Cooperation in Europe (OSCE), 6, 8, 108, 113, 115, 116, 118–121
Ottoman Empire, 16
Ozal, Turgut, 110, 111

P

Palestinians, 141, 149
Panakh Khan, 17
Parliamentary Assembly of the
    Council of Europe (PACE), 121
Pashinyan, Nikol, 122, 123, 125,
    155, 156, 158–160, 162–164,
    168–173, 176, 177, 184, 187,
    188, 197
Persia, 17, 19, 104
Pipes, Richard, 25
Putin, Vladimir, 135, 157, 158, 165,
    168, 169, 172, 177

Q

Quebec, 143

R

Rafsanjani Akbar Hashemi, 114
Rann of Kutch Arbitration, 140
Remedial secession, 142, 143, 192
Responsibility to Protect (R2P), 143
Russia/Soviet Union, 2, 3, 5–7,
    13–15, 17–25, 33–35, 38–43,
    45, 46, 48, 50, 52, 53, 56, 57,
    60, 61, 107–110, 113–115,
    118–122, 125–128, 130,
    154–158, 160–165, 167–170,
    172–178, 180, 182–185, 196
Rwanda, 143

S

Safavid (Persian Empire), 16
Schwimmer, Walter, 115
Scotland, 11, 146
Second Karabakh War, 2, 5, 8, 9, 11,
    27, 109, 113, 116, 124, 146
Security community, 125, 151
Self-defense, 197, 198

Self-determination, 4, 7, 8, 11–13,
    24, 101, 135–150, 193, 196–198
Sevres, Treaty of, 112, 122, 128, 188
Shahumian, Stepan, 24
Shusha, 17–20, 22–24, 29, 31, 115,
    131
Silk Road, 1, 15
Soft law, 142
South Africa, 141, 149
South Ossetia, 24, 138
South Sudan, 145, 149
Sovereignty, 11, 138, 139, 143, 145,
    147, 149
Stalin, Joseph, 21, 31
State succession, 137–140
Sultanov, Khosrov Bey (Bek), 21
Sumgait, 3, 9, 110
Sumgait riot, 45–49, 64
Sweden, 10, 26, 29, 110, 118, 121,
    130, 142, 145

T

Talsyh, 26
Tatars (Azerbaijanis), 19, 28
Temple of Preah Vihear Case, 140
Ter-Petrosyan, Levon, 109, 114, 121,
    122
Territorial integrity, 2, 4, 5, 7, 8,
    11–13, 16, 24, 135–145,
    147–150, 196–198
Tonoyan, Davit, 122
Treaty of Sevres, 159, 164
Turkey, 2, 6, 7, 13, 14, 22, 26, 63,
    100, 101, 108–114, 116,
    118–122, 125, 126, 128, 130,
    149, 188, 189, 191

U

Ukraine, 138, 146
Ukraine, Eastern, 11, 146
Umayyad, 16

UN Declaration of the Granting of
    Independence to Colonial
    Countries and Peoples, 136
UN Declaration on Friendly
    Relations, 148, 149
United Nations (UN), 13, 64, 116,
    124, 136, 137, 139, 141–143,
    145
United States (US), 2, 5, 9, 14, 111,
    115–119, 122, 128–130, 149
Uti possidetis, 11, 14, 23, 138–140,
    147

V
Vagif, 19
Vance, Cyrus, 116
Varanda, 17, 19
Versailles, Treaty of, 141

Victim identity, 85, 87, 176
Victim nationalism, 83
Victor identity, 69

W
Waal, Thomas de, 107, 113, 186, 192
War and nationalism, 73
Western Sahara, 11, 146, 149

Y
Yeltsin, Boris, 108
Yugoslavia (former), 137, 140

Z
Zangezur, 2, 15, 22–24
Zangezur (Meghri), 111
Zoroastrian, 16